Road Biking New Jersey

Road Biking™ Series

Road Biking
New Jersey

A Guide to the State's Best Bike Rides

Tom Hammell

Foreword by Governor Christine Todd Whitman

FALCONGUIDES ®

GUILFORD, CONNECTICUT
HELENA, MONTANA

AN IMPRINT OF THE GLOBE PEQUOT PRESS

FALCONGUIDES®

Copyright © 2009 Morris Book Publishing, LLC

Photos by Tom Hammell unless otherwise indicated.
Maps: Trailhead Graphics © Morris Book
    Publishing, LLC
Project Manager: John Burbidge
Layout: Maggie Peterson

Library of Congress Cataloging-in-Publication Data
Hammell, Tom.
Road biking New Jersey : a guide to the state's best
bike rides / Tom Hammell.
    p. cm. – (Falconguides)
Includes index.
ISBN 978-0-7627-4288-2
1. Bicycle touring–New Jersey–Guidebooks. 2. New
Jersey–Guidebooks. I. Title.

GV1045.5.N5H36 2009
796.6'409749–dc22   2009003200

Printed in the United States of America
10 9 8 7 6 5 4 3 2 1

Contents

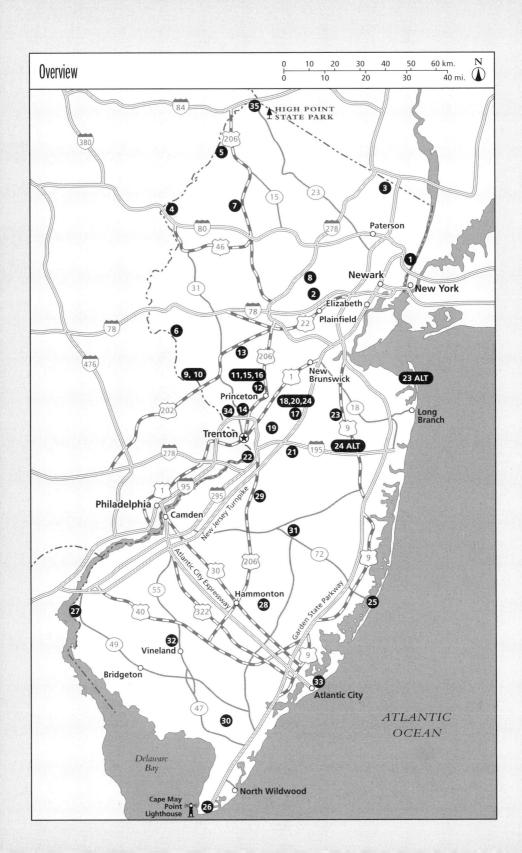

Overview

HIGH POINT
STATE PARK

Paterson

Newark
New York

Elizabeth
Plainfield

New Brunswick

Long Branch

Princeton

Trenton

Philadelphia
Camden

New Jersey Turnpike

Atlantic City Expressway

Hammonton

Garden State Parkway

Vineland

Bridgeton

Atlantic City

ATLANTIC OCEAN

Delaware Bay

North Wildwood

Cape May
Point
Lighthouse

Foreword

New Jersey is a state of many hidden treasures. With 127 miles of coastline, rolling hills, steep ascents, and large open spaces, it offers a variety of vistas and experiences that can often be best enjoyed from the seat of a bike. For several years as governor, I would take a group and bike across the state or down the coastline. It was not only a special chance to really enjoy the state, but it was also a way to encourage tourism and highlight some of the wonderful biking opportunities New Jersey has to offer. With his book *Road Biking New Jersey,* Tom Hammell has added immeasurably to the ability of cyclists to take advantage of all the biking opportunities in the Garden State.

Thoroughly researched, his work has something for everyone. Each ride description includes detailed information about length and difficulty, along with suggestions about what to see along the way. You can plan a day ride or a weekend getaway. With gas prices fluctuating and fitness becoming a focus of good health, taking time to ride a bike is a low-impact way to enjoy life while getting in shape. The wonderful part of *Road Biking New Jersey* is the enormous variety offered for bicyclists of every age, from beginners to experts. My only regret is that it wasn't available when I was planning my rides as governor, but it's never too late to learn, and *Road Biking New Jersey* is where I will go!

Governor Christine Todd Whitman

Preface

New Jersey is the most crowded and congested state in the United States. It is also a bicycler's paradise. These seemingly contradictory statements sum up the multiple personality disorder that is New Jersey. The New Jersey that is portrayed on television and in movies shows the crowded neighborhoods of the northeast with its run-down industrial towns and broken-down highways. New Jersey's reputation is often the subject of comedians' jokes. (Oh, you're from New Jersey. What exit?)

It is easy to understand where this impression comes from—many people's first sight of New Jersey is from the New Jersey Turnpike or some other major highway. These highways, especially in the northeast around Newark and Elizabeth, are some of the most unattractive roadways in the nation. But if you get off the highway, you will see a much different state.

Those of us who live here know the state's faults, but we wouldn't want to live anywhere else. New Jersey is a great state, with a lot of beauty and diversity in a small package (the fourth-smallest state in the union). Situated between New York City and Philadelphia, the variety of things to do in this state is endless. You can go hiking in the mountains by High Point, spend a romantic weekend in Cape May, hang out on the ocean at Belmar, or shop for antiques in the historic towns along the Delaware. The list goes on and on, and the best thing is, they are all within an hour or two drive.

For bikers, the smallness and variety means there are a lot of fun places to ride through and see, all within easy reach of a recreational rider. The state's long history and crowded nature actually help make biking better in this state. Since New Jersey has been around for more than 200 years and has always had a large population, an extensive network of roads has been built up. There are usually two or three ways to get between any two places without getting on highways or main roads. This makes it easy to find a good bike ride in almost any part of the state.

New Jersey may be crowded, but the worst congestion is confined mostly to the northeast by New York and the west-central section by Philadelphia. In between these places are large areas of rural towns and quiet roads. With a little research, it is easy to find roads where traffic and congestion are not a problem. The rural areas of the state surprise people and remind them of upstate New York or western Pennsylvania. The truth is, there are a lot of great roads in New Jersey; any biker, no matter his or her ability or preference, would find it a great place to ride.

Writing a book like this is not an easy task, and it would not be possible without the collected effort of a number of people.

First and most important, I have to thank my wife, who allows me to pursue my passion for biking and is always supportive. She also was very helpful with some of the more tedious aspects of preparing the manuscript. I am a fortunate man to have her.

I have a good bunch of friends who enjoy getting on bikes and exploring new roads. I would like to thank them for allowing me to drag them to different parts of the state in search of the best roads to ride. I would like to especially thank Laura Lynch for sharing her knowledge of the Sourlands and making me proud to be a Hill Slug, and Michael Heffler for showing me the better roads around Frenchtown and beyond and for helping me to learn that riding hills can actually be fun. I would like to thank Herb Cohen for his willingness to go anywhere, even though it usually meant getting lost and getting home late.

I encountered many fellow bikers while riding around the state who share a passion for riding. It was great sharing stories with them and helped keep me going week after week. I don't know any of their names, but their advice and companionship were greatly appreciated.

Lastly I want to thank Governor Whitman for writing the Foreword, and all the people at The Globe Pequot Press and FalconGuides for their hard work and dedication in making this book.

Introduction

This book is about bike riding in New Jersey and contains thirty-five great rides you can do. Researching the rides for this book has been a lot of fun and has reaffirmed my belief that this state has a lot to offer bikers. Writing this book has helped me rediscover some routes I haven't done in years and find some new ones that will now be part of my regular routine. I have lived in this state my whole life and been riding bikes a large part of it, and I was surprised at how many new places I found to ride while writing this book. If you try some of these rides, I'm sure you too will understand the joy of biking in New Jersey.

The rides in this book cover a variety of distances, terrain, locations, and traffic conditions. There are short rides (12 to 25 miles), medium rides (25 to 50 miles), long rides (50-plus miles), and even one marathon 232-mile ride. In the northwest you will find some challenging hilly rides; in the central and south you will find some rolling to flat rides. No matter what your ability or preference, you should be able to find a ride here that will fit your style.

The rides in this book were designed with the average recreational rider in mind—you don't need to be an elite athlete to complete any of them. With a little training and some miles, any healthy person should be able to enjoy these rides. The rides were also designed with touring in mind. Most rides overlap one or two other rides, so you can shorten or lengthen them to accommodate your ability and desired number of miles. It's also easy to use the rides in this book to put together a multiday state tour.

Besides the rides, this book also contains some brief words on bike safety, bike handling and maintenance, and a list of resources for bike maps, bike clubs, and other things that will help you explore and enjoy bicycling in New Jersey. Lastly you'll find a small section on how to go beyond the rides in this book to further explore the state on your own.

How to Use This Book

Organization

The rides in this book are grouped into three geographic areas of the state: north, central, and south. This was done so that you can choose a ride by the area you want to explore. The north part of the state tends be more hilly, especially in the western part. The central part of the state has the most varied terrain, from very hilly in the west by Frenchtown to mostly flat in the east by the ocean. The southern part of the state is fairly flat and the most rural. It is filled with endless farmland and nice, quiet roads.

Ride Format

All the rides in *Road Biking New Jersey* are presented in the same format. Each ride's name indicates the relative degree of difficulty.

Rambles are the easiest rides—less than 35 miles and on flat to rolling terrain. These rides should be easy for riders of any ability to complete within a day.

Cruises are intermediate rides of 25 to 50 miles. The terrain on these rides will be flat to rolling and possibly include some climbing. Experienced riders should be able to easily complete these rides in a day.

Challenges are more difficult intermediate rides of 40 to 70 miles. These rides are either long-distance marathons or intermediate-distance hilly rides. The terrain can be anything from flat to extremely hilly, with some tough climbs. Experienced riders who have some miles under their belt and have done some hill training should be able to complete these rides in a day. Less-experienced riders may want to do some distance or hill training before attempting these rides or possibly break these rides up over multiple days.

Classics are the most difficult rides—hard, hilly, long-distance marathons. The classic rides in this book range from 68 to 232 miles and go through all types of terrain, hilly to rolling to flat. Very experienced riders with enough training can complete any of these rides in a single day. (Yes, there are people insane enough to think riding 232 miles on a single day is a fun thing to do.) Saner or less-experienced riders may want to break these rides into multiple days.

Below the title is a brief summary of the ride, followed by more details about the ride:

Start tells you where the ride begins.

Distance gives the length of the ride in miles as well as the type of ride—loop, out-and-back, or one-way.

Terrain is the type of terrain you will encounter on this ride—flat, hilly, etc. This section also notes the vertical distance of the ride's major climbs.

Traffic and hazards give you an idea of the type of traffic you will encounter as well as any other things you need to look out for along the way.

Getting there provides directions to the ride's starting point.

This information is followed by a complete **description** of the ride, including a description of the route's roads and turns plus some of the things you will see along the way.

Miles and Directions provides turn-by-turn directions for the ride, with cumulative mileage from the start point.

The last section of each ride contains useful information about the area you are riding in. This section includes information about **events or attractions, restaurants,** and **accommodations** in the area. This is not meant to be a complete travel guide but will give you a starting point when looking for more information about the area around the ride. This section also lists references to maps of the area. Most rides will have two map references. The *DeLorme: New Jersey Atlas and Gazetteer* reference lists the pages containing the roads of the ride. The second reference lists the relevant New Jersey Bike Map. For those not familiar with New Jersey Bike Map, it provides

Crossing the Mullica River on the Batsto Village ride

free online maps (www.njbikemap.com) designed and maintained to help bikers find good roads to ride on. The appendix contains more information on New Jersey Bike Map and how to use the Web site.

Each ride is accompanied by a map of the route that shows an overview of the roads of the ride and the surrounding area. The route is clearly marked on the map, including symbols to mark the start and end of the ride and the miles at each turn. (See the map legend for a complete list of the symbols used.) Some of the routes contain alternative starting points that will let you turn a long ride into a shorter ride or take the easy way around some tough hills.

The write-up for each ride should give you enough information to complete the route as long as you take some time to prepare. If you are familiar with the roads of the ride, then the Miles and Directions section should be all you need to follow the route.

If you are unfamiliar with the area of the ride, spend some time preparing for it. The map provided with each ride is meant to give you an overview of the route. It is not a full street map but does show most of the major roads and towns and should provide sufficient points of reference for completing the route.

Bike rides always looks different when you're actually riding the route. Two-dimensional maps cannot fully communicate the actual route, so if you are riding in an unfamiliar area, it is recommended that you also bring along other, more-detailed maps in case you get lost. Good choices are printouts of the relevant New Jersey Bike Map or a Hagstroms County Map.

The route directions contain mileage for each turn on the ride. Although the actual miles on your bike computer may be slighter higher or lower than those provided, you should be able to calculate the distance to the next turn and know pretty quickly when you go off course.

VIRTUAL RIDES

If you really want to prepare for the ride and make sure you don't get lost, you can do a quick virtual bike ride to check out the route. Go to Google Maps (http://maps.google .com/) and type in the city and state where the ride is starting. You will be presented with a map of the area. If you click on the "Satellite" button on the map, you will see a satellite view of the area with the roads overlaid on the map. You can zoom in or out and move the map to view the roads of the ride.

The satellite images available for New Jersey are quite detailed, and you can really get a good idea of the type of roads you will be riding on. Sometime you can even tell whether the road has a shoulder. The satellite images can be five to ten years old, so they don't show the current conditions. But since most roads don't change that often, the images are usually pretty accurate. The one thing that is hard to tell from the satellite view is the type of terrain and how hard a particular climb is. Other than that, the Google Map is the next best thing to doing the ride.

The key to having a good ride is knowing both the route and your abilities. Taking the time to study the route directions and map will make it much easier to follow the route when you do the ride. I recommend clipping the ride directions onto the handlebars so that you can easily get the information about the next turn. Some of the turns are bunched together and come up quickly, so it's good to know the distance for the next two or three turns so that you don't ride by them. You should also keep the any additional maps in an easy-to-reach place in case you get lost or need to make a detour.

If you know your abilities on the bike, you will know the distance, terrain, and speed that you can handle and never start a ride that you will regret.

Above all, ride safely and have fun.

Ride Terms

In the ride description and Miles and Directions, I have tried to be consistent with the terms used to describe the turns, roads, and traffic conditions. Below is a list of the terms.

- For turns besides the usual turn left or right (bear left or right), you will sometimes see acute or hard left or right to indicate that the turn is greater then 90 degrees. Turns will also be marked quick left or right to indicate that the next turn is very close to the last turn (usually within 0.25 mile).

- All major climbs are indicated in the ride description and Miles and Directions sections. A major climb is anything over 100 feet in the central and northern part of the state and anything over 50 feet in the southern part of the state. The ride description will contain the word uphill to indicate terrain that is not considered a climb but will still cause you to downshift a few gears.

- To describe traffic conditions I have used the words light, moderate, and heavy or busy. Light traffic means that on average you will encounter a car every two to five minutes. Moderate traffic means that you will encounter a car every minute or two and there may be short periods when there will be a constant flow of cars. Heavy traffic means a constant flow of cars. These estimates are subjective and can change over time as certain areas become more populated. It is good to be constantly on the lookout, even on roads that have almost no traffic.

Your Mileage Will Vary

Every effort has been made to make the ride mileage as accurate as possible. The distance between each turn should be accurate to better than 0.1 mile, and the overall ride distance should be within 1 percent. The mileage that you will see on your bicycle computer will most likely be a little higher or lower. This is caused by a couple of factors.

First, most bicycle computers are not as well calibrated as a car's odometer. To calibrate the odometer on your bicycle computer, you have to accurately measure the circumference of the front wheel to a millimeter or small fraction of an inch and enter this number into the computer. If this number is off just a little, it can make a big difference in how accurate the odometer is. For example, say that your calibration is off by just 0.5 percent. This means that each mile you ride you will be off by 0.05 mile. This may not sound like a lot, but after 10 miles your odometer will be off by 0.5 mile, by 20 miles it will off by 1 mile, and by 40 miles it will be off by 2 miles.

The other main factor that contributes to your mileage being off is that you will probably not do the ride exactly as it is mapped out. You may reset your odometer in the parking lot before the mileage for the ride starts. You may have to turn around to retrieve a dropped water bottle. At the rest stops you may walk or ride your bike 0.1 mile or so. If you miss a turn, you have to double back. All these little things add a tenth of a mile here or there, and before long you are a mile or two off.

As long as you understand the difference between the mileage you see on your bicycle computer and the mileage provided in Miles and Directions, you should have no problem using it along with the road signs and landmarks described in the ride narrative to find your way along the route without getting lost.

Road and Traffic Conditions

About New Jersey Hills

People who are not familiar with New Jersey think it is a very flat state. While it is true that New Jersey doesn't have the large elevation changes of Colorado or other Rocky Mountain states, there are some very steep climbs that would challenge even experienced hill climbers. The northwest part of the state is particularly hilly, and although there aren't many individual climbs greater than 400 or 600 feet, there are a lot of ups and down and very few places where the road is flat. The series of hills can be constant and unrelenting and will have a cumulative effect over the course of the ride.

A lot of the roads in New Jersey were created from old farm roads and trails, so some roads are much steeper than would be created for cars today. This surprises a lot of people who are unfamiliar with the state, so keep this in mind when deciding which rides to do.

This book does contain some hilly rides that will challenge experienced riders, but I have avoided some truly tough hills, like Fiddlers Elbow, that are very steep and can be dangerous for all but elite riders. Some of the rides in this book do go very close to these hills, so if you enjoy the pain of a tough climb, it would be easy to make a detour to satisfy your desire.

How hard a particular climb is can be very subjective. A 200-foot climb that one person considers easy may cause another rider to run out of gears and have to walk up the last part. The description in this book of the toughness of each climb is based on how it felt to me. I consider myself an average climber. At 5 feet 11 inches and average weight for my size, I am not one of those skinny people who can just spin up any hill. I would like to add thirty pounds to the back of their bike and then see how well they climb. Although there are some tough hills here, with a little training and the right gearing, anybody should be able to climb most of the hills in the state.

The Weird Roads of New Jersey

People who drive the back roads of New Jersey know how confusing, strange, and downright weird they can be. Many roads are known by one or two different names, and sometimes roads of the same name actually meet each other, so when the ride directions say "make a left turn from River Road onto River Road," it's not a typo but just another messed-up set of roads that are so common here. The problem is that

Barnegat Lighthouse, one of New Jersey's many scenic delights ▶

most of the back roads in New Jersey weren't planned. They just sort of happened as early settlers created trails to connect towns to one another. These trails eventually became the chaotic mess of roads that we have today.

This mess that is the New Jersey road system is actually a good thing for bikers. There are lots of interconnected roads far from the main highways that are fun to ride and have some real character. Almost every road has an interesting history and a story to tell. This is why New Jersey is the birthplace of weirdness as documented in the popular cult magazine *Weird NJ* (www.weirdnj.com) and its various spin-offs.

To help you navigate the roads, I include the route number (if the road is a county road) along with the road name. When there is a major change in the road name, this is indicated in the Miles and Directions. I also include alternative road names in parentheses when a road may be known by another name. New Jersey's back roads are strange and confusing, but they are a lot of fun to explore.

Going Beyond the Rides

These rides have been designed to help show you the best roads to ride in as many areas of the state as possible. There is a lot of variety to the types of rides in this book. There are short, long, flat, and hilly rides and everything in between, so there is no doubt that you will find a ride that fits your style. A lot of rides in this book are close to or partially overlap another ride. This makes it easy to combine short rides to make longer ones or combine pieces of two or three rides to make a new ride.

There are many other rideable roads around the routes shown in this book. Using a resource like New Jersey Bike Map, it is easy to find some other roads to lengthen or shorten the ride, go around a tough hill, find a hard hill to climb, or locate an interesting landmark.

The thirty-five rides in this book cover a good part of the state, but I know there are many more rides out there. Even though New Jersey is a small state, there are more than a hundred unique rides that you could do in this state and still not see it all.

Using a combination of New Jersey Bike Map, some kind of mapping program, and Google Maps, it is easy to plan your own route. New Jersey Bike Map will help you find starting points, food stops, and the best roads to ride on. Using the "Satellite" view on Google Maps, you will be able to view a street-level map superimposed on detailed satellite images that will help you get a feel for the types of road you will be riding on.

You can then use an online mapping tool like MapMyRide.com or a dedicated program like Street Atlas USA by DeLorme or Microsoft's Streets and Trips to plot out the exact route of your ride and print out route directions and maps.

Expanding the area you ride in and exploring new routes breaks the monotony of doing the same rides over and over again. Exploring is infectious. Once you get started it's hard to stop, and it's even more fun if you can find others who will join you for the journey.

Safety and Comfort on the Road

Bike riding, like any other sport, comes with its own set of problems and safety risks. These risks can be greatly reduced by following some simple rules and using common sense.

- Be visible. The most important safety rule is to always be visible. Accidents happen when people don't see what's coming. In addition to wearing bright colors and reflective material, make sure that you can be seen from all angles when you are riding. Never shadow a car around a corner or weave in, out, or around parked or moving cars.

- Signal your intentions. Besides being visible, it's important that other people on the road know where you are going and when you are going to make a turn. This includes the usual hand signals for left and right turns as well as signaling for stopping and changing lanes. I prefer to signal left turns with the left arm pointed left and right turns with the arm pointed to the right. I don't like using the left arm pointed up at the elbow to signal right turns because it confuses some people. Clearly signaling your intentions will help you earn some respect from other motorists and also let the other riders on the ride know where you are going. It's also not a bad idea to yell out "Right turn," "Left turn," or "Stopping," as some riders tend to look around at intersections and may miss the hand signals.

- Ride predictably. When riding, especially in traffic, it is important to be predictable so that other vehicles on the road know where you are going. Try to ride in a straight line in the same part of the road as much as possible. Do not weave in and out, even when riding around parked cars. As the road gets wider or narrower, anticipate the change and slowly drift in or out.

- Anticipate and call out hazards. When riding on any road, you will have to navigate around potholes, bumps, grates, and other hazards. Try to keep your eyes constantly scanning ahead for hazards so that you don't have to make any sudden moves. Call out and point to the hazards as you go by them so that other bikers in the group are aware of them and can adjust their line accordingly to avoid them.

- Wear a helmet. A helmet is the most important piece of safety gear to wear while riding. If you ride enough miles, eventually you will take a fall. And when you do, you have a much better chance of getting up and riding away if you're wearing a helmet. It's also a good idea to wear glasses to keep the rocks, bugs, and other debris out of your eyes. I also highly recommend having a mirror on your helmet, glasses, or handlebars. A mirror allows you to see behind you quickly without having to turn your head around.

- Know and obey the law. Like every other state, New Jersey has a set of laws that apply to bicyclists. It's good to be familiar with the laws and try to abide by them. (See the appendix for a link to the New Jersey bike laws.) For the most

Sharing the road when entering Sandy Hook

part, bicyclists must follow the same laws as a car and must obey all traffic signs and signals.

- Know the traffic patterns. When riding on busy roads, it is good to know the traffic patterns so that you know when to avoid certain roads. If you are unfamiliar with the roads you think may have a lot of traffic, plan to avoid them during rush hour on weekdays, which is usually between 7:00 and 9:00 a.m. and 5:00 and 7:00 p.m. Saturday and Sunday mornings are usually the best time to ride to avoid traffic.

- Beware of other bikers. The most dangerous thing on the road is not cars but other bikers in your own group. Far more bikers get hurt by riding into one another than get hit by cars. When riding in a group, a split second's inattention can lead to bumping wheels or clashing handlebars, and then down goes the whole group. Avoid this by riding in an orderly manner and continually calling out signals as you turn, slow down, and stop.

- Don't do stupid things. A lot of bike accidents are caused by people doing stupid things. I have seen bikers run red lights, make sudden or illegal turns, weave around cars at a stoplight, and many other things that can get them—and others—hurt. Eventually their luck will run out. Remember to ride with common sense and good road manners, and you'll have a lot better chance of having a safe ride.

Riding in Traffic

Every effort has been made to design the rides in this book to uses the quietest back roads possible, but there will be times when traffic can't be avoided. During these times there are a few things you can do to reduce your risk of getting in an accident.

Riding in traffic is an art that is learned over time. Novice riders can be easily overwhelmed by traffic and make bad decisions. By using common sense and some best practices, you can greatly reduce your chances of being in an accident.

- **Ride defensively.** When riding in traffic, it is best to assume that no car can see you and that if they can see you then they are trying to hit you. This is a very paranoid attitude, but it will help you anticipate problems before they occur and have a plan to get out of any bad situation.

- **Communicate with the traffic.** As you ride, make sure you are communicating your intentions to the cars around you. This includes not only signaling turns and lane changes but also moving to the right when you see them coming up behind you, waving them around you when you are stopped, and thanking them for letting you make a turn. Do not use the one-finger wave to express your displeasure with someone's driving skills. As good as this gesture might feel, it almost always makes the situation worse.

- **Share the road.** Sharing the road works both ways. Just as car drivers should be courteous to bikers on the road, bikers need to be polite to cars by staying as far to the right as is safe, riding single file, and letting cars pass when possible. When riding in a group, never ride more than two abreast. If you see a car coming from behind, get into single file so that the car can easily pass the group. This will show drivers that you are trying to be courteous.

- **Learn to take the lane.** There will be times when you need to block a lane of traffic to safely negotiate an intersection. This is especially true when making a left-hand turn. The idea is to stay in the middle of the lane so that you are visible to the traffic that you are traveling with as well as to oncoming and cross traffic. To take a lane, first make sure it is clear, then signal your move with a hand signal and slowly move into the middle of the lane. Stay in the middle of the lane so that no cars can get around you. Once you negotiate the intersection, slowly slide back to the right to let cars get past you again.

- **Beware of parked cars.** When riding by parked cars, try to keep a door's width away. This may annoy some drivers who are trying getting past you, but it will prevent you from being taken out by somebody opening a car door without looking.

- **Maintain eye contact.** While riding in traffic, make sure you can see the eyes of anyone in a car that may cross your path. If you can see their eyes, then they can probably see you and are less likely to hit you.

- **Focus on riding.** It is easy to get distracted when riding in traffic, especially if you are riding though the center of a town. If you are looking at the sights or watching people on the street, you are not focusing on how best to get through the traffic. A moment's distraction can get you in trouble.

If you use these practices as you ride in traffic, they will become second nature and automatic over time. As you continue to ride in traffic, it will get easier. You will soon become comfortable and know how to handle any situation that occurs.

Planning for a Trouble-free Ride

Nothing is worse than a ride ended prematurely by a mechanical or physical breakdown. Although some problems are hard to avoid, with a little preventive maintenance and planning, you can be prepared to handle most problems and be able to ride home every time.

A trouble-free ride begins with preventive maintenance. Regular maintenance does not take much time, but it needs to be done on a regular basis. Before each ride you should:

- Pump up your tires. High-pressure tires lose a small percentage of pressure every day. If you don't pump up your tires before each ride, they are more likely to go flat.
- Check your brakes. It is a good idea to spin each tire and press the brakes to make sure the brakes work and the tires are not rubbing the brakes or the frame.
- Inspect the tires. Quickly check each tire for wear and pieces of debris that may be stuck in it.
- Inspect the gears. Look over your gears by the chain ring and the rear derailleur, and freewheel to make sure there is nothing stuck in the gears and there are no loose screws or frayed cables.

Every week or two you should perform the following maintenance and safety check on your bike:

- Lubricate your chain. Keeping your chain well lubricated will reduce wear on your drive train and help it last longer.
- Lubricate any other components on a bike that need it, such as pedals.
- Clean out the gunk. After miles of riding, dirt tends to accumulate on the underside of the down tube by the brakes and a few other places. Take a few minutes to knock off the dirt so that it doesn't corrode or wear out the moving parts.

Once or twice a season, spend some quality time with your bike and give it a full detailed cleaning, inspection, and adjustment. If you are not mechanically inclined, find a good bike mechanic to help you keep your bike properly adjusted and maintained.

Rides at a Glance

(Listed by category and distance)

Rambles

10–50 miles	New York Views Ramble/Challenge, Ride 1
11–70 miles	Sandy Hook Ramble/Challenge, Ride 23
12 miles	Atlantic City Boardwalk Ramble, Ride 33
14–35 miles	Long Beach Island Ramble, Ride 25
16 miles	Cape May Ramble, Ride 26
16 miles	Covered Bridge Ramble, Ride 10
18 miles	Great Swamp Ramble, Ride 2
18–30 miles	Twist and Tumble Ramble/Challenge, Ride 9
20 miles	Assunpink Park Ramble, Ride 17
23 miles	Princeton Tour Ramble, Ride 12
25 miles	Saddle River Ramble, Ride 3
27 miles	Mendokers' Bakery Ramble, Ride 20
28 miles	D&R Canal Ramble, Ride 11
28/84 miles	Belmar and Back Ramble/Classic, Ride 24

Cruises

30 miles	Sourlands Valley Cruise, Ride 13
32 miles	Jockey Hollow Hilly Cruise, Ride 8
38 miles	Rues Road Roller-Coaster Cruise, Ride 19
40 miles	Kittatinny Cruise, Ride 7
40 miles	Lindbergh Long Hill Cruise, Ride 15
40 miles	Clarksburg Cruise, Ride 18
41 miles	The Gap Cruise, Ride 4
43 miles	Hill Slug Cruise, Ride 14
43 miles	Rova Farm Cruise, Ride 21
45 miles	Medford Lakes Cruise, Ride 29
45 miles	Pine Barrens Cruise, Ride 31
50 miles	Batsto Village Cruise, Ride 28
54 miles	Zoo Cruise, Ride 32

Challenges

42 miles	High Point Hill Challenge, Ride 5
50 miles	New York Views Ramble/Challenge, Ride 1
50 miles	Milford to Merrill Creek Challenge, Ride 6
54 miles	Basic Training Challenge, Ride 22

The covered bridge on the Covered Bridge Ramble

Map Legend

══════════	Limited Access Freeway
▬▬▬▬ / ▬▬▬▬	U.S. Highway/ Featured U.S. Highway
———— / ————	State Highway/ Featured State Highway
———— / ————	County or Local Road/ Featured Road
✪	Capital
○	Town
🛡95	Interstate Highway
⬡1	U.S. Highway
⬡17	State Highway
■	Point of Interest
⊞	Picnic Area
❶	Starting Point
➤ 10.0	Mileage Marker
→	Directional Arrow
⬭	Reservoir or Lake
♠	State Park/Recreation Area
~~	River or Creek
/////////////	Large Park or Forest
≈≈≈	Swamp

North Jersey

North Jersey is usually divided into two parts: the northeast and the northwest. The northeast part of the state, where it borders New York City, is the most densely populated part of the state. If you want a quick tour of the congested part, just watch the opening credits of *The Sopranos* and you will see the chemical plants, highways, warehouses, and crowed neighborhoods of the northeastern New Jersey. Of course this doesn't give you the real view of the northeast. Yes, the region is crowded and congested and contains more than its share of ugly places, but this doesn't mean that you can't find a good bike ride. Bicycling is alive and well here.

Just head to the George Washington Bridge on a nice weekend morning, and you will see hundreds of people riding over the bridge to explore the roads in this area of New Jersey. Keep heading west into Bergen County and you will find a steady stream of bikers on the roads around the lakes and large houses that are part of this area. Just 26 miles from Manhattan is the Great Swamp, yet another great place to ride. This area of the state is a bit of an urban jungle, but as long as you're comfortable riding with a little traffic, there is plenty of biking to be found here.

The farther west you travel in the north, the more rural the area becomes. It's surprisingly empty at the northwest edge of the state, with a lot of quiet roads and scenic views of the rivers, hills, and valleys. This is a hilly area, so you will need some low gears and strong muscles to get around here. Don't let the hills keep you from this part of the state, though. Some of them are hard, but the views in this area are worth the pain.

1 New York Views Ramble/Challenge

New York, New York, a hell of a town. It can also be a crowded and congested place to try to ride a bike. There are, however, a few places along the Hudson River that are easy to ride and will give you spectacular views of New York City. This ride doesn't have a set route, but it does highlight the bike paths and rideable roads around the George Washington Bridge. You can easily put together a ride to fit your abilities.

Start: Hudson Terrace underneath the George Washington Bridge, Fort Lee, or Ross Dock Picnic Area.

Length: 10 to 50 miles out and back.

Terrain: If you stay on the bike paths by the Hudson River, the terrain is mostly flat. If you want to go a little farther north toward the Tappan Zee Bridge, you will have to climb the Palisades cliffs, which are short but steep. Once you are atop the Palisades, the terrain is mostly rolling hills.

Traffic and hazards: This is a very congested area of the state, especially at rush hour. These roads are best ridden on weekends, when there is much less traffic. The bike path by the Hudson will have no motorized traffic, but it can be crowded with hikers and bikes on nice summer days. The other roads outlined in this ride will always carry some kind of traffic. These roads are wide and for the most part have wide shoulders that make riding easy, no matter the traffic. These roads are also very popular with bikers riding out of New York, so cars are used to sharing the road. The worst part of this ride will be getting there. The George Washington Bridge approaches are busy no matter what time of day it is, so if you plan to ride in this area, your best bet is to do it early in the morning on weekends.

Getting there: From New Jersey take Interstate 80, the New Jersey Turnpike, or Route 4 and head east toward the George Washington Bridge. Eventually all these roads merge together to become Interstate 95. Stay in the local lanes and get off at the Fort Lee exit just before going over the bridge into New York. After the exit, head toward the Hudson River on Bridge Plaza South. This road parallels the roads going over the bridge and eventually ends at a T. The road in front of you is Hudson Terrace (County Road 505). To your left is the George Washington Bridge. Depending on the ride you want to do, there are a couple of places to park. For a totally flat ride, turn right onto Bigler Street. At the stop sign, turn left (east) onto Main Street, then keep in the right lane to bear right (south) at River Road. The southern park entrance will be on the left. Follow Henry Hudson Drive about 1 mile to the Ross Dock circle and follow signs (1A). To ride across the George Washington Bridge, turn left and park on Hudson Terrace as close to the bridge as possible (1B). The Palisades Interstate Park Web site (see this ride's Local Events/Attractions) includes directions to these parking areas and other parking areas on Henry Hudson Drive.

The roads described here will allow you to have some nice rides along the Hudson River with good views of New York City and the Palisades cliffs. There are three main routes you can use to create a bike ride that fits your ability and desire. All three routes are more or less out-and-back rides where you follow a road or bike path one

George Washington Bridge from the New York side

way and then just turn around and retrace your route to return. This will allow you to control the length of the bike ride—from a few miles to 50.

There are three easy-to-ride roads near the George Washington Bridge:

Henry Hudson Drive runs right along the Hudson River from the Edgewater–Fort Lee border, just south of the George Washington Bridge, to the Alpine Boat Basin, about 7 miles north. The road goes through Palisades Interstate Park and usually has no traffic on it.

Hudson Terrace more or less parallels Henry Hudson Drive but is more congested and carries a lot more traffic. The road is wide enough to accommodate both cars and bikes. It is also one of the main roads used by bikers coming out of New York to get to and from other roads in the area.

Route 9W parallels the Palisades Parkway. It's a busy road but has a wide shoulder. It's a designated state bike route, so even with traffic there is no trouble riding this road.

Route 1: Riding across the George Washington Bridge into the City

One of the best ways to get a great view of New York City is to ride across the George Washington Bridge. The entrance to the bridge sidewalk is on Hudson Terrace, just under the bridge. There are two sidewalks on the bridge, one on the north side and one on the south. The south sidewalk is usually the one that is open to bikers. There

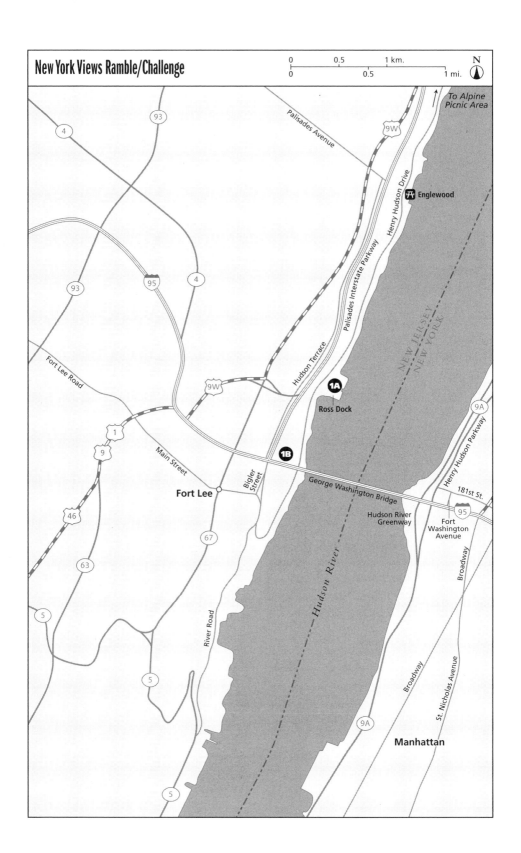

New York Views Ramble/Challenge

0   0.5   1 km.
0   0.5   1 mi.

N

To Alpine
Picnic Area

Palisades Avenue

9W

Henry Hudson Drive

Englewood

Palisades Interstate Parkway

NEW JERSEY
NEW YORK

4

93

95

4

93

Fort Lee Road

Hudson Terrace

9W

1A

Ross Dock

9A

1

9

Main Street

1B

46

Bigler Street

George Washington Bridge

181st St.

Henry Hudson Parkway

Fort Lee

63

67

Hudson River
Greenway

95

Fort
Washington
Avenue

5

Broadway

River Road

Hudson River

Broadway

5

9A

St. Nicholas Avenue

Manhattan

5

is a ramp from Hudson Terrace to the south sidewalk, so you can ride right onto the bridge. If the south sidewalk is closed, you will have to use the north one. To get to the north sidewalk, you have to climb a few flights of stairs from Hudson Terrace.

The sidewalk on the bridge is used by bikers, walkers, and runners and can be a little busy at times, so ride slow and watch out for others. If you're going to stop to take a picture, make sure you stay out of the way of other people using the sidewalk.

When you get to the other side of the bridge, go down a spiral ramp to 178th Street. There is a bike path close by on 181st Street called the Hudson River Greenway. To reach the greenway, head east (away from the river) on 178th Street for a couple of blocks and then turn left onto Fort Washington Avenue. Go a couple of blocks to 181st Street and make another left, going toward the river. Although you are riding on the streets of New York, as long as you don't ride these streets during rush hour, it's not too bad. Fort Washington Avenue even has a bike lane to ride in.

Make a left onto 181st Street, and go downhill toward the river. At the end of the street turn right and go down a walkway that leads to the Hudson River Greenway. This walkway is steep in parts, so keep it slow and watch out for people coming the other way. This walkway winds around, over, and under the Henry Hudson Parkway and eventually gets you to the greenway by the bridge.

The Hudson River Greenway is a multiuse path that runs along the river. From the George Washington Bridge you can ride north to the Cloisters Museum or south all the way to the south end of Manhattan. Like most areas in the city, the Hudson River Greenway can get congested pretty quickly on a nice day. It is best to ride this path as early in the morning as possible.

There are a couple of places where you can leave the greenway and explore other parts of the city. For example, on 90th or 78th Street you can ride a bike lane to Central Park. I would not recommend trying to ride on the streets of New York unless you are an experienced urban rider and are comfortable riding on busy urban streets. If you are up to the challenge, take a look at the excellent map put together by the NYC Department of City Planning (www.nyc.gov/html/dcp/html/bike/cwbm .shtml). The map shows the best streets and park paths to use when trying to ride in the city.

When you done exploring the city, just retrace your steps back to the George Washington Bridge and head back to your starting point.

Although you probably won't do this ride on a regular basis, it's fun to try for a change of pace.

Route 2: Flat Ride along the Hudson

If you want to stay in New Jersey and want a short, flat ride, then ride along the Hudson River on Henry Hudson Drive. This road runs from the Edgewater–Fort Lee border, just south of the George Washington Bridge, to the Alpine Boat Basin, about 7 miles north. There are a couple of places to park to ride this road. At the southern end you can park at the Ross Dock Picnic Area. At the northern end you can park at the Alpine Picnic Area and Boat Basin.

If you want to park at the midpoint Henry Hudson Drive, then park in the Englewood Picnic Area and Boat Basin. This is the best place to park if you are just going to ride the drive. From here you can ride a pretty flat road south toward the George Washington Bridge or north toward the Alpine Boat Basin.

If you choose to ride north, you will have to climb a steep hill for a little more than 0.25 mile until the road branches off and flattens out. From the parking lot of the Englewood Picnic Area and Boat Basin, climb a couple of switchbacks to get to Henry Hudson Drive. At the top of the second switchback, a road to your right heads north along the Hudson River. This is Henry Hudson Drive. (Continuing up the rest of the switchbacks would take you to Palisades Avenue, which connects to Hudson Terrace and Route 9W.) The advantage of parking at the Englewood Picnic Area and Boat Basin is that you are near all the rideable roads in the area and can choose whether you want to do any hills.

Besides the hill at the Englewood Picnic Area and Alpine Boat Basin, Henry Hudson Drive is relatively flat. This is a very scenic road to ride, with the Palisades cliffs on one side and the Hudson River on the other. This road goes through the center of Palisades Interstate Park—a narrow stretch of land on the Hudson that is 12 miles long and 0.5 mile wide at its widest, with 2,500 acres of wild Hudson River shorefront and uplands. The park contains a number of picnic areas and boat basins. With numerous hiking trails and scenic lookouts, it can be a great place to spend a day.

One thing you should know about Henry Hudson Drive is that because it runs along the Palisades cliffs, mudslides and falling rocks occasionally block the road. The park commission is good about updating the Web site with any road closing, so it's good to check the site before trying this ride.

Route 3: Hilly Ride on Route 9W

If you want a more challenging ride and don't mind a few hills, you can ride along Route 9W toward New York state and the Tappan Zee Bridge. For this ride it is recommended that you start at the southern part of Henry Hudson Drive and park at Ross Dock Picnic Area.

From here you can ride north on Henry Hudson Drive all the way to the Alpine Boat Basin. You will then take Alpine Approach Road to 9W. Alpine Approach Road goes from the Hudson River to the top of the Palisades, so you will do a little climbing. The climb is about a 7 percent grade for about a mile, in which you will climb about 400 feet. Watch out for oncoming bikers, who usually come down the hill at a high rate of speed. You know you are coming to the end of the climb when you see the park headquarters buildings on your right. Just past this point is the entrance to the Palisades Parkway. You can't ride on the Palisades Parkway, so bear left and then turn left and go under the parkway. The road comes to a T; this is Route 9W.

From here you can ride as far north as you want. The road is easily rideable all the way up to the Tappan Zee Bridge and beyond. Route 9W is a designated bike route and has nice wide shoulders to ride in. It's a very popular road with bikers, and many use it to get out of the New York area to some nice roads in northern New Jersey and southern New York. The road goes along the top of the Palisades cliffs and is a little hilly, and you will encounter a number of rolling hills as you ride north.

You can also ride south on 9W from the Alpine Approach Road to Palisades Avenue. There is a wide shoulder most of the way. However, south of East Clinton Avenue the shoulder disappears and you have to ride in the right lane of a two-lane road. This can be OK if you are riding in a group but can be tough if you are riding alone. Avoid this section of 9W if you can. Continuing south past East Clinton Avenue, you eventually run into Palisades Avenue. This is where you need to get off 9W—it is no longer a designated bike route and becomes really congested. Make a left here; go east (toward the river) and take Hudson Terrace or Henry Hudson Drive back to your starting point.

Miles and Directions

0.0 Starting point: N40° 51.286' / W73° 57.771'

NOTE: There are no miles and directions for this ride.

Local Events/Attractions

Palisades Interstate Park lies along the Hudson River by the George Washington Bridge. It's 12 miles long and 0.5 mile wide at its widest, with 2,500 acres of wild Hudson River shorefront and uplands, including some of the most impressive sections of the Palisades. The park has a number of different picnic areas, hiking trails, and boat launch ramps, and Henry Hudson Drive is a great road for biking. For more information, visit www.njpalisades.org.

Accommodations

Hilton Fort Lee: 2117 Route 4 East, Fort Lee; (201) 461-9000; www.hilton.com.

Holiday Inn: 2339 Route 4 East, Fort Lee; (201) 944-0623 or (800) 972-3160; www .ichotelsgroup.com/h/d/hi/1/en/hotel/FTLEE

Maps

DeLorme: New Jersey Atlas and Gazetteer: Pages 33 B21 and 27 N22.

New Jersey Bike Maps: Central Park, Yonkers, Nyack; www.njbikemap.com.

New York City Bike Map: www.nyc.gov/html/ dcp/html/bike/cwbm.shtml. This map shows all the best streets and park paths to use when riding in New York City.

The Great Swamp

2 Great Swamp Ramble

The Great Swamp sits in the southeast part of Morris County. This 7,600-acre eco-logical preserve is home to many plants and animals and provides a stopover for migrating birds. The area in and around the Great Swamp is one of the flatter parts of Morris County and a good place to ride. This ramble takes you on an easy 18-mile loop around the swamp.

Start: The ride starts at the intersection of New Vernon and Meyersville Roads in Meyersville.
Distance: 18-mile loop.
Terrain: The terrain around the Great Swamp is mostly flat, although you will have to go over a few small hills. None of the hills are hard to get over; most are short and not very steep.
Traffic and hazards: Most of the roads don't have any shoulders, but traffic is light. Southern Boulevard has moderate traffic but does have a shoulder. These roads can be busy during rush hour, but weekend traffic is light.

Getting there: From Interstate 287 take exit 30A (Basking Ridge/North Maple Avenue) and bear right onto North Maple Avenue. Go through the traffic light at Madisonville Road (ignore the refuge sign pointing left at Madisonville Road) and continue on North Maple. North Maple bears left after 1 mile and becomes South Maple Avenue. Continue on South Maple Avenue for 1 mile and turn left onto Lord Stirling Road. Continue on Lord Stirling through a short gravel section and then go over a bridge. The road becomes Whitebridgr Road. A couple of miles after the bridge, make a right onto New Vernon (Long Hill) Road. Continue south into the village of Meyersville. Parking is available at the tennis courts just before the intersection of New Vernon and Meyersville Roads.

In 1959 the land that is now the Great Swamp was proposed as the fourth airport for the New York area. Fortunately, through the efforts of a lot of volunteers, enough money and objections were raised to turn the land into wildlife refuge. The Great Swamp, situated just 26 miles west of Manhattan's Times Square, is now a beautiful ecological preserve that's home to a wide variety of bird and animal species, wildflowers, and other plants.

The mileage for the ride starts at the intersection of New Vernon and Meyersville Roads in Meyersville. There is a little mini-circle here in the center of the village. Start the ride by heading west on Meyersville Road. The roads in this area are relatively quiet, with a few gentle ups and downs. There is a little hill on Long Road, but it's short.

At the end of Carlton Road you will come to a T. The bridge to your left goes over the Passaic River and leads to Lord Stirling Park. Turn right here onto Whitebridge Road and enter the Great Swamp. After about 2 miles turn left onto New Vernon Road and head through the heart of the swamp. The name of the road changes to Long Hill Road—no relation to the Long Hill Road that you were on.

In about a mile you will see a gravel parking lot for the Wildlife Observation Center on your left. This is a good place to stop if you want to do a little hiking to observe the flora and fauna. There are usually some volunteer guides at the center who will give you maps and answer any questions you have.

Continue past the Wildlife Observation Center and cross two small bridges. To the right of these bridges are some of the wetland areas where birds congregate. It's a good place to stop and enjoy the view.

Before Long Hill Road actually becomes hilly, turn right onto Pleasantville Road and ride along the northern part of the swamp. Once you make a right on Village Road and the next right on Green Village Road, you will be out of the Great Swamp.

When you make a right onto Green Village Road, the sign may read SPRING VALLEY ROAD, since that road is just to the left. In a couple more turns, pass a small shopping center and then make a right onto Southern Boulevard.

Southern Boulevard is a moderately busy road, but there is a good shoulder to the right that you can ride in. Watch the mileage, and don't miss your right at a light onto Fairmount Avenue. This road is not as wide as Southern Boulevard, but it has less traffic. In just under 2 miles, turn right onto Meyersville Road. This can be an easy turn to miss. If you cross River Road, you went too far. Once on Meyersville Road, it's just over 2 miles to where you started.

If you want to explore the Great Swamp some more, check out the Wildlife Observation Center on Long Hill Road. Since the Great Swamp contains some

Great Swamp Ramble

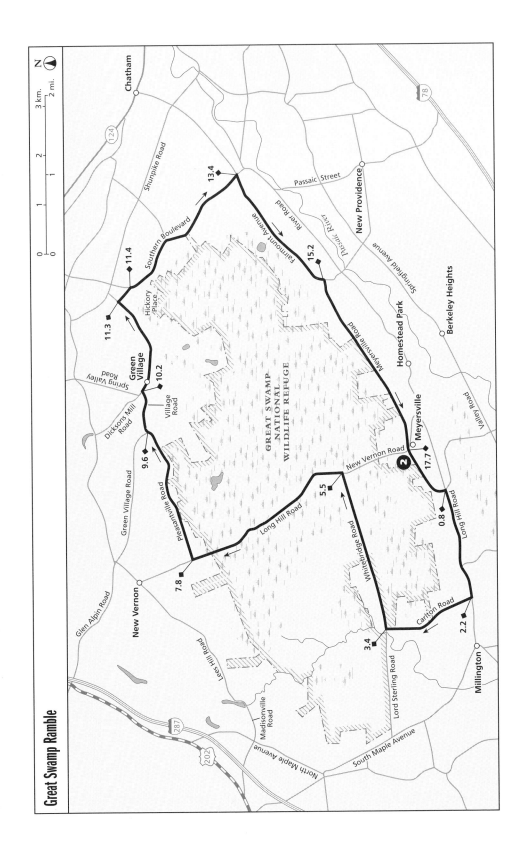

swampland, it is also home to a large number of insects—a fact not mentioned in the brochures. Most of these insects are more than happy to suck your blood, so if you're going to walk around, remember to bring some good bug repellent.

Miles and Directions

0.0 Start at intersection of Meyersville and New Vernon Road. Turn right onto Meyersville Road and head west. GPS: N40° 41.424' / W74° 28.264'

0.8 Turn right onto Long Hill Road.

2.2 Turn right onto Carlton Road.

3.4 Turn right at the T onto Whitebridge Road.

5.5 Turn left onto New Vernon Road.

5.9 New Vernon Road becomes Long Hill Road.

7.8 Turn right onto Pleasantville Road.

9.6 Turn right onto Village Road.

10.2 Turn right on to Green Village Road (road sign may say SPRING VALLEY).

11.4 Turn right onto Hickory Place.

11.4 Turn right onto Southern Boulevard.

13.4 Turn right at the stoplight onto Fairmount Avenue.

15.2 Turn right onto Meyersville Road.

17.7 Finish your ride in the town of Meyersville.

Local Events/Attractions

Great Swamp National Wildlife Refuge is an ecological preserve located in Morris County. The refuge comprises 7,600 acres of varied habitats and is home to more than 244 species of birds, plus fox, deer, muskrat, turtles, fish, frogs, and a wide variety of wildflowers and plants. The refuge contains numerous hiking trails for exploring the refuge and observing the flora and fauna. For more information on the refuge, visit www.fws.gov/northeast/greatswamp.

Restaurants

Casa Maya: 615 Meyersville Road, Meyersville (908) 580-0799. Delicious, authentic Mexican food doled out at this "funky little BYO" in the middle of the Great Swamp.

J. W. Ginty's, The Olde Meyersville Inn: 632 Meyersville Road, Gillette; (908) 647-6302. An upscale Irish pub in the historic Meyersville Inn.

Accommodations

Olde Mill Inn: 225 U.S. Highway 202 and North Maple Avenue, Basking Ridge; (800) 585-4461; www.oldemillinn.com.

Maps

DeLorme: New Jersey Atlas and Gazetteer: Page 31 L18.

New Jersey Bike Maps: Chatham, Bernardsville; www.njbikemap.com.

3 Saddle River Ramble

Bergen County is the most populated county in New Jersey. Its extensive network of roads and proximity to New York City make it a popular and expensive place to live. Although this is a high-population area, the roads are well designed and easily rideable, especially on Sunday, when the blue laws are in effect. This ramble will take you on a quick tour of the northeast part of the state and show you some of the reservoirs and large houses in the area.

Start: Parking lot of Lyons Park on Lake Street in Upper Saddle River.

Distance: 24.4-mile loop.

Terrain: Rolling, with a few small hills. There are no major climbs on this route, but there are lots of ups and downs. There is one short but steep climb of about 200 feet and a couple of easier 100+-foot climbs, but nothing that is terribly difficult.

Traffic and hazards: This is a busy area of the state with moderate to heavy traffic, so you will be doing some urban riding. The roads are fairly wide, making it easy for cars and bicycles to share the road. As long as you are comfortable riding in traffic, you'll have no problem riding here. On Sunday the blue laws close all the shopping malls, causing a noticeable reduction in traffic.

Getting there: Take the Garden State Parkway north to exit 172. At the end of the exit ramp turn left onto Grand Avenue. Follow Grand Avenue (which will eventually turn into Lake Street) for 1.6 miles to the entrance to Lyons Park, on your right just after you cross East Saddle River Drive.

The Saddle River area is filled with expensive homes, including the homes of a number of actors and sports stars. Although densely populated, the area is still very rideable for a number of reasons. First, the roads in Bergen County are, for the most part, very wide. This makes it easy for cars and bikes to share the road. There are also lots of roads, so it is easy to find ones with less traffic. During the week a lot of these roads are very busy, but on weekends—especially Sunday—there is much less traffic. Bergen County is one of the few places in the United States that still have blue laws, forcing most stores to close on Sunday.

Although there aren't a lot of rural roads to ride here, as long as you are comfortable riding with traffic, this area has a lot to offer. The best time to ride is early in the morning, especially on Sunday.

To start the ride, turn left out of Lyons Park onto Lake Street and cross over the Saddle River. The river lies in a valley, so once you cross it, the only way is up. After crossing East Saddle River Road, you have a short but steep 200-foot climb up the toughest hill you will have to climb on this ride. After this hill the road becomes Grand Avenue; there will be a few more rollers ahead.

Just before you cross Chestnut Ridge Road, Grand Avenue changes to a two-lane road with no shoulder. This stretch is tough to ride during rush hour, when people

One of the smaller mansions in Upper Saddle River

are entering or leaving the office buildings here, but riding this area early on week-ends is no problem.

After crossing Spring Valley Road, Grand Avenue turns back to a wide single-lane road. Be careful going through the town of Montvale; there can be a lot of traffic here at times. Almost 5 miles from the start of the ride, Grand Avenue ends at a T. Turn right onto Middletown Road, followed by a quick left onto Blue Hill Road.

The next couple of turns take you around Lake Tappan, a reservoir that provides drinking water to New Jersey. The northern part of Lake Tappan that you are riding around is actually in New York, so you have crossed the state line.

After crossing a bridge over the reservoir you will be riding on Hunt Road, which you take to Blaisdell Road. After riding on Blaisdell Road for about 0.5 mile, you will be back in New Jersey and the road becomes Orangeburgh Road.

When you make the right onto Old Tappan Road you will see a shopping center; watch the traffic here. Turn right onto Washington Avenue. You are back on a quiet road, viewing Lake Tappan again from the southwest end. Washington Avenue winds along Lake Tappan, then bends left away from the reservoir and changes names to Poplar Road. Make a couple of turns and go through a residential neighborhood and past a golf course. Be careful when you are on Broadway. This road can be a little busy at times, especially by the small group of stores.

Saddle River Ramble

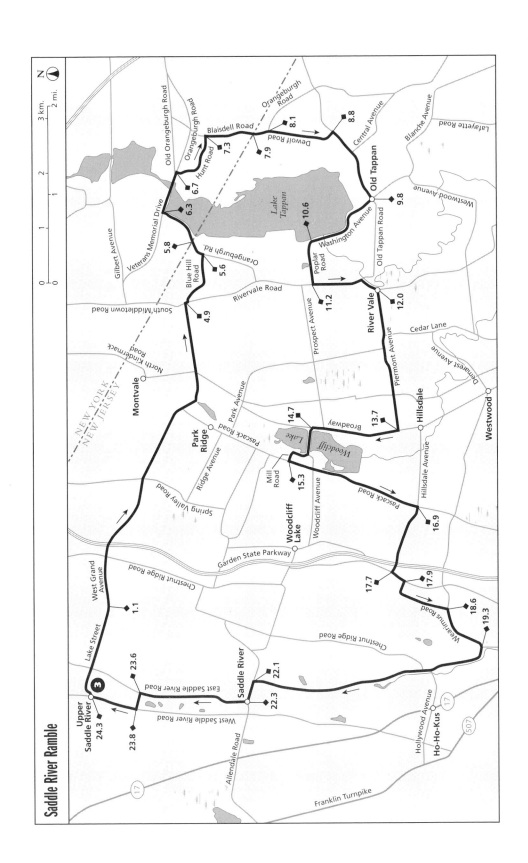

Woodcliff Avenue takes you across Woodcliff Lake, another of the area's reservoirs. After crossing the lake, turn right onto Mill Road, which follows the lake for a little bit. This road ends at a T where it meets Pascack Road (unsigned). The roads in this area are moderately busy at times but are wide enough to allow cars and bikes to share the road as long as you stay to the right.

Hillsdale Road takes you up a little climb over the Garden State Parkway. Turn left at the light onto Wearimus Road, followed by a quick right and a climb up a small hill to stay on Wearimus. Wearimus Road curves around a little, coming to a T after 0.7 mile. The street sign on the corner may say WASHINGTON AVENUE, but when you make a right here, the road is still called Wearimus. The road now traverses a nice downhill. At the bottom of the hill the road makes a long bend to the right. East Saddle River Road comes in from the left; watch for cars entering the road here. At this point the road you're on becomes East Saddle River Road.

You are now riding north through the lower part of Saddle River. The river itself is just to your left, and you will see glimpses of it as you ride along the road. This is an expensive residential area, and you will see a number of nice homes on both sides of the road. This is a popular road, so expect to see a number of other bikers.

Go through the town of Saddle River and continue on East Saddle River Road, heading into Upper Saddle River. Take some time to look around; there are some nice homes here.

A little less than 1.3 miles after you go through town, Locust Lane is on your right. Turn left here onto Upper Cross Road (which is not well marked). This road crosses over the river and ends at a T where it meets West Saddle River Road. Turn right here and continue riding north for about 0.5 mile to a traffic light. Turn right here onto Lake Street. This road goes downhill slightly and curves left then right. At the apex of the right curve is the entrance to the park where you started. Turn left into the park to finish the ride.

Although this is a high-population area, there is no reason that you can't ride here. There are many other places to ride around here, especially if you head north into New York. Search the Web for additional routes. (Check the link under Local Events/Attractions for a number of routes in the Hudson Valley.)

Miles and Directions

0.0 Start at the Lyons Park parking lot in Upper Saddle River, and turn left onto Lake Street. N41° 3.565' / W74° 5.759'

1.1 The road changes names to Grand Avenue; stay on Grand.

4.9 Turn right onto South Middletown Road.

4.9 Make a quick left onto Blue Hill Road.

5.6 Turn left onto Orangeburgh Road.

5.8 Cross into New York; the road again becomes Blue Hill Road.

6.3 Turn right onto Veterans Memorial Drive.

6.7 Turn right onto Hunt Road.

7.3 Turn right onto Blaisdell Road.

7.9 Cross back into New Jersey; Blaisdell Road becomes Orangeburgh Road.

8.1 Bear right onto Dewolf Road.

8.8 Turn right onto Old Tappan Road.

9.8 Turn right onto Washington Avenue.

10.6 The road bends to the left and becomes Poplar Road.

11.2 Turn left onto Rivervale Road.

12.0 Turn right onto Piermont Avenue.

13.7 Turn right onto Broadway.

14.7 Turn left onto Woodcliff Avenue.

15.0 Turn right onto Mill Road.

15.3 Turn left onto Pascack Road (unsigned).

16.9 Turn right onto Hillsdale Avenue.

17.7 Turn left onto Wearimus Road.

17.9 Turn right to stay on Wearimus Road.

18.6 Turn right to stay on Wearimus Road.

19.3 The road name changes to East Saddle River Road.

22.1 Turn left onto Allendale Road.

22.3 Turn right onto East Saddle River Road.

23.6 Turn left onto Upper Cross Road.

23.8 Turn right onto West Saddle River Road.

24.3 Turn left onto Lake Street.

24.4 Turn left into Lyons Park to complete the loop.

Local Events/Attractions

Bike Hudson Valley: (www.roberts-1.com/ bikehudson/index.html). This Web site contains a lot of good information on bike routes in this part of New Jersey and New York.

Restaurants

Saddle River Inn: 2 Barnstable Court, Saddle River; (201) 825-4016. French and New American food in the casual elegance of a 150-year-old rustic barn.

Accommodations

Best Western The Inn at Ramsey: 1315 Route 17 South, Ramsey; (201) 327-6700 or (800) 678-5683 (reservations).
Residence Inn by Marriott Saddle River: 7 Boroline Road, Saddle River; (201) 934-4144 or (800) MARRIOTT (reservations); www.residenceinnsaddleriver.com.

Maps

DeLorme: New Jersey Atlas and Gazetteer: Pages 26 D13 and 27 D15.
New Jersey Bike Maps: Park Ridge, Nyack; www.njbikemap.com.

4 The Gap Cruise

The Delaware Water Gap is a cut in the Appalachian Mountains where the Delaware River traverses the ridge. The river in this area is surrounded by the Delaware Water Gap National Recreation Area, which comprises more than 70,000 acres of unspoiled wilderness. The gap is a popular place for canoeing, hiking, camping, and fishing. This out-and-back ride takes you through several different regions. There aren't many roads here, but the ones available are very scenic and a joy to ride. Because this is an out-and-back route, you can adjust the ride to fit whatever distance you are in the mood for.

Start: Parking lot of Kittatinny Point Visitor Center, underneath the Interstate 80 bridge.
Distance: 41.1 miles out and back.
Terrain: Even though you will be riding near the Delaware River, the terrain is moderately hilly. By Millbrook Village there is a good steep climb of 200 feet outbound and 400 feet

inbound that will have you shifting into your lowest gears.
Traffic and hazards: Delaware Water Gap is a popular area on a nice summer day. The area by the visitor center will have moderate traffic on nice weekends, but traffic will lighten considerably once you travel a few miles north.

Getting there: From I-80 west take exit 1. At the bottom of the ramp, turn left and head back under I-80 into the Kittatinny Point Visitor Center parking lot. If you're heading east on I-80, the visitor center will be at the bottom of the ramp.

The Delaware Water Gap and surrounding park is one of the biggest recreation areas in the Northeast. This area has a lot to offer those who enjoy the outdoors, including canoeing, camping, hiking, fishing, and of course biking. (Check out www.nps.gov/DEWA for information on the park's facilities.)

Because this is a rural part of the state and most of the area is devoted to parkland, there aren't many roads here. The main road you will be riding is Old Mine Road (County Road 606), thought to be one of the oldest roads in the country. It was used in colonial times to transport ore from the copper mines along to the Delaware all the way up to what is now Kingston, New York. Much of the original road has been modernized and is now part of U.S. Highway 209. However, the part by the gap has been kept undeveloped and maintains most of its rural charm.

This ride starts at the Kittatinny Point Visitor Center. Before leaving the parking lot, make sure you have enough food and water for the ride you are planning. There are a couple of historic villages and campgrounds along the route where you can probably find water, but it is best to be self-sufficient for this ride.

To start the ride head north back toward I-80 from the visitor center parking lot. Pass under the bridge and continue straight, watching out for traffic entering from your right off I-80. There is a stoplight ahead, which seems strange since there is no intersection at the light. The light is used to alternate the north- and southbound

Riding along Old Mine Road

traffic on the one-lane road ahead. Please obey the traffic signal—the road ahead is narrow in places, and oncoming traffic will have a hard time seeing you.

Once through the light, you'll climb a small hill. Although maps show Old Mine Road (CR 606) following the Delaware River, this does not mean the road is flat or right next to the river. Old Mine Road runs slightly above the Delaware on a ridge, so you will only have occasional glances rather than a constant view of the river. Although the road has a number of ups and downs as it follows the ridge along the Delaware, there are no major climbs along the next 12 miles, just a series of rolling hills.

As you continue north you will go through Worthington State Forest. This thickly wooded area is really beautiful and quiet. There are a number of parking areas, campgrounds, and boat ramps, but for the most part this area is just empty forest. The only cars on the road will be the ones going to the campgrounds or hauling canoes upstream. You will mainly have the road to yourself.

After about 9.5 miles you will climb a pretty long uphill section before intersecting another road at 12 miles. Turn left at the T onto Millbrook Flatbrook Road (Old Mine Road on some maps). You will see Millbrook Village on the right just after the turn.

Millbrook Village is a re-created 1800s community where aspects of pioneer life are exhibited and occasionally demonstrated. If you need a break, feel free to take a walk around. There are restrooms here, and you can probably get some water.

If you are looking for a short, easy ride, this is a good place to turn around—a couple of real climbs lie ahead.

Beyond Millbrook Village is a steep climb of about 200 feet over 0.5 mile. You will then cruise along the ridge for a while, with occasional views to your left of the valley below. Right after Blue Mountain Lakes Road, there is a general store where you might be able to get some food. The store doesn't have set hours, so there is no guarantee that it will be open. After you pass Blue Mountain Lakes Road, there is a steep downhill ending at a T. Watch your speed here.

At the T you have a choice of which way to go. Going left will keep you on Old Mine Road and along the Delaware. The only problem with this route is that the last 2 miles of the road are packed gravel. If you're on a mountain bike or hybrid, this won't be problem, but the packed gravel can be a little annoying if you are on a road bike. It's not impossible to ride packed gravel on a road bike, and a number of road bikers ride the gravel here on a regular basis.

If you are uncomfortable riding on packed gravel, turn right at the T onto Walpack Flatbrook Road. Both roads merge in about 6 miles, so no matter which way you go, you will end up at the same place.

If you choose to go left, you will be on one of the most remote roads in the area. Old Mine Road continues along the Delaware, affording occasional glimpses of the river. There are very few houses on this road and almost no cars or people, just the surrounding forest. The views along the road are extremely scenic, and after a few miles you feel very remote, almost in a scary way (think Blair Witch). Five miles after the turn, the packed gravel begins at a Y. The road to the left is part of the original Old Mine Road and is not well maintained. Bear right and continue up a hill. This road is unmarked, but on maps it is called Pompey Road. After about 2 miles on the gravel, intersect County Road 615 (Walpack Flatbrook Road). Turn left here and continue north.

If you turned right back at the T, you will ride for a little while along Big Flat Brook and will probably see a number of people fishing. You are now riding though the Walpack Wildlife Management Area, encountering a few hills as you continue. After 5.5 miles the road bears left and goes down a nice hill. At the bottom is the gravel road you would have come out of had you turned left at the T.

Continue on CR 615 for a little less than a mile to the Walpack Inn. This is the northernmost point of this ride and where you will turn around and start heading back. The Walpack Inn is one of the only restaurants in the area, but the food here is good and the people friendly. It's a good place to stop for lunch. Even if you don't want a full lunch, you can probably use the restroom and get some water.

Once you are ready to head back, just start riding south on CR 615. Even though you are retracting the same roads back to the start, the scenery in this area is worth a second look. Option: If you took the gravel part of Old Mine Road on the way up, you can stay on CR 615 and ride through the Walpack Wildlife Management Area for a change of scenery.

The Gap Cruise

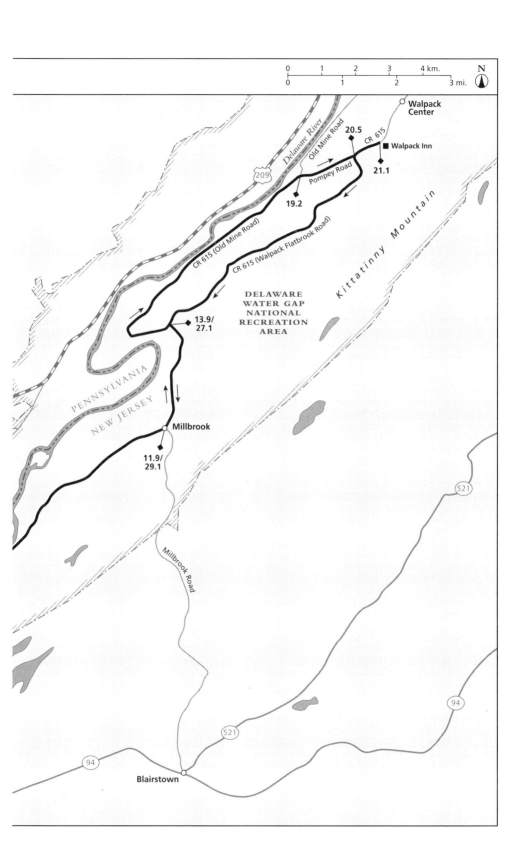

0   1   2   3   4 km.

0   1   2   3 mi.

N

Delaware River

Walpack Center

209

Old Mine Road

CR 615

20.5

Walpack Inn

Pompey Road

21.1

19.2

CR 615 (Old Mine Road)

CR 615 (Walpack Flatbrook Road)

Kittatinny Mountain

DELAWARE WATER GAP NATIONAL RECREATION AREA

13.9/ 27.1

PENNSYLVANIA

NEW JERSEY

Millbrook

11.9/ 29.1

Millbrook Road

521

521

94

94

Blairstown

On the way back you will have the hardest climb of the ride. After about 6 miles of heading south on CR 615 from the Walpack Inn, you are back at the intersections of CR 615 and Old Mine Road. Turn left here and cross the bridge, heading back toward Millbrook Village. This is a steep climb—about 400 feet in only a little over 0.5 mile. The top of the climb is by the general store. If it is open, it's a good place to take a break.

After the climb, ride along the ridge for a short stretch before reaching a steep downhill that ends by Millbrook Village. Turn right after the village and continue heading south on Old Mine Road. It's now a straight shot back to the start. You will have some rolling hills for the next 12 miles, but they will seem small after the last climb.

Back at the visitor center, head down to the beach for a closer look at the river and the gap. You can even take a swim if you want to cool off. The Delaware Water Gap is a great place for outdoor activities, so if you enjoy hiking and canoeing, it can be a great place to spend a couple of days.

Miles and Directions

0.0 Head north out of the visitor center parking lot and pass under I-80. N40° 58.322' / W75° 8.016'

0.3 Go straight at the traffic light. You are now on CR 606 (Old Mine Road).

11.9 Turn left toward Millbrook Village to stay on Old Mine Road.

13.9 Climb a steep 200-foot hill and then head steeply downhill. At the bottom of the hill turn left onto Old Mine Road. The last part of this road is gravel. (Option: To avoid the gravel, turn right here onto CR 615 (Walpack Flatbrook Road), which will intersect the route at Mile 20.5.)

19.2 Bear right at the Y where the road turns to gravel onto an unmarked road (Pompey Road).

20.5 Turn left at the T onto CR 615. (If you didn't take the gravel road, this is where you return to the route.)

21.1 Arrive at the Walpack Inn, your turnaround point. (This is a good place to get a good meal and take a break before the return ride.)

21.1 Head south from Walpack Inn on CR 615 (Walpack Flatbrook Road).

27.1 Turn left onto Old Mine Road. There's a steep 400-foot climb here followed by a steep decent after 1.5 miles.

29.1 Turn right after Millbrook Village to stay on Old Mine Road.

41.1 Arrive back at the visitor center.

Local Events/Attractions

Delaware Water Gap National Recreation Area is a 77,000-acre wilderness area administered by the National Park Service. There are numerous campgrounds, boat launch ramps, hiking trails, and historic areas throughout the park. For more information about all there is to do at the gap, visit www.nps.gov/dewa.

Restaurants

Walpack Inn: Route 615, Walpack Center; (973) 948-3890. A nice country restaurant with good food and friendly service. The inn is located in one of the most scenic parts of the Delaware Water Gap National Recreation Area, so the views from the restaurant are wonderful.

Accommodations

Budget Inn & Suites: I-80 exit 308, East Stroudsburg, Pennsylvania; (800) 597-2914

New Jersey Bike Maps: Stroudsburg, Portland, Bushkill, Flatbrook, Lake Maskenozha; www .njbikemap.com.

Maps

DeLorme: New Jersey Atlas and Gazetteer: Pages 18 N5, 22 I7, and 23 E15.

5 High Point Hill Challenge

For those who like to climb, there is a certain appeal to finding the highest point in the state. At 1,803 feet, High Point State Park is that place in New Jersey. The park offers scenic views of Pennsylvania, New York, and New Jersey. This ride takes you on a loop from Dingmans Ferry on the Delaware River to High Point and back. This is a hilly ride, which is why it is designated a challenge, but the ride should be accessible to an average hill climber who doesn't mind a few 300+-foot climbs.

Start: Dingmans Ferry Bridge parking lot, Dingmans Ferry, Pennsylvania.
Alternative starting point: Dingmans Falls Visitor Center parking lot, Dingmans Ferry, Pennsylvania.
Distance: 42.1-mile loop.
Terrain: Rolling to hilly. This is the hilliest region of New Jersey, so there will be a lot of ups and downs. There are a couple of climbs of around 300 feet and a number of steep 100+-foot

climbs. The hilliest part of the ride is the 4.4 miles on Deckertown Road, which has a series of climbs. No single climb is that hard, but the cumulative effect makes this ride tough.
Traffic and hazards: This is a very rural area, so traffic will be light for the most part. There are some towns and intersections that will be busy. Four miles of this ride are on Route 23, which can be a busy road, but it does have a shoulder to ride in.

Getting there: Take U.S. Highway 206 to Tuttles Corners, at the junction with Dingmans Road (County Road 560). Take CR 560 west and cross the Dingmans Ferry Bridge over the Delaware River. Make the first left into the parking lot and pay the fee. To avoid the parking fee, you can park at Dingmans Falls Visitor Center. To reach the Dingmans Falls parking lot, continue on CR 560 after crossing the Dingmans Ferry Bridge. Turn left onto U.S. Highway 209, followed by the next right onto Johnny Bee Road. The visitor center parking lot is a mile up the road. To start the ride, retrace your route back to the Dingmans Ferry Bridge.

At 1,803 feet, the highest point in New Jersey isn't very high, but it's high enough to make this ride a challenge. The ride starts out in Dingmans Ferry, Pennsylvania, which is at 400 feet. If you do the math, you will be climbing at least 1,403 feet. Of course the cumulative amount of climbing will be a little more because of the ups and downs along the way.

High Point Hill Challenge

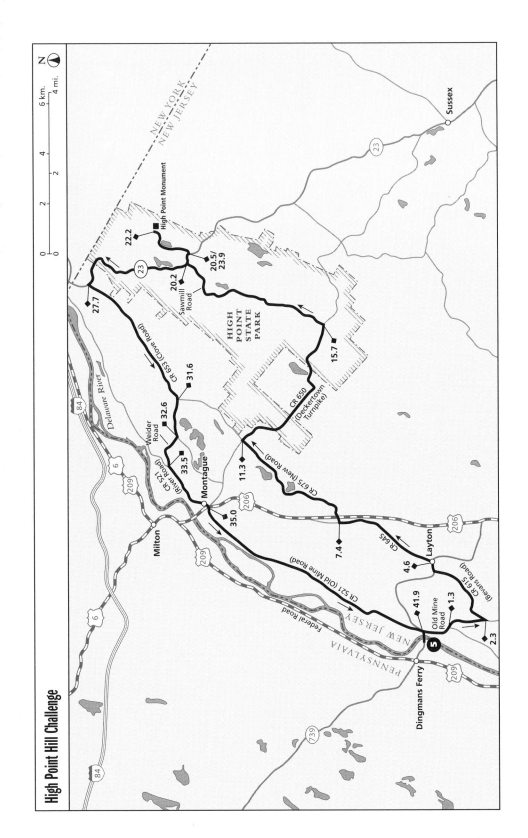

All downhill from here

There are many tough climbs in the area, but this ride was designed with the average biker in mind. None of the individual climbs is overwhelming. This ride should be in reach of any bike rider who has done some hill training and doesn't mind doing a few 300- or 400-foot climbs.

This ride starts on the Pennsylvania side of the Dingmans Ferry Bridge, in the parking lot on the left just after you cross the bridge. To start the ride, take the path out of the parking lot on the south side, turn right onto the road, and head back over the bridge into New Jersey. The Dingmans Ferry Bridge is one of the last privately owned toll bridges in the country. This beautiful, nostalgic bridge may be old, but it is well maintained and has survived a number of floods over the years. The toll keeper stands in the middle of the road on the Pennsylvania side, but there is no charge for bikers crossing the bridge.

After you cross the bridge, make a hard right at the next intersection onto Old Mine (Walpack) Road. There are no road signs here, so just follow the signs toward Peters Valley. There is not much time to warm up as the road immediately begins to climb. The climb is about 300 feet, followed by a few more little rollers. This road ends in the middle of Peters Valley, where three roads meet—Walpack, Kuhn, and Flatbrook. Peters Valley is widely known as a craft center; many craftspeople teach their varied crafts and display their work here. Except for the annual fall craft fair, this area is pretty quiet. From here you will continue on to the town of Layton. There is a general store as you enter the town if you want to take a break. The next few turns have you riding though some rolling hills and nice farmland.

When you make the right onto Deckertown Turnpike, the real climbing begins. The road starts out with a steep little 80-foot climb followed by an easier but longer 300-foot climb and then a series of smaller ups and downs that are somewhere between 80 and 100 feet. Deckertown doesn't have many flat sections, but it gets a little easier as you continue on. After 4.4 miles on Deckertown, you will see a road on your left at the bottom of one of the hills. This is Sawmill Road and has signs pointing you toward High Point.

Sawmill is the best road of the ride. This is a nice forested area with almost no traffic. In 2.5 miles pass picturesque Sawmill Pond. It's worth a quick stop here to enjoy the view.

Sawmill Road eventually takes you to Route 23. This can be a busy road at times, so stay in the shoulder and be careful when you make the left into High Point State Park.

There is no park entrance fee for bikers, so there is nothing stopping you from reaching the monument except a little more climbing. Continue on the park road and follow the signs to the monument. There are a number of restrooms along the road if you want to stop for a break or to get some water.

The steepest part of the ride is the climb right after the lake as you go around the back of the hill up to the monument. You will be using your lowest gears, but it is a short section and you should be able to tough it out. If it is a clear day you will have some spectacular views of New Jersey, New York, and Pennsylvania from the monument. A snack stand at the bottom of the monument offers a small selection of food and drinks.

Now that you have reached the monument, the phrase "It's all downhill from here" is almost true. Although there are some rolling hills to come, for the most part there are no more major climbs for the rest of the ride.

To return to the ride's starting point, follow the park road to Route 23 and head toward Port Jervis. Route 23 will have moderate traffic, but it has a shoulder to ride in. Some parts of the road are a little steep, so watch your speed. Toward the bottom of the hill, after 3.8 miles, you will turn left onto Clove Road (County Road 653). You are now back in the valley and will be on quiet, scenic roads for most of the way back.

Just before you make the right turn onto Weider Road, there is a little strip mall on your left that contains a deli and is a good place to take a break. As you approach US 206, bear left at the Y then cross US 206. Old Mine Road is straight ahead just off to your left. Once on Old Mine Road, you have a nice, quiet 7-mile ride back to the Dingmans Ferry Bridge. Although the Delaware River is just to your right, you really won't get a good view of it.

After 6.7 miles on Old Mine Road, intersect County Road 560. Turn right here and go back over the Dingmans Ferry Bridge. The road and bridge are narrow, so watch out for cars as you make the turn. After you cross the bridge, turn left back into the parking lot and return to your start point. If you still have some energy left, Dingmans Falls are a mile away just off Johnny Bee Road. The falls are worth the trip if you have the time.

Miles and Directions

0.0   Start by turning right out of parking lot. Cross the Dingmans Ferry Bridge back to New Jersey. N41° 13.196' / W74° 51.704'

0.4   Make a hard right turn at the first intersection onto Old Mine Road (County Road 521). Head toward Peters Valley and the 280-foot climb ahead.

1.3   The road's name changes to Walpack Road. (Old Mine Road turns right here and becomes gravel.)

2.3   Make a hard left at the center of Peters Valley onto County Road 615 (Kuhn Road), which becomes Bevans Road.

4.3   Turn right at the town of Layton onto CR 560 (Rahoche Lane). Stop at the general store on the left if you need a break.

4.6   Turn left onto County Road 645 (Layton Haineville Road).

7.4   Turn right onto Country Road 675 (deli in strip mall on left). Be careful as you cross US 206.

11.3   Turn right onto County Road 650 (Deckertown Road). There's a tough series of climbs ahead.

15.7   Turn left onto Sawmill Road and head toward High Point.

20.2   Turn right onto Route 23. This is a busy road, so stay in the shoulder. There's a short climb here.

20.5   Turn left into High Point State Park.

22.2   Follow the park road to High Point Monument. There are some short but steep climbs right after the lake.

22.2   Take a picture to prove you made it, then ride back to entrance of the park. It's almost all downhill from here. (Really!)

23.9   Turn right onto US 23. This is another busy road; stay in the shoulder. There are long downhill stretches ahead.

27.7   Turn left onto Clove Road (CR 653).

31.6   Bear right where Clove Road meets New Road to stay on Clove. There's a food store on the left just before the turn onto Weider Road.

32.6   Turn right onto Weider Road.

33.5   Turn left onto County Road 521 (River Road).

35.0   Bear left at the Y and then cross US 206 onto Old Mine Road.

41.7   Turn right where Old Mine Road meets CR 560.

41.9   Cross Dingmans Ferry Bridge into Pennsylvania.

42.1   Turn left into the parking lot to complete the ride.

Local Events/Attractions

Delaware Water Gap National Recreation Area is a 77,000-acre wilderness area administered by the National Park Service. There are numerous campgrounds, boat launch ramps, hiking trails, and historic areas throughout the park. For more information about all there is to do at the gap, visit www.nps.gov/dewa.

Dingmans Falls and Visitor Center: Dingmans Ferry, Pennsylvania, (570) 828-2253. Dingmans Falls is one of the most popular waterfalls in northeastern Pennsylvania. Easy-to-traverse trails, bridges, and even a boardwalk make access to Dingmans Falls, Silver Thread Falls, and other neighboring waterfalls very accessible. For more information visit www.nps.gov/DEWA/planyourvisit/dingmans-falls.htm.

High Point State Park Sussex County, is the location of the highest point in New Jersey. In addition to the monument at High Point, the park has a beautiful lake for swimming, camping facilities, a number of hiking trails, plus cross-country skiing in the winter. For more information, visit www.state.nj.us/dep/parksandforests/parks/highpoint.html.

Restaurants

Walpack Inn: County Road 615, Walpack Center; (973) 948-3890. A nice country restaurant with good food and friendly service. The inn is located in one of the most scenic parts of the Delaware Water Gap National Recreation Area, so the views from the restaurant are wonderful.

Accommodations

Red Carpet Inn: 240 U.S. Highway 6, Milford, Pennsylvania; (570) 296-9444; www.redcarpetinnpa.com.

Maps

DeLorme: New Jersey Atlas and Gazetteer: Pages 18 H9 and 19 D15.
New Jersey Bike Maps: Lake Maskenozha, Culvers Gap, Milford, Port Jervis South; www.njbikemap.com.

⑥ Milford to Merrill Creek Challenge

Warren and Hunterdon Counties have some of the most scenic vistas in the state. These vistas are best seen from the top of the hills. This challenging, hilly ride takes you from the Delaware River in Milford up to the Merrill Creek Reservoir and back. Along the way you will have some great views of the countryside as you climb your way up the mountains.

Start: Parking lot in front of church on Church Street, Milford.
Distance: 50.3-mile loop.
Terrain: This is one of the hilliest rides in the book. The ride starts out flat as you ride along the Delaware River, but the climbing begins once you head east. There are numerous 100-foot climbs, a couple of 400-foot climbs, and one long 640-foot climb up to Merrill Creek. There are also some steep downhills that require caution but are a lot of fun.
Traffic and hazards: This is a very rural area, so traffic will be light. There may be moderate traffic in the towns of Milford and Bloomsbury.

Getting there:
From New Hope, Lambertville, and south: From the Lambertville side of the Delaware River, drive north on Route 29 (North Main Street). Continue north on Route 29 through Stockton to Frenchtown, where the road ends. At the stop sign turn left onto Bridge Street, then take the first right

onto Harrison Street (Route 619). Turn left at the first traffic light onto Bridge Street and then turn right onto Church Street (1 block before the Delaware River bridge, with a drive-in bank on the corner). Park in the lot on your left in front of the church.

From New York City, Newark Airport, Clinton, and points east and north: Take Interstate 78 west to exit 11 (Pattenburg). Go off to the right (BE CAREFUL TO YIELD) and curve around left over the expressway to the only stoplight. Once through the light you are on the Pattenburg Road (Route 614). Stay on Route 614 through Pattenburg and Little York (5.2 miles) to Joseph's Little York Tavern. You must go left there to stay on Route 614. Continue 2.7 miles, passing a church on the right and then heading downhill toward a stop sign. Turn left onto Route 519 (Milford-Warren Glen Road). In about 3 miles pass the Milford Oyster House on the left. In just a couple of blocks, come to the only stoplight in Milford. Turn right at the light onto Bridge Street and pass some stores and restaurants. Look for Church Street (1 block before the Delaware River bridge, with a drive-in bank on the corner). Turn right onto Church Street and park in the lot on your left in front of the church.

Merrill Creek Reservoir is located in the hills of Warren County. It's a good, quiet place for fishing and hiking. This is a hilly area that provides pleasant scenic vistas. Riding here is very enjoyable as long as you don't mind climbing a few hills. If the idea of 2-mile-long 400- and 600-foot climbs doesn't scare you, then this is a ride you will want to try. The hills on this ride can be long and moderately steep in places, but if you are an experienced bicyclist who climbs on a regular basis, none of the hills on this ride should pose a serious challenge. There are much harder hills in the area, like Fiddler's Elbow (which would have made this ride a real challenge), but those roads were left off the route to keep it accessible to the average hill climber.

This ride starts in Milford on the parking lot on Church Street. Turn left out of the parking lot entrance where you came in, and follow Church Street toward the Delaware River.

For the first 9 miles you will be riding scenic if sometimes bumpy roads along the Delaware. There are some interesting cliffs to your right that have plants growing on them, including some cactus. When you get to Riegelsville, look for a bridge over the Delaware to your left. This small, interesting-looking suspension bridge was built by John Roebling, builder of the Brooklyn Bridge.

When you make the right onto Snyders Road (unmarked), the climbing begins. Most of the terrain from here on will be rolling to hilly. Still Valley Road starts with a steep 100-foot climb, so make sure you get into the right gear before making the turn here.

When you cross Route 173, the mountain you see ahead of you is where Merrill Creek is. If you look close you will see some radio towers at the top—that's where you are headed.

Eventually you'll enter the town Stewartsville and turn right at the center of town onto Washington Street. There is a food store on the far left corner if you need a break. This is the last spot for a break for the next 17 miles.

The intersection at Route 57, where you make a right followed by a quick left onto Montana Road, can be a busy intersection; use caution here.

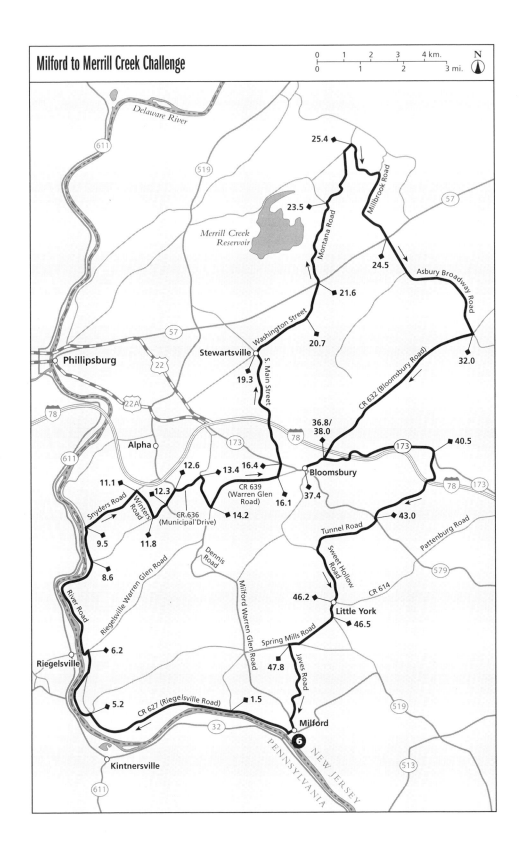

Milford to Merrill Creek Challenge

0   1   2   3   4 km.
0   1   2   3 mi.

N

Delaware River

611

519

25.4

Millbrook Road

57

23.5

Merrill Creek Reservoir

Montana Road

24.5

Asbury Broadway Road

21.6

57

20.7

Washington Street

32.0

Phillipsburg

22

Stewartsville

S. Main Street

CR 632 (Bloomsbury Road)

22A

19.3

78

36.8/38.0

40.5

22

Alpha

173

173

12.6

13.4

16.4

78

173

11.1

12.3

CR 639 (Warren Glen Road)

Bloomsbury

Snyders Road

Winters Road

CR 636 (Municipal Drive)

16.1

37.4

43.0

14.2

Tunnel Road

Pattenburg Road

9.5

11.8

Dennis Road

Sweet Hollow Road

579

8.6

River Road

Riegelsville Warren Glen Road

CR 614

46.2

Milford Warren Glen Road

Little York

46.5

6.2

Spring Mills Road

Riegelsville

Javes Road

47.8

5.2

CR 627 (Riegelsville Road)

1.5

32

Milford

6

Kintnersville

PENNSYLVANIA

NEW JERSEY

519

513

611

Riding along River Road

Once on Montana, the real climbing begins. What lies ahead is a 620-foot climb over about 1.5 miles. The grade is more or less constant. There are no really steep spots, just a few places where the grade gets a little tougher. Just find a comfortable gear, and grind up the hill. The best way to find the right gear is to listen to your lungs and legs. If your legs hurt, shift down to ease the strain. If your lungs hurt, shift up to try to reduce your heart rate. If both your legs and lungs hurt, suck it up and make a mental note to do more hill training. Unfortunately, the only way to get better at climbing is to do a lot of it. Even with a lot of training, it never feels great to climb—it just feels less bad.

The nice thing about Montana Road is that it is tree covered, so even on a hot day you are in shade while you are climbing. Once you get toward the top, the trees thin out and you get some nice views of the valley below. Eventually you will see Richline Road. If you want to see the reservoir, turn left onto Richline and then left onto Merrill Creek Road and go to the visitor center. It's worth a stop on a nice day.

To skip the visitor center, continue on Montana Road to Millbrook. This road starts with a little downhill section then a surprising little uphill before a monster 640-foot downhill section. Watch your speed and be careful here—the tree cover makes it hard to see any bumps or potholes in the road. At the bottom of the hill by a light, cross Route 57 and enter the valley again. Just ahead is a 400-foot climb. This is not a steep climb, but it is annoying. It twists enough to look like there is just 50 feet left until you get around the next turn, only to see there is more climbing ahead.

Once over the top and around the hill, you're treated to some nice views of the surrounding farms and countryside. There are supposed to be some eagles in the area; if you get lucky you may see one.

The next few turns take you through some rolling hills toward the town of Bloomsbury. After you cross under I-78 and come to a T, turn left onto Route 173. This is a busy road, so stay to the right. In less than a 0.1 mile Brunswick Avenue merges into Route 173 from the right. Make a hard right turn onto Brunswick and follow it in to the town of Bloomsbury. There is a general store on the far right corner where Brunswick intersects Church Street. This is a nice place to stop, with tables out front where you can sit and relax.

When you're done with your break, follow Brunswick Avenue back to Route 173 and continue east. Since this is by an I-78 exit ramp, there is a lot of activity here. This is not a real pretty place for riding, but it is the only way out of this area. After a little while the shoulder gets better and the traffic becomes light. There are a number of ways out of Bloomsbury, most of them pretty; and since Bloomsbury sits in a valley, all ways out require a major climb. The easiest ways out are Turkey Hill and Tunnel Road. Both require about a 500-foot climb. Turkey is a little more scenic but has a couple of steep spots. For this ride, continue on Route 173 until you see Tunnel Road. Make a right here and start the climb. This nice, constant grade lasts over 2 miles. There are no real steep sections, so just find a comfortable gear and grind up the hill.

Tunnel Road ends at a T. Turn left then make a quick right onto Sweet Hollow. You now have a beautiful 3-mile winding, scenic stretch of mostly downhill road. It almost makes all the climbing worth it.

After enjoying Sweet Hollow, continue through some scenic back roads and end up back in the town of Milford on at Church Street. No doubt, after all the climbing you're ready for a good meal. Milford has a number of nice little places to eat. Check out the Lovin' Oven for a quick bite or the Ships Inn for a beer.

Miles and Directions

0.0 Start at the parking lot on Church Street. Turn left out of the parking lot and follow Church Street around to the left. N40° 34.091' / W75° 5.822'

0.1 Turn right onto Spring Garden Street.

0.3 The road's name changes to River Road.

1.5 The road's name changes to Riegelsville Road (County Road 627).

5.2 Turn left onto Old River Road.

6.1 Turn left onto Riegelsville Road (CR 627).

6.2 Make an acute left turn onto Riegelsville Warren Glen Road.

6.6 Turn right onto River Road.

8.6 Turn left at T and then bear right to stay on River Road.

9.5 Turn right onto Snyders Road (unmarked). The climbing begins (120 feet).

11.1 Turn right onto Winters Road.

11.8 Turn left onto Creek Road.

12.3 Bear left and merge with County Road 519.

12.6 Turn right onto Municipal Drive.

13.4 Turn right onto Still Valley Road. There's a steep little 100-foot climb here.

14.2 Turn left onto County Road 639 (Warren Glen Road).

16.1 Turn left onto Maple Drive. (Follow sign for County Road 637.)

16.4 Cross Route 173. The road's name changes to South Main Street (CR 637).

19.3 Turn right in the middle of Stewartsville onto Washington Street. There's a food stop on the far left corner and a small climb ahead.

20.7 The road's name changes to Stewartsville Road.

21.6 At the end of Stewartsville Road make a right then a quick left onto Montana Road. There's a long 620-foot climb ahead.

23.5 Bear right at Richline Road. (Option: If you want to see Merrill Creek, make a detour here. Turn left onto Richline and then left onto Merrill Creek Road to the visitor center.)

25.4 Turn right onto Millbrook Road. There are some nice downhills ahead; use caution.

28.5 Cross Route 57 at the light. The road's name changes to Asbury Broadway Road.

29.4 Start a 400-foot climb followed by some nice rolling hills.

32.0 Turn right onto County Road 632 (Bloomsbury Road).

36.7 Turn left after passing under I-78 onto Route 173.

36.8 Make an acute right turn (almost a right U-turn) onto Brunswick Avenue.

37.4 Stay on Brunswick Avenue until it intersects Church Street (general store on far-right corner).

38.0 After your stop, take Brunswick back to Route 173 and continue east. This is a busy road; stay in the shoulder.

40.5 Turn right onto Tunnel Road. Start a 480-foot climb out of Bloomsbury.

43.0 Turn left at the T onto Route 579 (Bloomsbury Road), followed by a quick right onto Sweet Hollow Road. There's a beautiful 3-mile downhill ahead.

46.2 Go through the town of Little York. The road becomes County Road 631 (Little York Mount Pleasant Road).

46.5 Bear right onto County Road 614 (Spring Mills Road).

47.8 Turn left onto Javes Road.

49.8 Turn left onto County Road 519 (Water Street).

50.1 Turn right at the light onto Bridge Street.

50.3 Turn right onto Church Street and back to the parking lot where you started.

Local Events/Attractions

Merrill Creek Reservoir is a 650-acre reservoir surrounded by a 290-acre environmental preserve. This beautiful outdoor area provides great fishing, hiking, bird watching, and a number of other activities that allow people to interact with the natural environment. The visitor center offers a number of public programs. For more information, visit www.merrillcreek.com.

Restaurants

The Lovin' Oven: 17 Bridge Street, Milford; (908) 995-7744. This tiny, funky cafe in the heart of Milford serves breakfast and lunch every day except Monday and Tuesday. The baked goods are always fresh and delicious, as are the sandwiches and salads.

The Ships Inn: 61 Bridge Street, Milford; (908) 995-7744. This was the first brewpub in New Jersey and serves good food and drink with a British accent. It's a great place to enjoy a whole meal or just a simple snack.

Accommodations

Chestnut Hill on the Delaware: 63 Church Street, Milford; (908) 995-9761 or (888) 333-2242; www.chestnuthillnj.com. This elegant antique bed-and-breakfast right on the Delaware River was named the Best Overall Bed-and-Breakfast in North America in 2006.

Maps

DeLorme: New Jersey Atlas and Gazetteer: Pages 34 E9 and 28 N7.

New Jersey Bike Maps: Frenchtown, Riegelsville, Easton, Belvidere, Bloomsbury; www.nj bikemap.com.

7 Kittatinny Cruise

"Hope" and "tranquility" are two words that may come to mind as you ride in this quiet section of New Jersey. Maybe that's why they are also the names of some roads and towns in this rural area. There are also a lot of weird and scary legends about the area, so you will find Shades of Death Road and pass by Ghost Lake. The landscape is very scenic, so if you don't mind a few hills and some spooky places, this ride may help you achieve inner peace.

Start: Parking lot off Goodale Road, Kittatinny Valley State Park, Andover.

Distance: 40.2-mile loop.

Terrain: Rolling to Hilly. There are no major climbs on this route, but there aren't a lot of flat stretches either. There will be hills on both sides of you, and the valley you will be riding through has a lot of little ups and downs of 30 to 80 feet and a couple 100-foot climbs. There

are steep hills on both sides of this route, so if you want to do some real climbing, you can make some detours along the way.

Traffic and hazards: This is a very rural area, so traffic will be light. A couple towns and intersections will be busy, especially for the mile that you have to ride on U.S. Highway 46, but for the most part you will have to road to yourself.

Getting there: From Interstate 80, take U.S. Highway 206 north approximately 8 miles through Andover Borough. Do NOT turn right onto Limecrest Road where a sign directs you to Kittatinny Valley State Park. Continue 0.9 mile and turn right onto Goodale Road; follow it approximately 1 mile to the park entrance on the right.

Glacial lakes, rural landscapes, and quiet roads make this a beautiful area to ride through. It is especially nice in the fall when the leaves are changing. It is a hilly area, so you will have some ups and downs along the way. Because this route avoids most of the major hills in the area, this ride should be accessible to most riders. If you enjoy hills and want to make this ride more challenging, there are plenty of tough climbs on either side of this route that you can easily detour to.

Riding by the farms on the Kittatinny Cruise

This ride starts in Andover in the parking lot of Kittatinny Valley State Park. To start the ride, turn right out of the parking lot onto Goodale Road, a narrow road through the forest and farmland around Kittatinny. It's a quiet road with almost no traffic and a good way to start the ride. The road has some mild ups and downs, which characterize most of the roads that you will be riding. You'll wind around a few roads and eventually cross US 206. Here the road becomes County Road 611 (Springdale Greendale Road), which will have light to moderate traffic, depending on the time of day. The road has a small shoulder most of the way, so any traffic is not a problem. Continue to travel through some nice meadows and farmland.

When you get to County Road 519 (Dark Moon Road) you will be between the towns of Hope and Tranquility, which is a nice place to be. This road eventually passes through a small tunnel as you continue to follow CR 519 toward the town of Johnsonburg.

Once you pass around Johnsonburg, you have a nice 2.6-mile cruise on Bear Creek Road. This quiet road winds past some more forest and farmland, ending at a T where it meets the famous Shades of Death Road.

The first thing you will notice about the road is the road sign. It is not your usual pole with a sign atop it. As you can imagine, a road sign saying SHADES OF DEATH makes a popular souvenir, so the ones the town put up didn't last long. The traditional sign has been replaced with a metal post with the road names painted on it.

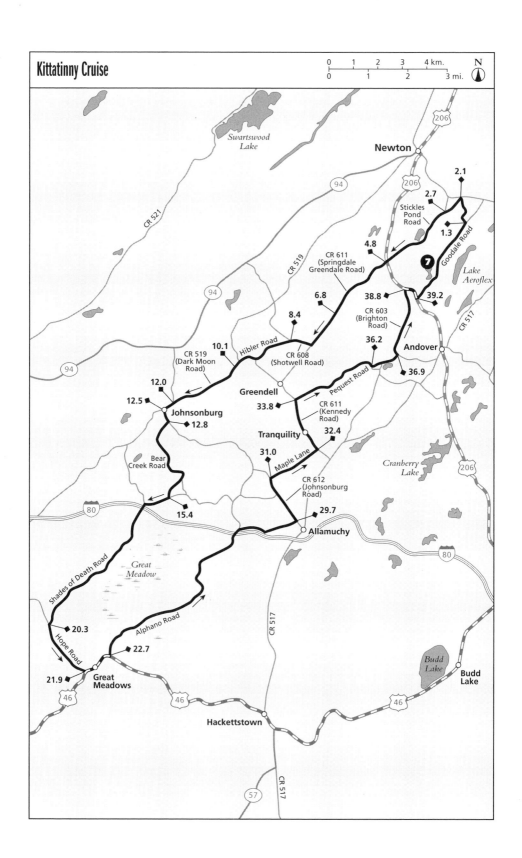

Kittatinny Cruise

0 1 2 3 4 km.
0 1 2 3 mi.
N

206

Swartswood
Lake

Newton

94

2.1

206

2.7

Stickles
Pond
Road

1.3

Goodale Road

4.8

CR 519

CR 611
(Springdale
Greendale Road)

7

Lake
Aeroflex

94

6.8

38.8

39.2

CR 603
(Brighton
Road)

CR 517

8.4

36.2

Andover

Hibler Road

CR 608
(Shotwell Road)

36.9

10.1

94

CR 519
(Dark Moon
Road)

Greendell

Pequest Road

12.0

33.8

CR 611
(Kennedy
Road)

12.5

Johnsonburg

12.8

Tranquility

32.4

Bear
Creek Road

31.0

Maple Lane

Cranberry
Lake

206

CR 612
(Johnsonburg
Road)

80

15.4

29.7

Allamuchy

80

Great
Meadow

CR 517

Shades of Death Road

Budd
Lake

Budd
Lake

20.3

Alphano Road

Hope Road

22.7

21.9

Great
Meadows

46

46

46

Hackettstown

57

CR 517

Turn right at the T and head down Shades of Death. Despite the name, this is a pretty road to ride. No one knows exactly how the road got its name, but there are many legends and ghost stories surrounding this road—all of which involve horrible unexplained deaths and warnings to stay out of this area. This has made this road one of the more popular subjects of *Weird NJ* magazine.

As you continue down the road you will pass Ghost Lake, named for the wraith-like vapor that forms on the lake on cool morning. Of course this has led to people reporting seeing actual ghosts, which has only deepened the weirdness surrounding this area and Shades of Death Road.

Shades of Death is a pretty tree-covered road, despite the legends, so enjoy the ride (but watch your back just in case). This road has some rollers, so you have some ups and downs. After about 3 miles, climb a 100-foot hill and then enjoy a nice downhill. At the bottom of the hill Great Meadow is to your left. This large meadow surrounded by hills has been used for farming since the time of the Lenni-Lenape Indians. To your right are the hills of Jenny Jump State Forest.

Shades of Death ends at a T; turn left here onto Hope Road (Route 611). (If you're interested in doing some hills, you can turn right here to do a loop through Jenny Jump State Park, which has some 200+- and 400+-foot climbs.)

Hope Road is a main road in this area, so traffic will be moderate to busy; stay to the right. Turn left onto US 46 to get through the town of Great Meadows. There will be traffic here—be careful. There is a liquor store on the right halfway through town if you need a break. You should be able to get some water and snacks there if you need them, but there is a better place to stop in 7 miles if you can wait.

After leaving town, turn left onto Alphano Road, another quiet country road. To your left is Great Meadow again and you will get some more views of it. Alphano continues to climb slowly around the valley. The road passes under I-80 and then parallels it for the next 2 miles until the road ends at a T. Turn left here onto County Road 612. If you need a break, there is a general store in the opposite direction on CR 612 about 0.25 mile up the hill in the center of Allamuchy. The town is by I-80 exit 19 and makes a good alternative starting point.

Once on CR 612, make a series of turns onto Maple Lane, Kennedy Road, and then Pequest Road and go through the town of Tranquility. There are some nice views around here as you cross small rivers and streams.

Continue to ride through some nice country on Pequest Road and go through another tunnel. Watch the directions, and make sure to keep turning to stay on Pequest until you reach County Road 603 (Brighton Road). This road will take you back to US 206, a busy road with a good shoulder. Be patient and careful making the left onto Goodale Road; this can be a hard road to cross at times. Once on Goodale Road, it is just a mile back to the parking lot in Kittatinny State Park. If you have some energy left, there are some hiking trails here. The short walk to the lake is a nice way to unwind after a ride.

Miles and Directions

0.0 Start at the parking on Goodale Road in Kittatinny State Park. Turn right out of the lot onto Goodale Road. N41° 1.036' / W74° 44.618'

1.3 Turn left onto Luchetti Way.

2.1 Turn left onto Yates Avenue.

2.7 Merge with Stickles Pond Road.

4.8 Cross US 206. The road's name changes to Springdale Greendale Road (CR 611).

6.8 The road's name changes to Wolfs Corner Road (CR 611).

7.9 Turn right onto Shotwell Road (County Road 608).

8.4 Turn left onto Hibler Road.

10.1 The road's name changes to Dark Moon Road (CR 519).

12.0 Turn left to stay on CR 519 where the road meets (Johnsonburg/Ramsey Road).

12.5 Turn left onto County Road 612 (Allamuchy Road).

12.8 Turn right onto Bear Creek Road.

15.4 Turn right onto Shades of Death Road. (Watch out for ghosts!)

20.3 Turn left onto Hope Road.

21.9 Turn left onto US 46. (You may be able to get some water and a snack at the liquor store on the right.)

22.7 Turn left onto Alphano Road.

29.7 Turn left onto Route 612 (Johnsonburg Road).

31.0 Turn right onto Maple Lane.

32.4 Turn left onto Kennedy Road (CR 611).

33.8 Turn right onto Pequest Road.

36.2 Turn left to stay on Pequest Road.

36.5 Turn left to stay on Pequest Road.

37.0 Turn left onto Brighton Road (CR 603).

38.8 Turn right onto US 206.

39.2 Turn left onto Goodale Road.

40.2 Turn right into the Kittatinny State Park parking lot to complete the loop.

Local Events/Attractions

Glacial lakes, limestone outcroppings, former railroads, and a small airport are features of **Kittatinny Valley State Park.** This scenic property is home to a variety of wildlife and is a great place for hunting, hiking, mountain biking, birding, fishing, and boating. For more information, check out www.state.nj.us/dep/parksandforests/parks/kittval.html.

Restaurants

Andover Diner: 193 Main Street, Andover; (973) 786-6641. Good local spot for a meal.
Bella Italia Pizzeria & Restaurant: 448 U.S. Highway 206, South Andover; (973) 940-8600; www.bellaitalia8600.com. Simple Italian cuisine.

Accommodations

Econo Lodge: 448 U.S. Highway 206 South, Newton; (973) 383-3922; www.econolodge.com

Maps
DeLorme: New Jersey Atlas and Gazetteer: Pages 23 G28, 24 G2, and 29 A19.
New Jersey Bike Maps: Newton East, Newton West, Tranquility, Blairstown; www.njbikemap .com.

8 Jockey Hollow Hilly Cruise

Jockey Hollow, just outside Morristown, is where George Washington and his troops spent two tough winters. He chose this location because the area's hills gave him an easy place to defend. This moderately hilly ride takes you around some of the hills in the area and shows you some nice parts of Morris and Somerset Counties.

Start: First parking lot after entering the park, Jockey Hollow, Morristown National Historical Park, Morristown.
Distance: 32.4-mile loop.
Terrain: The terrain in this area is hilly, and there aren't many flat parts. You will spend most of the ride going up and down a series of rolling hills. Plus there are two or three moderate climbs of around 250 feet. The main hilly parts are on Bernardsville Road and then on Tempe Wick Road on your way back to Jockey Hollow. None of the individual climbs is particu-larly difficult, but the cumulative effect of the rolling hills and moderate climbs can be tough if you are not use to hills. There are some really fun downhills to help you forget about some of the climbs. The middle of the ride through part of the Great Swamp is flat and will provide a nice change of pace.
Traffic and hazards: Most of the roads along this route don't have any shoulders, but traffic is light. The town of Basking Ridge can have heavy traffic, depending on the time of day you go through.

Getting there: From Interstate 287 South or North, take exit 30B (Bernardsville). At the traffic light turn right onto U.S. Highway 202 north. Turn left at the light for Tempe Wick Road (Route 646). (Note that the road has a different name on the right side; don't let this confuse you.) Continue on Tempe Wick Road for about another 1.5 miles. The entrance to the Jockey Hollow unit of Morristown National Historical Park is on your right. Park in the first lot on the left after entering the park.

In January 1777, after victories at Trenton and Princeton, General George Washington picked the town of Morristown for his troops to spend the winter. He picked the hills of Jockey Hollow for his encampment. Today Jockey Hollow is part of a national park that helps preserve some of the history of the Revolutionary War.

The mileage for the ride starts in the parking lot farthest from the visitor center. To start the ride, go back down the road you came in on and turn right onto Tempe Wick Road. The road starts out with a nice downhill. Enjoy it while you can, because no good downhill goes unpunished. Ahead of you is a steep little 80-foot climb on

End of the ride at Jockey Hollow

Talmage Road followed by some rollers then a downhill on Hilltop Road. This is a long, steep downhill, so be careful. Hilltop takes you to Bernardsville Road, where you start a long climb of about 240 feet and then go through some more rollers.

Bernardsville is home to a number of wealthy people, which is evident by the look of the houses along the road. The downhill once you make the left onto Lloyd will help you forget about the recent climb. Turn right onto Hardscrabble Road and enjoy 2 miles of winding down hills. This road is a little narrow, so keep an eye out for oncoming traffic.

Make a few turns, go under I-287, and enter the town of Basking Ridge. Watch out for traffic here. This is a good place to stop for a break; there are a number of delis and other places to get a quick snack. As you leave town, you make a couple of turns that head you toward the Great Swamp.

Once you get to Whitebridge Road, you enter the Great Swamp. After about 2 miles turn left onto New Vernon Road and head through the heart of the Great Swamp. The name of the road changes to Long Hill Road—no relation to the other Long Hill Road you were on.

In about a mile there's a gravel parking lot for the Wildlife Observation Center on your left. This is a good place to stop for a little hiking to observe the flora and fauna. There are usually some volunteer guides at the center who will give you maps and answer any questions you have.

Continuing past the Wildlife Observation Center, cross two small bridges. On the

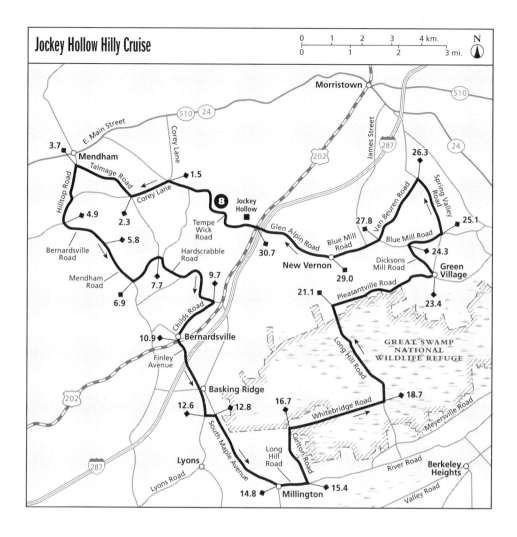

Jockey Hollow Hilly Cruise

0 1 2 3 4 km.
0   1   2   3 mi.   N

Morristown

510 24
510
24

E. Main Street
Corey Lane
James Street
287
26.3

3.7
Mendham
Talmage Road
202

Van Beuren Road
Spring Valley Road

1.5
Corey Lane
8 Jockey Hollow
27.8
25.1

4.9
2.3
Tempe Wick Road
Glen Alpin Road
Blue Mill Road
Blue Mill Road
24.3

5.8
Hardscrabble Road
30.7
New Vernon
Dicksons Mill Road
Green Village

Bernardsville Road
9.7
21.1
29.0
23.4

Mendham Road
7.7
Pleasantville Road

6.9
Childs Road

GREAT SWAMP NATIONAL WILDLIFE REFUGE

10.9
Bernardsville
Long Hill Road

Finley Avenue
Meyersville Road

202
Basking Ridge
18.7

12.6
12.8
16.7
Whitebridge Road

Lyons
South Maple Avenue
Long Hill Road
Carlton Road
River Road
Berkeley Heights

287
Lyons Road
14.8 Millington 15.4
Valley Road

Hilltop Road

right side of these bridges are wetland areas where birds congregate—good places to stop and enjoy the view.

Before Long Hill Road actually becomes hilly, turn right onto Pleasantville Road and ride along the northern part of the swamp. Once on Green Village Road, you are out of the Great Swamp.

Continue riding along relatively quiet scenic roads as you head back toward Jockey Hollow. The roads get a little hillier as you continue on. When you get to Glen Alpin Road, you start to encounter a few rolling hills. After crossing US 202, you start climbing. Although you have only a couple miles until the end of your ride, it will feel longer because you will be climbing most of the way. You can see why Washington chose Jockey Hollow. Anybody attacking him here would be too tired to fight once he climbed the hills.

At the entrance to Jockey Hollow, turn right and head up the last little hill to where you parked. If you have the energy left and want to ride a few more miles, take a loop on the tour road and explore some of the historic buildings in Jockey Hollow.

Miles and Directions

0.0 Make a right out of the entrance road that you came in. N40° 45.640' / W74° 32.572'

0.3 Turn right onto Tempe Wick Road.

1.5 Turn left onto Corey Lane.

2.3 Turn right onto Talmage Road. There are some moderate climbs here.

3.7 Turn left onto Hilltop Road. Watch your speed on the steep downhill here.

4.9 Turn left onto Bernardsville Road. There's more climbing ahead.

5.8 The road's name changes to Mendham Road.

6.9 Turn left onto Lloyd Road. There are some nice downhills ahead.

7.7 Turn right onto Hardscrabble Road, a narrow winding road.

9.7 Turn right onto Childs Road.

10.7 Make a left to stay on Childs Road.

10.9 Cross US 202. The road's name changes to Finley Avenue.

12.0 Cross Oak Street; the road becomes South Finley Avenue. You are in the middle of Basking Ridge.

12.6 Turn left onto Collyer Lane.

12.8 Turn right onto South Maple Avenue.

14.2 The road becomes Basking Ridge Road; there's another climb ahead (120 feet).

14.8 Bear left at the five-point intersection onto Long Hill Road.

15.4 Turn left onto Carlton Road.

16.7 Turn right onto Whitebridge Road. You are entering Great Swamp.

18.7 Turn left onto New Vernon Road.

19.2 The road's name changes to Long Hill Road.

21.1 Turn right onto Pleasantville Road.

22.9 Turn right onto Village Road.

23.4 Turn left onto Spring Valley Road and then bear left onto Dicksons Mill Road.

24.3 Turn right onto Blue Mill Road.

25.1 Turn left onto Spring Valley Road.

26.3 Turn left onto Van Beuren Road.

27.8 Turn right onto Blue Mill Road.

29.0 Bear right and then turn right onto Glen Alpin Road.

30.7 Cross US 202; the road's name changes to Tempe Wick Road. It's now a constant climb to the finish.

32.1 Turn right into Jockey Hollow.

32.4 Climb the entrance road back to the parking lot to complete the ride.

Local Events/Attractions

Great Swamp National Wildlife Refuge is an ecological preserve located in Morris County, New Jersey. It consists of 7,600 acres of varied habitats and is home for more than 244 species of birds, as well as fox, deer, muskrat, turtles, fish, frogs, and a wide variety of wildflowers and plants. The refuge contains numerous hiking trails that can be used to explore the refuge and observe the flora and fauna. For more information, visit www.fws.gov/northeast/greatswamp.

Lord Stirling Environmental Education Center: 190 Lord Stirling Road, Basking Ridge; (908) 766-2489. This center on the western side of the Great Swamp provides a number of different environmental education programs for children of all ages. The center is also a good place to access some of the many trails in the Great Swamp. For more information, visit www.somersetcountyparks.org/programs/EEC/eec_main.htm.

Morristown National Historical Park (Jockey Hollow) contains a number of historic buildings and exhibits related to the Revolutionary War. Visit www.nps.gov/morr for more information.

Restaurants

Cappia Cafe: 19 Market Street, Morristown; (973) 267-8787. Casual deli; open for breakfast and lunch.

George and Martha's American Grille: 67 Morris Street, Morristown; (973) 267-4700. American cuisine in a casual colonial-style setting.

Accommodations

Olde Mill Inn: 225 U.S. Highway 202 and North Maple Avenue, Basking Ridge; (908) 221-1100; www.oldemillinn.com.

Maps

DeLorme: New Jersey Atlas and Gazetteer: Pages 30 H14 and 31 L15.

New Jersey Bike Maps: Chatham, Bernardsville, Mendham, Morristown; www.njbikemap.com.

⑨ Twist and Tumble Ramble/Challenge

Frenchtown is a charming little town on the Delaware River in western New Jersey. The town has a number of great places to eat and shop and makes a great stopping point for a bike ride. This ride takes you from Bull's Island to Frenchtown two different ways—flat and easy or hilly and hard.

Start: Bull's Island Recreation Area parking lot, Route 29, Stockton.

Distance: 18.1 miles out and back (ramble); 29.5-mile loop (challenge).

Terrain: The route for the ramble is simply Route 29. This road follows the river and is relatively flat, with only some gentle ups and downs. The route for the challenge is very hilly and climbs the toughest hills between Bull's Island and Frenchtown. There are three climbs of 400 feet, as well as a number of smaller climbs.

Traffic and hazards: Although Route 29 has some traffic, it has a wide shoulder that you can ride in. Once you get off Route 29, you are on backcountry roads where you will encounter only an occasional car.

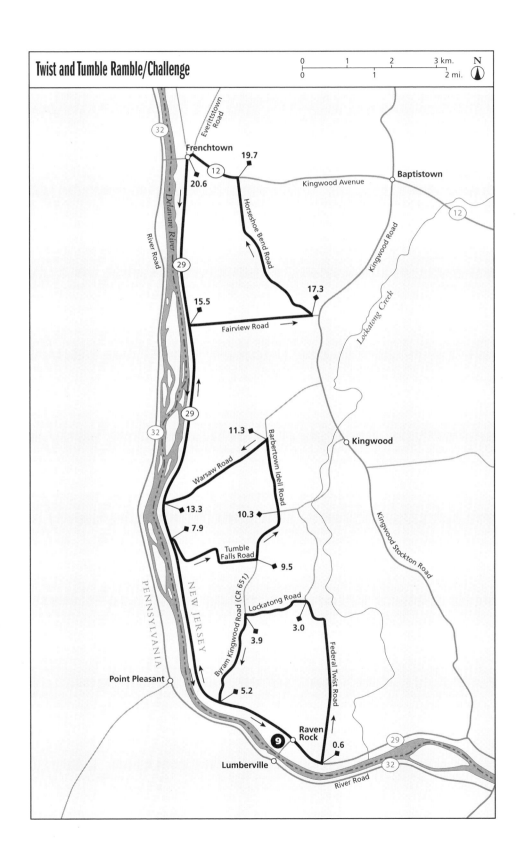

Twist and Tumble Ramble/Challenge

0   1   2   3 km.

0   1   2 mi.

N

32

Everittstown Road

Frenchtown   **19.7**

12

20.6

Kingwood Avenue

Baptistown

12

29

Horseshoe Bend Road

River Road

Delaware River

Kingwood Road

17.3

Lockatong Creek

15.5

Fairview Road →

29

32

11.3

Barbertown Idell Road

Kingwood

Warsaw Road

13.3

10.3

Kingwood Stockton Road

7.9

Tumble Falls Road

9.5

Lockatong Road

3.0

PENNSYLVANIA

NEW JERSEY

Byram Kingwood Road (CR 651)

3.9

Federal Twist Road

Point Pleasant

5.2

9

Raven Rock

0.6

29

32

Lumberville

River Road

The first part of the Federal Twist climb

Getting there: Bull's Island Recreation Area is on Route 29 in the northwest part of Stockton. From the south take Interstate 95 south toward Pennsylvania and get off at exit 1, the last exit before crossing the Delaware River. Follow Route 29 north for about 17 miles. The entrance to Bull's Island is on your left.

From the north take Interstate 287 or U.S. Highway 22 to the intersection with U.S. Highway 202 in Somerville. Follow US 202 south for 26 miles to the exit for Route 29 north. Travel north for about 6 miles. The entrance to Bull's Island is on the left.

Frenchtown is a favorite rest stop for a lot of bike riders on any given Saturday or Sunday. The easiest way to Frenchtown is to ride along Route 29. This is a busy road, but it has a wide shoulder to ride in and offers some nice views of the river. Staying on Route 29 is the safe and easy way to get to Frenchtown. If you want a more challenging ride, try climbing some of the hills off Route 29. There is a lot of nice scenery east of Route 29, but in order to see it you have to endure some tough climbs.

The route for the ramble is very simple: Just turn right out of the parking lot for Bull's Island and follow Route 29 to and from Frenchtown. Route 29 carries constant traffic, but it has a wide shoulder to ride in. From Bull's Island take Route 29 for almost 9 miles until it ends in Frenchtown where it meets Bridge Street. When

Route 29 gets narrower, you are about 0.75 mile from Frenchtown. On Saturday or Sunday, Frenchtown can be a busy place, so watch out for the cars that will be cruising the streets.

At the end of Route 29 turn left onto Bridge Street. There are a number of places to eat in town. One of the best is the Bridge Cafe, which is on the left just before you cross the Delaware River. They have nice baked goods and some tables right by the river. It's a good place to hang out.

When you are done with your break, just retrace the route and follow Route 29 back to Bull's Island. Although you will be going back the same way you came, the views along the Delaware are worth a second look.

For the challenge route, head east on Route 29 and quickly start climbing. The challenge route zigzags around the hills above the river and returns to Route 29 a couple of times, so you can choose to do some or all of the climbs depending on how you are feeling.

To start the challenge route turn right out of the parking lot for Bull's Island onto Route 29. After 0.5 mile turn left onto Federal Twist Road and begin climbing. The Federal Twist climb is not continuous but comes in a couple of sections. The first part starts right after you turn onto the road. The road flattens out for a little bit after you pass Raven Rock Road and then starts a second, steeper climb. There is then a little downhill followed by a more gentle uphill section. The road gets a little narrower here and twists around a little.

From Federal Twist Road make a few turns and work your way back down the hill. Watch your speed at the bottom of the hill on Byram Kingwood Road—you want to be able to stop before making the right onto Route 29.

Continue north on Route 29. After 2.6 miles turn right onto Tumble Falls Road and start climbing again. This is a 440-foot climb on a narrow road that climbs steeply with a number of twists. The first 0.5 mile is the toughest part of the hill, which gets less steep as you continue. After the climb you ride along the ridge for a while and then start heading downhill again when you turn left onto Warsaw Road. This road follows a small stream down the hill. The lower part of the road is tree covered and beautiful, especially in fall when the leaves are turning.

Warsaw Road ends at the bottom of the hill where it meets Route 29. Turn right onto Route 29 and continue toward Frenchtown. If your legs are still willing, there is one more major climb before Frenchtown.

Continue on Route 29 for 2.5 miles, then turn right onto Fairview Road. This 380-foot climb is a more or less constant grade. It is a little steeper at the bottom. The climb lasts about 1.5 miles, so try to find a comfortable pace to grind up the hill. From Fairview make a hard left onto Horseshoe Bend Road, and continue on some more rolling hills with more downs than ups. There is a downhill that gets very steep right before Horseshoe Bend ends. Keep your speed down—Route 12 can be a busy road, and you want to come to a complete stop before making the left turn.

Route 12 will take you into Frenchtown, where the road ends at a T in the middle of town. Turn left at the T and follow the road around to the right. On Saturday or Sunday Frenchtown can be a busy place, so watch out for the cars that will be cruising the streets. There are a number of good places to stop and take a break here. One of the best spots is the Bridge Cafe, which is on the left just before you cross the Delaware River. It's a great place to take a break and watch the river go by.

When you are done with your break, you have a nice flat ride back to Bull's Island. Just head away from the river on Bridge Street and turn right onto Route 29. Route 29 starts off a little narrow, but after 0.75 mile it gets wider and has a nice shoulder to ride in. It's just about 9 miles back to Bull's Island. Although the road has some gentle inclines and declines, it is a relatively flat and easy ride. This is a good road to do some sprints and work on your cadence. You will have some nice views of the river and the surrounding area as you ride along. Once back at Bull's Island, you can relax by the river or check out some of the park's trails.

Ramble Miles and Directions

Note: These mileages not shown on map.

0.0 Turn left out of the Bull's Island parking lot onto Route 29 (Daniel Bray Highway). N40° 24.650' / W75° 2.055'

8.9 Turn left at the T onto Bridge Street.

9.0 Bridge Cafe is on the left before the bridge over the Delaware River.

9.1 Head away from the river and turn right onto Route 29 to retrace your route.

18.1 Turn right into the parking lot at Bull's Island to complete your ride.

Challenge Miles and Directions

0.0 Turn right out of the Bull's Island parking lot onto Route 29 (Daniel Bray Highway). N40° 24.650' / W75° 2.055'

0.6 Turn left onto Federal Twist Road (380-foot climb).

3.0 Turn left onto Lockatong Road.

3.9 Turn left at the T onto Byram Kingwood Road (County Road 651).

5.2 Turn right at bottom of hill onto Route 29.

7.8 Turn right onto Tumble Falls Road (440-foot climb).

9.5 Turn left at the T onto CR 651 (Byram Kingwood Road).

10.3 Continue straight onto Barbertown Idell Road where CR 651 goes right.

11.3 Turn left onto Warsaw Road. Enjoy a nice scenic downhill.

13.0 Turn right onto Route 29.

15.5 Turn right onto Fairview Road (380-foot climb).

17.3 Make a hard left onto Horseshoe Bend Road.

19.7 Turn left onto Route 12 (Kingwood Avenue). There is a steep downhill before this turn.

20.3 Turn left at the T onto Race Street. The road bends to the right and becomes Bridge Street.

20.5 Bridge Cafe is on left before the bridge.

20.6 Head away from the river and turn right onto Route 29.

29.5 Turn right into the parking lot at Bull's Island to complete your ride.

Local Events/Attractions

Bull's Island Recreation Area is a small, forested island surrounded by the Delaware River and the Delaware and Raritan Canal. It's a good place for camping, fishing, hiking, and biking. For more information, check out www.state.nj.us/dep/parksandforests/parks/bull.html. **Delaware and Raritan Canal State Park** is one of central New Jersey's most popular recreational corridors for canoeing, jogging, hiking, bicycling, fishing, and horseback riding. The canal and the park are part of the National Recreation Trail System. This linear park is also a valuable wildlife corridor connecting fields and forests. For more information, visit www.dandrcanal.com.

Restaurants

Errico's Market: 12 Bridge Street, Stockton; (609) 397-0049. Located in an old railroad station, this market sells baked goods and coffee, sandwiches, fried chicken, salads, and desserts.
The Stockton Inn: 1 South Main Street (Route 29), Stockton; (609) 397-1250. Historic inn established in 1710; serves lunch and dinner in a tavern setting.

Accommodations

The Stockton Inn: 1 South Main Street (Route 29), Stockton; (609) 397-1250.

Maps

DeLorme: New Jersey Atlas and Gazetteer: Page 34 N10.
New Jersey Bike Maps: Lumberville, Frenchtown; www.njbikemap.com.

10 Covered Bridge Ramble

This short but slightly hilly ride by the Delaware River takes you past some wonderful scenery and through the only covered bridge left in the state.

Start: Bull's Island Recreation Area parking lot, Route 29, Stockton.

Distance: 16-mile loop.

Terrain: There aren't many flat roads in this part of the state. Route 29 is flat, but you will hit some hills once you start heading east. This route tries to minimize the amount of climbing you have to do. There are some long, slow hills and a couple of very short but steep hills but nothing that is a real climb.

Traffic and hazards: Although Route 29 has some traffic, it has a wide shoulder that you can ride in. Once you get off Route 29, you are on backcountry roads where you will encounter only an occasional car.

Getting there: Bull's Island Recreation Area is on Route 29 in the northwest part of Stockton. From the south take Interstate 95 south toward Pennsylvania and get off at exit 1, the last exit before crossing the Delaware River. Follow Route 29 north for about 17 miles. The entrance to Bull's Island is on your left.

Riding along Rock Raven Road

From the north take Interstate 287 or U.S. Highway 22 to the intersection with U.S. Highway 202 in Somerville. Follow US 202 south for 26 miles to the exit for Route 29 north. Go north for about 6 miles. The entrance to Bull's Island is on your left.

This area of New Jersey is a picturesque place to ride. There are a number of small parks and towns along the Delaware River that provide scenic views of the river and surrounding area. Besides the Delaware River there is also the Delaware and Raritan Canal, a popular place to fish, kayak, canoe, or bike.

To start the ride exit Bull's Island and turn right onto Route 29 south. There is a wide shoulder here to ride in, so don't worry about the traffic and enjoy the nice view of the Delaware. After a little less than 3 miles, Route 29 makes a bend to the left followed by a right bend. When the road starts bending to the right, you will see County Road 519 (Kingwood Stockton Road). Turn left here and then right at the next Y onto Lower Creek Road. This fairly flat road along a creek is one of the most beautiful roads in the area. The covered bridge is to your left at the end of Lower Creek Road. From here turn right onto Rosemont Ringoes Road for a long, slow climb of about 160 feet.

Eventually ride through the town of Sergeantsville, make a few turns, and ride along the rural area of the lower ridges of the mountains. When you get to Covered

Covered Bridge Ramble

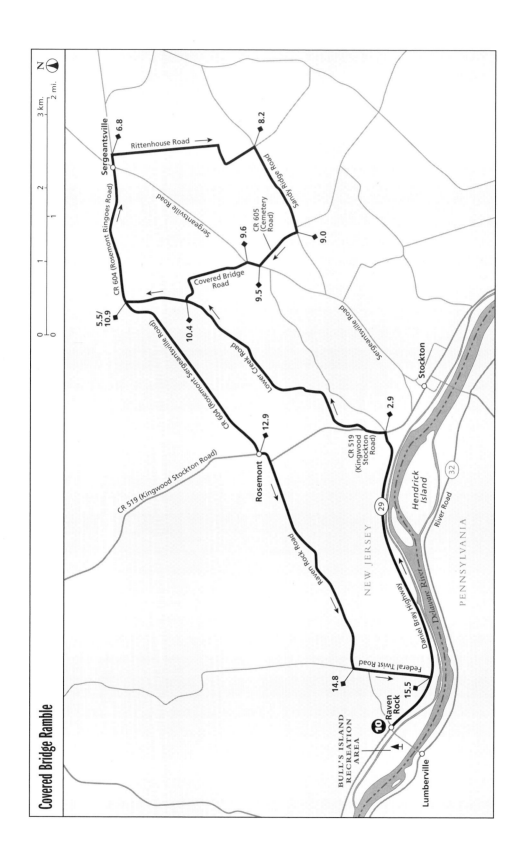

Bridge Road, you have a nice, winding downhill. This is a very scenic area with a lot of old houses; it probably looks like it did one hundred years ago. At the next T make a right onto Lower Creek Road. If this road looks familiar, it's because you were on it before. This time, turn left when you get to end of Lower Creek and ride across the covered bridge, then bear left onto Rosemont Ringoes Road (also called Rosemont Sergeantsville Road). This is another small, steady climb. Ride through another small town, up and down a few rollers, and past some nice farmland. When you get to Federal Twist Road, enjoy a screaming downhill. At the bottom of the hill is Route 29. Turn right here and head north back to Bull's Island. The entrance is ahead about 0.5 mile on your left. The towns of Lambertville and New Hope, Pennsylvania, are close by if you want to do some shopping or enjoy a good meal by the river.

Miles and Directions

- **0.0**   Start at Bull's Island Recreation Area. Turn right out of the parking lot onto Route 29 (Daniel Bray Highway). N40° 24.650' / W75° 2.055'
- **2.8**   Turn left onto CR 519 (Kingwood Stockton Road).
- **2.9**   Bear right at the Y onto Lower Creek Road.
- **5.5**   Turn right at the covered bridge onto County Road 604 (Rosemont Ringoes Road).
- **6.8**   Go through Sergeantsville then turn right onto Rittenhouse Road.
- **8.2**   Turn right at the T onto Sandy Ridge Road.
- **9.0**   Turn right after a church onto Cemetery Road (County Road 605).
- **9.5**   Turn right onto County Road 523 (Sergeantsville Road).
- **9.6**   Make a quick left onto Covered Bridge Road.
- **10.4**   Turn right onto Lower Creek Road.
- **10.9**   Turn left and then bear left onto Rosemont Ringoes Road (CR 604).
- **12.7**   Turn left onto Kingwood Stockton Road (CR 519).
- **12.9**   Bear right onto Raven Rock Road.
- **14.8**   Turn left at the T onto Federal Twist Road.
- **15.5**   Turn right at the T onto Route 29.
- **16.0**   Turn left into Bull's Island to complete the loop.

Local Events/Attractions

Bull's Island Recreation Area is a small, forested island surrounded by the Delaware River and the Delaware and Raritan Canal. It's a good place for camping, fishing, hiking, and biking. For more information, check out www.state.nj.us/dep/parksandforests/parks/bull.html. **Delaware and Raritan Canal State Park** is one of central New Jersey's most popular recreational corridors for canoeing, jogging, hiking, bicycling, fishing, and horseback riding. The canal and the park are part of the National Recreation Trail System. This linear park is also a valuable wildlife corridor connecting fields and forests. For more information, visit www.dandrcanal.com.

Restaurants

Errico's Market: 12 Bridge Street, Stockton; (609) 397-0049. Located in an old railroad station, this market sells baked goods and coffee, sandwiches, fried chicken, salads, and desserts.

The Stockton Inn: 1 South Main Street (Route 29), Stockton; (609) 397-1250. Historic inn established in 1710; serves lunch and dinner in a tavern setting.

Accommodations

The Stockton Inn: 1 South Main Street (Route 29), Stockton; (609) 397-1250.

Maps

DeLorme: New Jersey Atlas and Gazetteer: Pages 34 N12 and 35 N16.

New Jersey Bike Maps: Lumberville, Stockton; www.njbikemap.com.

Central Jersey

The idea of Central Jersey really didn't exist until about twenty-five years ago. People were either from North Jersey (every town north of Trenton) or South Jersey. The population growth in the 1980s served to make this area less rural, especially along the U.S. Highway 1 and U.S. Highway 9 corridors. This served to give this area its own identity and character. Central Jersey is not as crowded as the northeast part of the state, but there are pockets of congestion that can be almost as bad. The pace of life is a little slower here, and even though new developments are continually devouring the farmlands and rural meadows, many towns here have been able to preserve their history and small-town charm.

This area has a lot to offer bikers, from the quiet rural hills of the Sourlands in the west to the beautiful beaches on the ocean in the east. There are some hills here, but they're not as bad as in the northwest. Head east and the land becomes much flatter, although there are still some rolling hills to keep it interesting. No matter what types of terrain or roads you like to ride, Central Jersey has them. There are also a lot of small towns here hidden on the back roads and waiting to be explored. If you want variety without the traffic, then this is a great place to ride.

11 D&R Canal Ramble

The Delaware and Raritan Canal is a great place to take a leisurely ride. This laid-back ride shows you some of the nicer parts of the canal just north of Princeton, as well as some good scenery at the base of the Sourland Mountains.

Start: Rocky Hill parking area, Delaware and Raritan Canal, Rocky Hill.
Distance: 27.2-mile loop.
Terrain: Mostly flat.
Traffic and hazards: The roads around the canal usually have light traffic, especially in the morning. This is a popular biking area, so cars are used to sharing the road with bikes. Parts of Amwell and Blawenburg Belle Mead Roads can have moderate traffic during rush hour.

Getting there: From U.S. Highway 1 in South Brunswick, take Ridge Road west through Kingston. Cross Route 27 and continue on. The Rocky Hill parking area is about 3 miles from US 1, on the left across from the rock quarry just before the light at County Road 518.

With its wooden bridges, cobblestone spillways, historic houses, and tree cover, the canal is a relaxing place to ride. The area around Rocky Hill and Griggstown offers a lot of different recreational activities, including fishing, canoeing, and biking.

The ride starts at the corner of CR 518 and Canal Road. To get there from the parking lot, follow the gravel path north toward CR 518. When you reach CR 518 turn left at the light onto Canal Road.

As you ride north on Canal Road, you will see the canal on your left through the trees. You will also notice a number of historic houses on both sides of the road. The road does not have shoulders, but traffic is usually light, so it's usually not a problem. As you continue to head north, you make lose sight of the canal for a while as you go through some farmland.

At around 5 miles you need to jog left to stay on Canal Road, which eventually turns into Elm Street. Make the first left from Elm onto Market Street. If you want to stop, there's a small market on the left side of the street a little ways up.

From Market Street turn left onto Amwell Road, which carries moderate traffic. Parts of the road have a shoulder; others don't, so stay to the right. From Amwell Road take Willow Road to Hillsborough Road and then ride a short stretch on U.S. Highway 206. Usually I don't like to ride on major roads like US 206, but there is a nice shoulder here and no other easy way to get to the base of the Sourland Mountains. Turn left onto US 206 and then a right at the next light just ahead. Watch out for cars entering and leaving the various stores and offices to your right.

For the next 4 miles you will be riding along the base of the Sourland Mountains. (If you are interested in going farther into the mountains, check out Rides 13, 14, and 15.)

After crossing US 206 at Mile 20.9, you are on Harlingen Road. After about 0.5 mile come to a T. You are now at the corner of Harlingen and Harlingen. No, this is

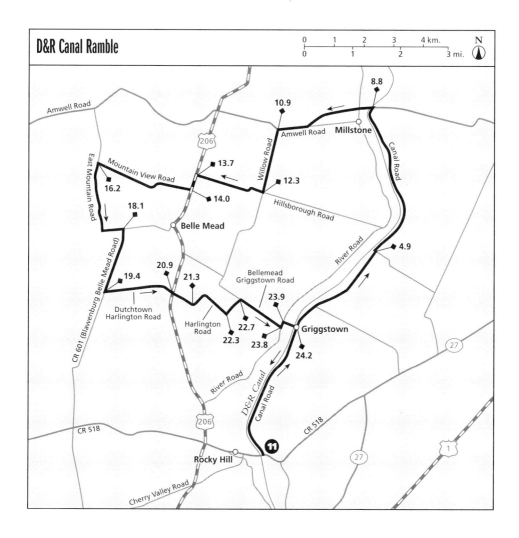

D&R Canal Ramble

0   1   2   3   4 km.
0   1   2   3 mi.

N

Amwell Road

206

8.8

10.9

Amwell Road   **Millstone**

Canal Road

East Mountain Road

Mountain View Road

13.7

16.2

Willow Road

12.3

18.1

14.0

Hillsborough Road

River Road

4.9

Belle Mead

Bellemead Griggstown Road

20.9

19.4

21.3

23.9

CR 601 (Blawenburg Belle Mead Road)

Dutchtown Harlington Road

Harlington Road

22.7

Griggstown

27

22.3   23.8

24.2

River Road

D&R Canal

Canal Road

CR 518

206

CR 518

27

1

Rocky Hill

11

Cherry Valley Road

not a misprint; it's just a result of poorly merging old and new roads. Turn left here and make another left in a mile to stay on this strangely disconnected road.

From here take Bellemead Griggstown Road to River Road to Griggstown Causeway. The first part of the Griggstown Causeway is a one-lane bridge, so watch out for oncoming traffic. From here just follow Canal Road to your starting point.

Miles and Directions

0.0   From the corner of CR 518 and Canal Road, turn left (north) onto Canal Road. N40° 23.951' / W74° 37.679'

4.8   Turn left at T where Canal Road meets Suydam to stay on Canal Road.

Crossing the bridge at Griggstown

8.6 Canal Road makes a hard right and turns into Elm Street. Turn left onto Market Street. There's a small deli just ahead on your right.

8.8 Turn left onto Amwell Road.

10.9 Turn left onto Willow Road.

12.3 Turn right onto Hillsborough Road.

13.7 Turn left onto US 206.

14.0 Turn right onto Mountain View Road.

16.2 Turn left onto East Mountain Road.

18.1 Turn right onto County Road 601 (Blawenburg Belle Mead Road).

19.4 Turn left onto Dutchtown Harlingen Road.

20.9 Cross US 206. The road becomes Harlingen Road.

21.3 Turn left at the T to stay on Harlingen Road.

22.3 Turn left to stay on Harlingen Road.

22.7 Turn right onto Bellemead Griggstown Road.

23.8 Turn left onto River Road.

23.9 Turn right onto the Griggstown Causeway.

24.2 Turn right onto Canal Road.

27.2 Finish your ride at the Rocky Hill parking area.

Local Events/Attractions

Delaware and Raritan Canal: www.dandrcanal
.com. The 70-mile Delaware and Raritan Canal
State Park is one of central New Jersey's most
popular recreational corridors for canoeing,
jogging, hiking, bicycling, fishing, and horseback riding. This linear park is also a valuable
wildlife corridor connecting fields and forests.
Griggstown Canoe and Kayak Rental: 1076
Canal Road, Griggstown; (908) 359-5970;
www.canoenj.com/index.htm. Great place
to rent canoes or kayaks to explore the canal
firsthand.

Restaurants

Washington Street Station: 153 Washington
Street, Rocky Hill; (609) 924-9872. Casual
American cuisine.

Accommodations

Holiday Inn Princeton: 100 Independence
Way, Princeton; (609) 520-1200.

Maps

DeLorme: New Jersey Atlas and Gazetteer:
Pages 36 N9 and 41 A9.
New Jersey Bike Maps: Rocky Hill, Monmouth
Junction; www.njbikemap.com.

12 Princeton Tour Ramble

Princeton is a beautiful historic town. Besides the university, which dominates the
town, there is also some nice scenery on the outskirts. This rambling ride takes you
around Princeton and shows you some of the sights.

Start: Carnegie Lake, Washington Road
(County Road 571), Princeton.
Distance: 23-mile loop.
Terrain: Rolling with few small hills. There are a
couple of slow, steady uphills and a few steep
but very short uphills, but no real climbs.
Traffic and hazards: Although two-thirds of the
ride is on the outskirts of Princeton with little
traffic, a couple sections will have moderate
traffic. The roads in Princeton are wide enough

to accommodate cars and bikes together, so
although you might encounter some traffic, as
long as you are courteous and give cars the
right-of-way, you should have no problems. The
roads in and around Princeton are well traveled
and in various states of repair. Most roads are
well maintained, but there are always a few
places where the road can be a little rough.
Just be prepared for a little urban riding.

Getting there: Washington Road is just off U.S. Highway 1. Take US 1 to the CR 571 Circle, then
go west on CR 571 (Washington Road). Once you are on Washington Road, there will be a large
field on your right with a number of soccer fields. At the west end of the fields is a parking lot, the
starting point for the ride.

This ride takes you through and around Princeton. The ride starts by Carnegie Lake,
heads out to Terhune Orchards, and then returns to the lake through some of the
beautiful back-end neighborhoods. This is a short ride, but it will give you a flavor
of the town.

Princeton Tour Ramble

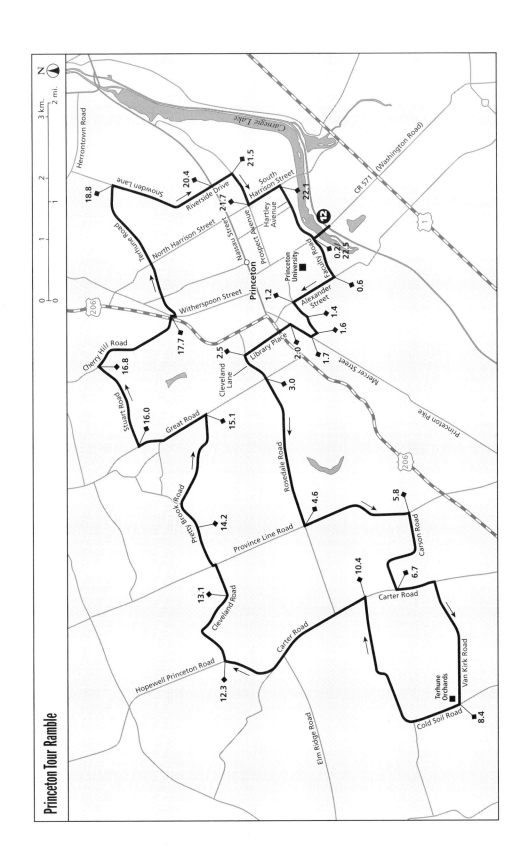

Princeton University

Princeton

Carnegie Lake

Herrontown Road

Snowden Lane

Riverside Drive

South Harrison Street

Hartley Avenue

North Harrison Street

Terhune Road

Nassau Street

Prospect Avenue

Witherspoon Street

Alexander Street

Faculty Road

Library Place

Cleveland Lane

Mercer Street

Princeton Pike

Cherry Hill Road

Stuart Road

Great Road

Rosedale Road

Pretty Brook Road

Province Line Road

Carson Road

Carter Road

Cleveland Road

Hopewell Princeton Road

Elm Ridge Road

Van Kirk Road

Terhune Orchards

Cold Soil Road

CR 571 (Washington Road)

0.2
22.5
0.6
1.2
1.4
1.6
1.7
2.0
2.5
3.0
4.6
5.8
6.7
8.4
10.4
12.3
13.1
14.2
15.1
16.0
16.8
17.7
18.8
20.4
21.5
21.7
22.1

206

1

N

0   1   2   3 km.

0   1   2 mi.

Start the ride by exiting the parking lot and turning right onto Washington Road. You are heading toward Princeton. Almost immediately cross a bridge over Carnegie Lake. To your left is the boathouse for the Princeton Crew. On most days you will see a number of people out rowing on the lake. From here take Faculty Road to Alexander Road. Alexander Road can be a busy road, especially at rush hour, so be careful here.

The next few miles of the ride take you through town and require some urban riding skills. After you cross US 206 the road gets a little wider and the traffic lightens up. The area has some good-looking homes that are beyond most people's price range.

Rosedale Road can be busy. If you don't want to ride on the road, there is a bike path to your right. When you get to Province Line Road you are at the south end of Princeton; the homes are a little more spread out here. As you continue, the area becomes more rural. When you get to Cold Soil Road, you are at the back end of the Terhune Orchards. The road bends around to the right, and the entrance to the orchards is on your right after about 1.5 miles. They have some really good produce, baked goods, cookies, and other good foods here, so it makes a nice stop. There are also restrooms here if you need them. Terhune's hosts a number of events throughout the year that can be fun for a family. Check the Web site (see Local Events/Attractions) for information.

After Cold Soil Road turn left onto Carter Road. This road can be busy at times, so stay to the right. From here take Cleveland Road to Pretty Brook Road. There are a few rolling hills here, but the scenery is nice and there are a number of large estates here.

When you make the left onto Great Road, you have another little uphill and may encounter a little traffic. There is a paved bike path along the road you can use to avoid the traffic. When you get onto Cherry Hill Road you will have a nice downhill. At the end of the road is a light. Go straight through the light and cross US 206. Go to the T and make a right and then a quick left onto Terhune Road. Watch the traffic here. Continue through some nice residential sections of town. As you continue on Snowden Lane, you may encounter a little more traffic as you head back to the center of Princeton. Be careful not to miss the turn onto Hartley Avenue. If you cross a bridge over Carnegie Lake, you have gone too far.

As you ride along Faculty Road, Carnegie Lake is to your left and some of the buildings of Princeton University are to your right. Eventually come to a light; this is Washington Road. Turn left at the light and make your way back to your starting point. The heart of Princeton is Nassau Street, which is too busy to ride a bike on. If you want to explore Princeton some more, take your car and drive back toward Carnegie Lake and go up the hill to Nassau Street. Find a place to park and walk around the town. There are a lot of nice stores and places to eat.

Boathouse on Carnegie Lake

Miles and Directions

0.0 Turn right out of parking lot onto Washington Road (CR 571). N40° 20.335' / W74° 38.845'

0.2 Turn left at the light onto Faculty Road.

0.6 After crossing the railroad tracks, turn right at the light onto Alexander Street. This is a busy road, so stay to the right.

1.2 Turn left onto College Road.

1.4 At the next Y keep right and stay on College Road.

1.6 Go through the gate and turn right onto Springdale Road.

1.7 Turn right onto Mercer Street. Stay to the right on this busy road.

2.0 Turn left onto Library Place.

2.5 Turn left onto Cleveland Lane.

3.0 At Elm Road go straight at the light. The name changes to Rosedale Road and there's a little more traffic.

4.6 Turn left onto Province Line Road.

5.8 Turn right onto Carson Road.

6.7 Turn left onto Carter Road.

7.1	Turn right onto Van Kirk Road.
8.4	Turn right onto Cold Soil Road. Terhune Orchards are on your right if you want to take a break
10.4	Turn left onto Carter Road.
12.3	After going through the light at Rosedale Road, continue on and turn right turn onto Cleveland Road.
13.1	The road becomes Pretty Brook Road.
14.2	Make a left followed by a quick right to stay on Pretty Brook Road.
15.1	Turn left onto Great Road.
16.0	Turn right onto Stuart Road.
16.8	Turn right onto Cherry Hill Road. Enjoy the downhill here.
17.7	Cross US 206 at the light. Go to the next intersection and turn right onto Mt. Lucas Road followed by a quick left onto Terhune Road.
18.8	Turn right onto Snowden Lane.
20.4	Cross Route 27 and continue straight onto Riverside Drive.
21.5	Turn right onto Prospect Avenue.
21.8	Turn left onto South Harrison Street.
22.1	Turn right onto Hartley Avenue, which becomes Faculty Road.
22.5	Turn left onto Washington Road (CR 571).
23.0	Cross the bridge and turn left into the parking lot where you started.

Local Events/Attractions

Terhune Orchards: 330 Cold Soil Road, Princeton; (609) 924-2310. The orchards host a number of family-oriented events throughout the year. For a list of events, check out their Web site: www.terhuneorchards.com.

Restaurants

PJ's Pancake House: 154 Nassau Street, Princeton; 609) 924-1353; www.pancakes .com. A restaurant in the heart of Princeton famous for their delicious pancakes. Also serves hot and cold sandwiches for lunch and dinner.

Triumph Brewing Company: 138 Nassau Street, Princeton; (609) 924-7855; www .triumphbrewing.com/indexfl6.html. Restaurant and brewery featuring eclectic American cuisine and hand-crafted freshly brewed beer.

Witherspoon Bread Company: 74 Witherspoon Street, Princeton; (609) 688-0188. Offers a great selection of sandwiches on a variety of breads and croissants.

Accommodations

Hyatt Regency Princeton: 102 Carnegie Center, Princeton; (609) 987-1234; www .princeton.hyatt.com/hyatt/hotels/index.jsp.
Nassau Inn: 10 Palmer Square East, Princeton; (609) 921-7500; www.nassauinn.com.
The Westin Princeton at Forrestal Village: 201 Village Boulevard, Princeton; (609) 452-7900.

Maps

DeLorme: New Jersey Atlas and Gazetteer: Page 42 E7.
New Jersey Bike Maps: Princeton; www.njbike map.com.

13 Sourlands Valley Cruise

The valley between the Sourlands and U.S. Highway 202 is dotted with rustic farm-land. It is a beautiful place to ride. This cruise takes an easy path through some of the nicer roads in the area. Although there are a few short hills on the route, this ride doesn't require any major climbing.

Start: Mark E. Singley Park parking lot, Wood-fern Road, Hillsborough.
Distance: 30-mile loop.
Terrain: Rolling hills with a few small climbs.
Traffic and hazards: You will be riding mostly in rural areas, so there should not be much traffic to deal with. The ride also touches some areas that are less rural. You may experience some moderate traffic on Amwell, Pleasant Run, and Wertsville Roads.

Getting there: From U.S. Highway 206 take Amwell Road west toward Neshanic Station. After 6.3 miles make a right onto Woodfern Road. The park is about 0.5 mile ahead on the right, next to the school.

The valley of Sourlands has a lot of undiscovered beauty. With a number of rural farms, hills, and streams, it can be a picturesque place to ride. The Hill Slugs Cruise (Ride 14) will climb and explore the ridge of the Sourlands Mountains. This ride explores the valley and keeps the hill climbing to a minimum. The terrain is still roll-ing with a few small hills, but it should be an easy ride for most people.

To start the ride leave the parking lot, turn right onto Woodfern Road, and then take your first left onto Three Bridges Road. This nice, quiet road follows the Raritan River. You will see the river on your right and will be crossing it a number of times on this ride. For the first 7 miles of the ride you are on some really nice rural roads with almost no traffic. They are also very scenic as you ride along rivers, past farmland, and over some old truss bridges that cross the Raritan.

There is a strange turn at Mile 7.1 where you make a left from River Road onto another River Road (which is marked as Opie Road on some maps). Not sure why two roads that meet have the same name—it's just another one of those oddities that you get used to and accept as you ride around New Jersey.

River Road is a good name for the roads, which follow and cross over the Raritan River. Continue to ride over and next to the river as you travel on Studdiford Drive and South Branch Road. When you get to Pleasant Run Road, one of the busier roads in the area, you may encounter a little light traffic.

When you make the left onto Old York you have a 120-foot climb. The slope is gentle, so the climb is not too difficult. Old York Road is one of the oldest roads in the area and was once a main road between Philadelphia and New York. This road has been replaced as a major thoroughfare by highways like US 202, so it's now a quiet road and good to bike on. Old York takes you into the town of Three Bridges. There is a food store on the left on the south end of town if you need a stop.

Church at the end of Rainbow Hill Road

After leaving the town, continue on Old York Road. Be careful at the intersection where Voorhees Corner Road enters from the right, which can be a little busy at times. From here take Clover Hill Road to Cider Mill Road and eventually be treated with views of some old rustic farms. When you make the left from Welisewitz Road onto Manners Road, you have a short but steep little climb of 140 feet—the hardest climb of the ride. After you make a left onto Wertsville Road (County Road 602), there's a nice little general store called Peacock's ahead on the right. It's the best place in the area for a break, and you will almost always find bikers here.

Wertsville Road can carry moderate traffic at times, so stay to the right. From Wertsville Road turn left onto Rainbow Hill Road. As the name implies, there is a hill here. The road starts with a short but reasonable 80-foot climb followed by a winding downhill. The road does have a few rough spots, so be careful on the downhill. From here you will ride through some nice scenic farmland, then take Amwell Road back to Woodfern Road and then back to the starting point.

If you don't mind a few hills, this is a beautiful area to ride in. Many other roads in the area are equally nice, so feel free to explore some more on your own.

Miles and Directions

0.0   Make right out of the park onto Woodfern Road. N40° 30.059' / W74° 45.695'

0.3   Turn left onto Three Bridges Road.

Sourlands Valley Cruise

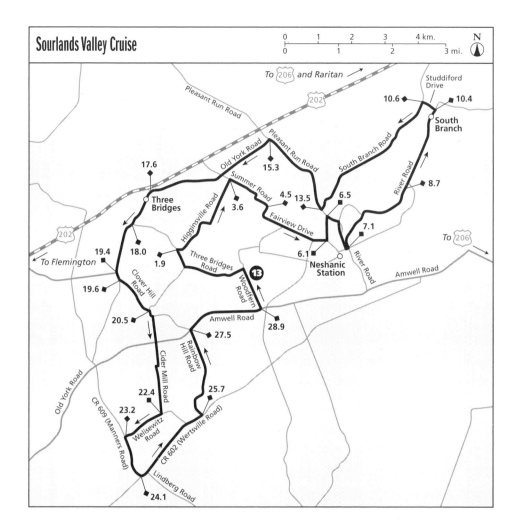

1.9 Make a hard right turn onto Higginsville Road.

3.6 Turn right at the T onto Summer Road.

4.5 Turn right at the T onto Fairview Drive.

6.1 Turn left at the T onto Pleasant Run Road.

6.5 Turn right at the T onto River Road.

7.1 Turn left from River Road onto another River Road. (Some maps may show this as Opie Road.)

10.4 Turn left onto Studdiford Drive.

10.6 Turn left onto South Branch Road.

13.5 Turn right onto Pleasant Run Road.

15.3 Turn left onto Old York Road.

17.6 Enter the town of Three Bridges. Old York Road becomes Main Street as it passes through town. There's a food stop at the south end of town on the left.

18.0 As you leave town, Main Street again becomes Old York Road.

19.4 Go straight where Voorhees Corner Road meets Old York Road. Watch out for cars coming from the right

19.6 Turn left onto Clover Hill Road.

20.5 Turn right onto Cider Mill Road.

22.4 Turn right at the T after crossing the bridge onto Welisewitz Road.

23.3 Turn left at the T onto Manners Road (County Road 609). There's a short, steep climb here.

24.1 Turn left at the T onto Wertsville Road (CR 602). Peacock's general store is on the right just ahead if you need a stop.

25.7 Turn left onto Rainbow Hill Road. There's a small climb ahead, then a nice downhill.

27.5 Turn right by the church onto Amwell Road.

28.9 Turn left onto Woodfern Road.

29.5 Turn right back into the park where you started.

Restaurants

Murphy's Crocodile Inn: 102 Woodfern Road, Neshanic Station; (908) 369-4012. Good food and drink in a friendly Irish pub setting.

Accommodations

Days Inn Hillsborough: 118 U.S. Highway 206 South, Hillsborough; (908) 685-9000 or (877) 717-6203 (hotel direct); www.daysinnhillsborough.com.

Maps

DeLorme: New Jersey Atlas and Gazetteer: Pages 35 H28 and 36 I1.

New Jersey Bike Maps: Rocky Hill, Hopewell, Flemington, Raritan; www.njbikemap.com.

14 Hill Slug Cruise

Hill Slug is a term for a biker who is a slow hill climber. This may seem like a derogatory term, but some bikers wear the appellation with pride. The truth is that in order to become a better biker, you have to climb hills. This ride takes you through the hills of the Sourlands. These aren't the hardest hills in the area, but they will give you a good workout.

Start: YMCA parking lot, Main Street, Pennington.

Distance: 43.2-mile loop.

Terrain: Rolling to hilly. This ride has a lot of ups and downs and not many flat roads in between. There are a number 100+-foot climbs as well as a few 200+-footers.

Traffic and hazards: You will be riding mostly in rural areas, so you shouldn't have much traffic to deal with. The beginning and end of the ride are through parts of Pennington, which will have moderate traffic. The ride touches areas that are less rural, so you may experience some moderate traffic on Amwell, Pleasant Run, and Wertsville Roads.

Hill Slug Cruise

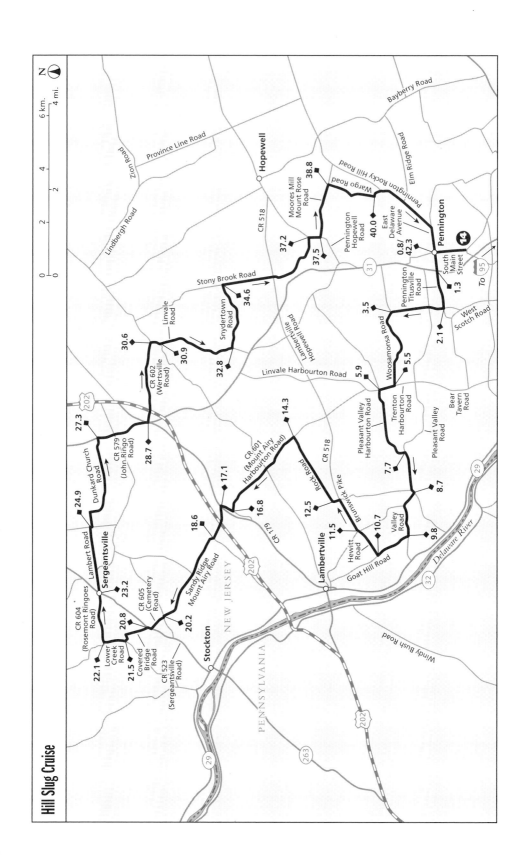

Getting there: Take Interstate 95 toward Pennsylvania to Route 31 north. After about a mile, come to a circle. Take the second right off the circle onto Pennington Road. Continue on Pennington Road for 0.6 mile until it turns into Main Street, and then make a right turn into a driveway where there is a building that looks like a school. If you reach the center of town, you went too far. Alternatively, you can park anywhere on Main Street.

The Sourlands have a lot of quiet rural roads with scenic vistas and a lot of little hills. Hill climbing is as much a state of mind as it is physical. Some bikers, especially beginners, fear hills, but there is really nothing to fear. Yes, your legs will hurt and your lungs will burn as you climb, and you may feel like you can't make it to the top, but most of the time you will. As a biker once said, "I haven't met a hill that I couldn't walk up"—a great attitude to have.

As you do more hills, you will get better and at some point even start to enjoy the hills. You don't have to be fast to do hills; you just have to lose the fear, do the climb, and accept the fact that you might not be the fastest one up the hill. Basically, to be a good hill climber, you first have to become a Hill Slug.

To start the ride, make a right turn out of the parking lot and head north on Main Street toward the center of Pennington. Pennington is a nice little town, but because there are a lot of little shops here, there will be some traffic until you cross Route 31. Once on Woosamonsa Road you have a little climbing and then go through some nice rolling farmland.

You have another short 80-foot climb on Valley Road. This climb will get you warmed up for Goat Hill, a 260-foot climb that lasts almost a mile. It's not real steep, but it is long. When you get to Brunswick Pike (CR 518) you will probably encounter some moderate traffic, so stay to the right.

From here you will wind around some roads along a ridge of the mountains just east of the Delaware River. The roads are a little flatter here, although you will still encounter a number of rollers. Go through the town of Mount Airy, turn right, and go down a little hill. At the bottom of the hill, this road meets County Road 179 at a strange angle that makes it hard to see traffic, so make the next turn with caution. What you want to do here is cross CR 179 and turn left onto the road just ahead of you to the right. This road is Queen Road (County Road 605) and will take you under US 202.

You have a couple of rollers here before the road changes names to Sandy Ridge Mount Airy Road. Then you have a long, slow, shallow climb of about 2 miles.

Sandy Ridge Mount Airy Road ends at a T by a beautiful little church. From here make a couple of quick turns to end up on Covered Bridge Road, a beautiful winding downhill. Some of the corners are sharp, so be careful and watch out for oncoming traffic.

Covered Bridge Road ends at a T. Turn left here onto Lower Creek Road. This is another nice road along a river. Lower Creek Road brings you to the only covered bridge in New Jersey. Turn right at this intersection away from the bridge, and start climbing again. This is a gentle 160-foot climb that isn't too hard. This road takes you into the town of Sergeantsville. There is a nice little general store here on the left by the light if you need a break.

Be careful not to miss the left turn at the Y onto Lambert Road after you pass through Sergeantsville. The road takes you to Dunkard Church Road, a beautiful road that winds along a stream through some quiet farmland for almost 2.5 miles. A few more turns from here gets you onto Wertsville Road.

Wertsville is one of the main east–west roads in the area, but it should only have light traffic. You are heading back toward the main Sourland Mountains and will start to do a little climbing as you continue.

Once on Linvale you have the last real climb of the ride. This is a 220-foot climb over about a mile. It's not real steep, but it will get your heart rate up. When you reach Mountain Road, you are at the end of the climb. Ride along the ridge of the mountain for a little while, then enjoy a well-deserved downhill on Stony Brook Road. At the bottom of the hill, you cross CR 518. This is a busy road, so be careful as you cross.

From here you will pass through some farmland on the back side of Hopewell. Take Pennington Rocky Hill Road back into the town of Pennington and to the YMCA parking lot where you started your ride.

Miles and Directions

0.0 Turn right out of the YMCA parking lot onto Main Street. N40° 19.021' / W74° 47.364'

0.8 Turn left at the light onto Delaware Avenue.

1.3 Cross Route 31. The road becomes Pennington Titusville Road.

2.1 Turn right onto Scotch Road, which becomes Burd Road.

3.5 Turn left onto Woosamonsa Road (100-foot climb).

5.5 Turn right onto Trenton Harbourton Road.

5.9 Turn left onto Pleasant Valley Harbourton Road.

7.7 Turn right onto Pleasant Valley Road.

8.7 Turn right onto Valley Road.

9.8 Turn right onto Goat Hill Road (260-foot climb).

10.7 Turn right onto Hewitt Road.

11.5 Turn right onto CR 518 (Brunswick Pike).

12.4 Turn left onto Hunter Road (Rock Road).

12.5 Turn right onto Rock Road.

14.3 Turn left onto County Road 601 (Mount Airy Harbourton Road).

16.8 Turn right at the T onto Mount Airy Village Road.

17.1 Cross CR 179, then make a quick left onto CR 605 (Queen Road).

18.6 The road's name changes to Sandy Ridge Mount Airy Road (long slow climb).

20.2 Turn left onto Sandy Ridge Road, and make a quick right onto Cemetery Road (CR 605).

20.7 Turn right onto County Road 523 (Sergeantsville Road).

20.8 Turn left onto Covered Bridge Road.

21.5 Turn right onto Lower Creek Road.

Back roads of the Sourlands

22.1 Turn right by the covered bridge onto County Road 604 (Rosemont Ringoes Road).

23.2 Enter the town of Sergeantsville. There's a general store on the left.

23.8 Bear left onto Lambert Road.

24.9 Turn right onto Sandbrook Headquarters Road.

24.9 Make an immediate left onto Dunkard Church Road.

27.3 Turn right onto County Road 579 (John Ringo Road).

28.7 Merge with CR 179, and then turn left onto Wertsville Road (County Road 602).

30.6 Turn right onto Rocktown Road.

30.9 Turn left onto Linvale Road (220-foot climb).

32.8 Turn left onto Snydertown Road.

34.6 Turn right onto Stony Brook Road.

37.2 Turn right onto Pennington Hopewell Road.

37.5 Turn left onto Moores Mill Mount Rose Road.

38.8 Turn right onto Wargo Road.

40.0 Turn left onto Titus Mill Road.

40.3 Turn right onto Pennington Rocky Hill Road.

41.6 Turn left onto East Delaware Avenue.

42.4 Turn left onto South Main Street.

43.2 Turn left into the YMCA parking lot to complete the loop.

Marco's Pizza: 2580 Pennington Road, Pennington; (609) 737-0072. Italian restaurant just off the Pennington circle.
Vitos: 2 North Main Street, Pennington; (609) 737-8520. Good pizza place in center of town.

Courtyard by Marriott: 360 Scotch Road, Trenton; (609) 771-8100

Maps
DeLorme: New Jersey Atlas and Gazetteer: Pages 35 N18 and 41 F27.
New Jersey Bike Maps: Pennington, Hopewell, Stockton, Lambertville; www.njbikemap.com.

15 Lindbergh Long Hill Cruise

The Sourlands offer quiet roads and scenic views of the forest, small streams, and rustic farmlands. This is a beautiful but hilly area to ride. This ride takes you through the nicer parts of the Sourlands and up a few of the tougher hills.

Start: Rocky Hill parking area, Delaware and Raritan Canal, Rocky Hill.
Distance: 39.6-mile loop.
Terrain: Rolling to moderately hilly, with a couple of tough climbs. There will be a couple of 200+-foot climbs and one tough 380-foot

climb up Dutchtown Zion.
Traffic and hazards: Most of the rides are on backcountry roads with little traffic. You will pass through a few town centers that can be a little busy.

Getting there: From U.S. Highway 1 in South Brunswick take Ridge Road west through Kingston. Cross Route 27 and continue on US 1. The Rocky Hill parking area is about 3 miles from US 1, on the left across from the rock quarry just before the light at County Road 518.

The ridge of the Sourland Mountains contains one of the largest contiguous forested areas in New Jersey. It is a beautiful place to ride. This ride goes from the canal, over the Sourland Mountains, into the valley, and back. You will see the variety the Sourlands have to offer as you climb up and down the mountains. There are a couple climbs of 200+ feet and one 380-foot climb. As long as you have done some hill training, none of these climbs should be too difficult.

The ride starts at the corner of County Road 518 and Canal Road. To get there from the parking lot, follow the gravel path north toward CR 518. When you reach CR 518 turn left and head west towards the town of Rocky Hill. Watch out for traffic as you go through the town, especially by the post office. You will be on U.S. Highway 206 for a couple of hundred feet on the way out of Rocky Hill. This is a busy road, so stay in the shoulder.

From US 206 make a couple of turns and go through a little park as you ride on Mill Pond Road. The next turn is a little confusing because of the road names. Mill

Peacock's rest stop at bottom of Lindbergh Road

Pond bends to the left and then and changes its name to Harlingen Road where Harlingen Road enters from the right. Continue on for another mile and turn right at the corner of Harlingen and Harlingen Roads to stay on Harlingen Road. It's easy to make a right onto the wrong Harlingen Road, but if you keep track of the mileage, it will be easier to make the correct turn.

After you cross US 206, the Sourland Mountains loom directly ahead. Continue for 1.5 miles before turning left onto County Road 601 (Blawenburg Belle Mead Road) followed by a quick right onto Dutchtown Zion Road.

You're about to do some climbing, and this ride puts the worst hill first. The best way to describe this hill is that it is just plain rude. It doesn't look like a bad climb when it starts with a few small rollers, but the hill gets slowly steeper. It also bends around a little, so it's hard to tell when it is going to end or flatten out. Unless you are a regular hill climber, you will be using your lower gears by the time you get to the top.

At the top of the hill turn left onto Pin Oak and then take Grandview to Hollow Road. You are now in the heart of the Sourlands forest. As you continue on Hollow Road, you are again climbing. This is a gentle climb with a couple of little bumps. At the end of Hollow Road, turn right onto Long Hill Road.

Long Hill Road is well named; after a short downhill you have a long, slow climb of about 200 feet with a few small downhills thrown in to the mix. Eventually the

Lindbergh Long Hill Cruise

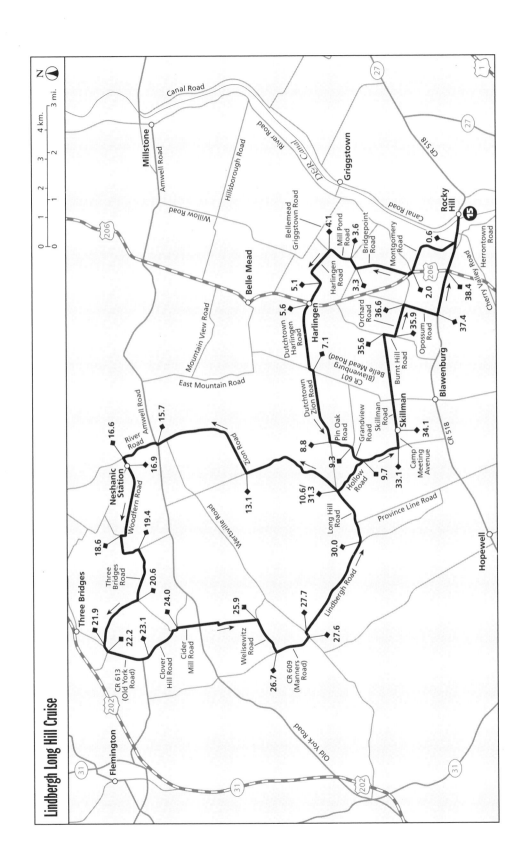

road flattens out and you ride along the ridge of the mountains on Zion Road. The end of Zion is a fun downhill that will get you into the Sourland Valley—just watch out for the usual potholes, which can really ruin your day.

At the bottom of the hill turn right onto Amwell Road, followed by an immediate left onto River Road. This can be a busy and confusing intersection, so be careful here. As you ride up River Road you are riding along the Raritan River. The next few turns will take you through Neshanic Station and then on through some quiet backcountry roads.

Three Bridges is an especially scenic road that follows the river and is a relatively flat ride. A few more turns will have you onto Cider Mill Road, which takes you past some farmland and provides some nice views of the surrounding mountains. When you make the left from Welisewitz Road onto Manners Road, you have a short but steep little climb of 140 feet. After your left turn onto Wertsville Road, there's a nice little general store called Peacock's ahead on the right where you turn onto Lindbergh Road. It's the best place in the area for a break, and you will almost always find bikers here.

When you're done with your break, begin climbing Lindbergh Road, an annoying 240-foot climb. It is a moderately steep hill—not that difficult, but a relatively long climb (about 1.5 miles) that just never seems to end. When you pass Ridge Road on the right, the main part of the climb is over. As you continue you are still climbing, but it won't be as hard except for a few steep bumps in the road.

At the top of Lindbergh Road bear left onto Zion Road and start a nice series of downhills. Eventually turn right onto Hollow Road and continue downhill along a small stream. This is an easy turn to miss. If you start going uphill, you have missed the turn.

Toward the bottom of the hill, make a left onto Camp Meeting House Road and start making your way back to the canal. When you turn right onto Opossum Road, you will see a sign that says ONE WAY DO NOT ENTER, so it may look like you're about to go the wrong way down a one-way street. The truth is that this is a two-way road (as the yellow line down the middle indicates). The only problem is a one-lane bridge about 600 feet down the road. As long as you watch for oncoming traffic while crossing the bridge there is no problem going down this road. Continue to CR 518 and follow it back through the town of Rocky Hill to your starting point.

Miles and Directions

0.0 From the Rocky Hill parking area, take CR 518 west into the town of Rocky Hill. N40° 23.962' / W74° 37.671'

0.6 Turn right onto Montgomery Road.

2.0 Turn right on to US 206; stay in the shoulder.

2.1 Turn right onto Bridgepoint Road.

3.3 Where road bends left, turn right onto Dead Tree Run Road.

3.6 Turn left onto Mill Pond Road.

4.1 The road bends left and changes its name to Harlingen Road where Harlingen and Mill Pond Roads meet.

5.1 Turn right to stay on Harlingen Road at the corner of Harlingen and Harlingen Roads.

5.6 Cross US 206. The road's name changes to Dutchtown Harlingen Road.

7.1 Turn left onto CR 601 (Blawenburg Belle Mead Road).

7.1 Turn right onto Dutchtown Zion Road; you have a 380-foot climb ahead.

8.8 Turn left onto Pin Oak Road.

9.3 Turn right onto Grandview Road.

9.7 Turn right onto Hollow Road.

10.6 Turn right onto Long Hill Road, a long slow climb.

13.1 Turn right onto Zion Road.

15.7 Turn right followed by a quick left onto River Road.

16.6 Turn left onto Elm Street and cross the bridge over the river.

16.8 Turn left onto Main Street.

16.9 Main Street becomes Woodfern Road.

18.6 Turn left to stay on Woodfern Road.

19.4 Turn right onto Three Bridges Road.

20.6 Bear right to stay on Three Bridges Road.

21.9 Turn left onto County Road 613 (Main Street).

22.2 The road becomes Old York Road.

23.1 Turn left onto Clover Hill Road.

24.0 Turn right onto Cider Mill Road.

25.9 Turn right after crossing bridge onto Welisewitz Road.

26.7 Turn left onto Manners Road (County Road 609) for a steep 140-foot climb.

27.6 Turn left onto Wertsville Road (Country Road 602).

27.7 Turn right onto Lindbergh Road (general store on the right as you make the turn), and prepare for a 240-foot climb.

20.0 Turn left onto Zion Road, which changes its name to Long Hill Road.

31.3 Turn right onto Hollow Road.

33.1 Turn left onto Camp Meeting House Avenue.

34.1 The road changes names to Skillman Road.

35.6 Turn right at the T onto Burnt Hill Road.

35.9 Turn left onto Orchard Road.

36.6 Turn right onto Opossum Road. Use caution going over the narrow bridge.

37.4 Turn left onto CR 518. Stay in the shoulder.

38.4 Cross US 206 at a busy intersection.

39.6 Turn right into the parking lot at Rocky Hill to complete your ride.

Local Events/Attractions

Delaware and Raritan Canal: www.dandrcanal.com. The 70-mile Delaware and Raritan Canal State Park is one of central New Jersey's most popular recreational corridors for canoeing, jogging, hiking, bicycling, fishing, and horseback riding. This linear park is also a valuable wildlife corridor connecting fields and forests.

Griggstown Canoe and Kayak Rental: 1076 Canal Road, Griggstown; (908) 359-5970; www.canoenj.com/index.htm. Great place to rent canoes or kayaks and explore the canal firsthand.

Restaurants

Washington Street Station: 153 Washington Street, Rocky Hill; (609) 924-9872. Casual American cuisine.

Accommodations

Holiday Inn Princeton: 100 Independence Way, Princeton; (609) 520-1200.

Maps

DeLorme: New Jersey Atlas and Gazetteer: Pages 35 I28, 36 N8, and 42 A9.
New Jersey Bike Maps: Rocky Hill, Hopewell; www.njbikemap.com.

16 Round Valley Reservoir Challenge

The beautiful blue water of the Round Valley Reservoir attracts boaters, fishermen, and campers to its shoreline. There are a lot of good quiet roads in this area. Although the terrain is hilly, the views are worth the work. This loop takes you from the Delaware and Raritan Canal in Rocky Hill to the Round Valley Reservoir and back.

Start: Rocky Hill parking area, Delaware and Raritan Canal, Rocky Hill.
Distance: 65.1-mile loop.
Terrain: Moderately hilly, with a few long climbs near the reservoir.

Traffic and hazards: Most of the ride is on backcountry roads with little traffic. You will pass through a few town centers that can be a little busy.

Getting there: From U.S. Highway 1 in South Brunswick take Ridge Road west through Kingston. Cross Route 27 and continue on Kingston. The Rocky Hill parking area is about 3 miles from US 1, on the left across from the rock quarry just before the light at County Road 518.

In the 1960s the New Jersey Water Authority constructed two dams and transformed a huge Hunterdon County ravine into what is today Round Valley Reservoir. Covering more than 2,000 acres and reaching depths of 180 feet, the reservoir is known for its pristine blue water. The reservoir is surrounded by 5,291 acres of unspoiled eastern woodlands. In addition to boating, Round Valley Reservoir offers campsites and hiking and mountain biking trails.

The ride starts at the corner of County Road 518 and Canal Road. To get there from the parking lot, follow the gravel path north toward CR 518. When you reach CR 518, turn left at the light onto Canal Road.

As you ride north on Canal Road you will see the canal on your left and some historic houses on both sides of the road. Continue over the Griggstown Causeway and then down River Road and across U.S. Highway 206. You will be heading over the Sourland Mountains, which means some climbing—that starts once you get to Hollow Road.

Hollow Road starts out flat, then begins a gentle climb of about 160 feet that follows a little stream. At the top of the hill turn left onto Long Hill Road. Continue a gentle climb as you ride to Zion and Lindbergh Roads.

Once you are on Lindbergh, the road continues uphill a little before giving you a nice long downhill. Be careful of oncoming traffic as you round the curves of this road. At the bottom of the hill is a nice general store called Peacocks—a good place to stop if you need a break. Turn left onto Wertsville Road, followed by a right onto Manners Road (County Road 609). The road starts off with a short, steep 100-foot climb followed by a steep downhill. Watch your speed on the downhill—you will have to make a right turn at the bottom onto Welisewitz Road. If you cross a bridge, you have missed the turn.

From here you will travel though part of the Sourlands Valley on nice quiet roads through some beautiful farmlands and eventually end up on Old York Road. One of the oldest roads in the area, Old York Road was once a main road between Philadelphia and New York. This road has been replaced as a major thoroughfare by highways like U.S. Highway 202, so it's now a quiet road that's good to bike on.

Continue on Old York Road for 3.25 miles. After about a mile, pass through the town of Three Bridges. It's a pretty quiet town, but there will be a little more traffic here. After passing through town, you have a small climb of about 80 feet and the road gets a little quieter. After another 3.25 miles on Old York Road, make a left onto Summer Road and climb a small, annoying hill. After climbing the hill, come to a traffic light. There is a convenience store at the right-hand corner if you need a break, but if you can wait 6 miles, there is a much better place to stop in Stanton. At the light go straight and cross US 202. Continue on some more nice back roads until you turn left onto Pleasant Run Road. This road does not have any shoulder and can carry moderate traffic at times, so stay single file and to the right.

After 1.25 miles Pleasant Run Road comes to an intersection where five roads meet. Go across the road and bear right onto Springtown Road. This is a pretty road with an uphill grade.

At the end of Dreahook and Stanton Mountain Roads is a T where you have a choice to make, depending on how strong you feel. If you need a break, turn left here to reach the Stanton General Store in 0.25 mile. It's a great rest stop with good food, including some of the best muffins in New Jersey.

Your other option is to turn right from Dreahook onto Stanton Mountain Road and begin to climb Stanton Mountain—about a 260-foot climb that is not too difficult. This is followed by a steep 400-foot downhill. The only problem with going this way, besides adding a climb, is the condition of the road. As of this writing, the downhill section is really beat up and dangerous to ride. Until the road is fixed, I don't recommend going this way. NOTE: If you do go this way, Stanton Mountain Road intersects Stanton Road (County Road 629) at Mile 33 of this ride, and you can continue on the route.

To avoid the rough Stanton Mountain Road, make a left from Dreahook onto Stanton Mountain and head for the general store. After you take a break at the store, turn right onto Stanton Lebanon Road (CR 629). This road can be a little busy, so stay to the right. You are now getting close to the reservoir. Your approach to the reservoir starts with a 260-foot climb followed by a few more rollers. You know are done climbing when you see Valley Crest Road on your left. I don't know how a valley can crest—I'm just happy to be at the top. To your right you start to get some good views of the reservoir and begin to appreciate its size and scenic beauty.

Right after you pass Valley Crest Road, there is an entrance to Round Valley Reservoir to your right. This road leads to some of the swimming areas but does not provide a way through the reservoir property. Continue on and take the next right into the reservoir. After making the right, you have some great views of the reservoir as the road zigzags along its shores. Eventually the road veers left away from the reservoir; make the next right onto Old Mountain Road.

There are a few rollers here and then a downhill where you cross some railroad tracks. Make a right immediately after the tracks onto Railroad Avenue. After a little less than 2 miles, this road comes to a T at Main Street in Whitehouse Station. You are now in the center of town; it can be very busy on weekend afternoons, so be very careful here. Turn right onto Main Street and then make the next left onto Kline. Away from the traffic again, continue along some beautiful, relatively flat back roads.

When you're on Pulaski you will pass the Solberg Airport (although you may not notice it). It's a very small airport, but it hosts the biggest balloon festival in the area every July. Reddington and Old York Roads will have moderate to heavy traffic. Old York has a nice shoulder, so traffic is not a problem; just be careful as you approach US 202.

After crossing US 202, make a few turns as you ride over and along the Raritan River. If you need a break, at Mile 52.24 stay on South Branch and go past the turn for East Mountain Road. Just ahead on the right is a deli and liquor store in what looks like an apartment building. Look close, because it's easy to miss. The entrance is in back.

You have just gone around the top end of the Sourlands Mountains and are riding south along the base of them on East Mountain Road.

After you cross US 206, the road's name changes to Harlingen Road. After about 0.5 mile come to a T. You are now at the corner of Harlingen and Harlingen Roads. No, this is not a misprint; it's just a result of poorly merging old and new roads. Turn left here and stay on Harlingen Road. The road wind around a little past a park; after about another mile, turn left onto, believe it or not, Harlingen Road.

Round Valley Reservoir Challenge

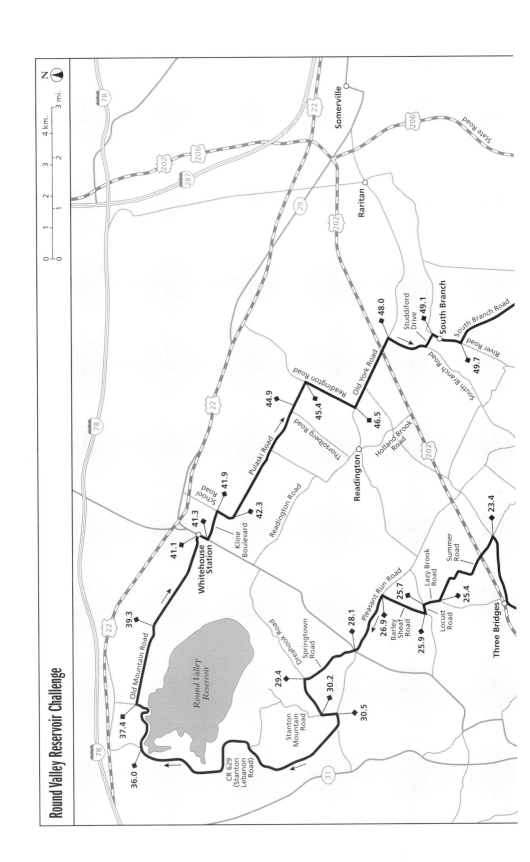

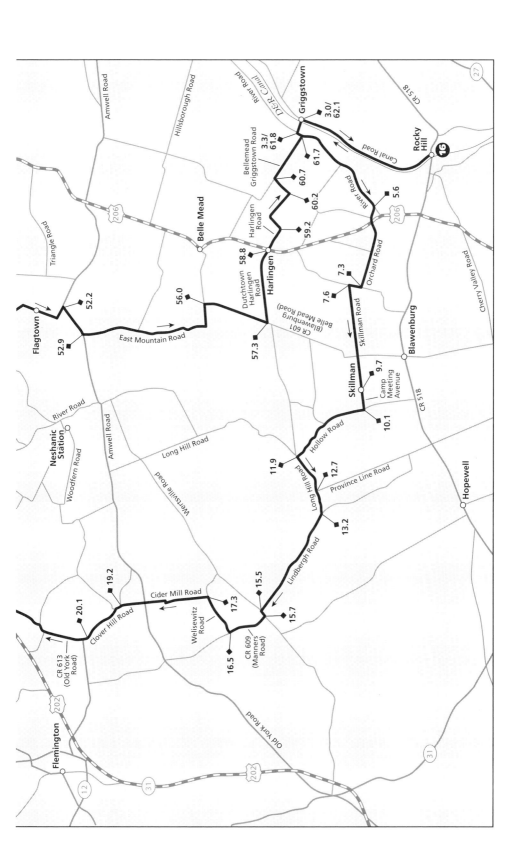

Come to a T after another 0.5 mile. This is the end of the strangely disconnected Harlingen Road. Turn right here onto Bellemead Griggstown Road and go downhill back toward the canal, then make a left onto River Road followed by a quick right onto the Griggstown Causeway. Watch the traffic here.

From the Griggstown Causeway turn right onto Canal Road. In about 3 miles you will hit CR 518 and be back at the starting point.

Miles and Directions

0.0 From the exit of the parking lot, turn right on CR 518 and go north on Canal Road. N40° 23.962' / W74° 37.671'

3.0 Turn left onto the Griggstown Causeway.

3.3 Turn left onto River Road.

5.6 Cross Bridgepoint Road; the road becomes Orchard Road.

7.3 Turn right at the T onto Burnt Hill Road.

7.6 Turn left onto Skillman Road.

9.7 Go over the railroad bridge; the road becomes Camp Meeting Avenue.

10.1 Turn right onto Hollow Road for a 160-foot climb.

11.9 Turn left at the T onto Long Hill Road.

12.7 The road becomes Zion Road.

13.2 Bear right and merge with Lindbergh Road. There's a long downhill ahead.

15.5 Turn left onto County Road 602 (Wertsville Road). (Peacocks general store is on the left if you need a break.)

15.7 Turn right onto Manners Road for a steep uphill followed by steep downhill.

16.5 Turn right at the bottom of the hill, before the bridge, onto Welisewitz Road.

17.3 Turn left onto Cider Mill Road.

19.2 Turn left onto Clover Hill Road.

20.1 Turn right onto Old York Road (County Road 613).

23.4 Turn left onto Summer Road. (There's a convenience store at top of hill by the stoplight.) Be careful crossing US 202.

25.4 Turn right onto Lazy Brook Road.

25.7 Turn left onto Locust Road.

25.9 Turn right onto Barley Sheaf Road.

26.9 Turn left onto Pleasant Run Road (CR 629). Stay to the right.

28.1 At the five- point intersection, cross the road and bear right onto Springtown Road.

29.4 Turn left at the T onto Dreahook Road.

30.2 Turn left onto Stanton Mountain Road. (Option: Turn right and climb Stanton Mountain. This road intersects the ride at Mile 33.)

30.5 Turn right onto CR 629 (Stanton Lebanon Road). The general store on the corner has good food.

36.0 Turn right into the second entrance to the reservoir to stay on CR 629. You will now get some good views of the reservoir on your right

Crossing the bridge on Cider Mill

37.4 Turn right on to Old Mountain Road. This turn is in the middle of a downhill, so it's easy to miss.

39.3 Turn right after the railroad tracks onto Railroad Avenue.

41.1 Turn right at the T onto Main Street (County Road 523) in Whitehouse Station. This is a very busy area, so stay to the right.

41.3 Turn left onto Kline Boulevard.

41.9 Turn right at the T onto School Road.

42.3 Turn left onto Pulaski Road.

44.9 Pass Solberg Airport; the road becomes Harlan School Road.

45.4 Turn right onto Reddington Road.

46.5 Turn left at the T onto Old York Road.

48.0 Turn right after crossing US 202 onto South Branch Road.

48.4 Turn left at the T to stay on South Branch Road.

48.9 Turn left onto Studdiford Drive.

49.1 Turn right onto River Road.

49.7 Turn left onto South Branch Road.

52.2 Turn right onto East Mountain Road. (There's a food stop on South Branch on the right in what looks like an apartment building just past the turn for East Mountain Road.)

52.9 Bear left at the light to stay on East Mountain Road.

56.0 Turn right onto County Road 601 (Blawenburg Belle Mead Road).

57.3 Turn left onto Dutchtown Harlingen Road.

58.8 Cross US 206. The road becomes Harlingen Road.

59.2 Turn left at the T to stay on Harlingen Road.

60.2 Turn left to stay on Harlingen Road.

60.7 Turn right onto Bellemead Griggstown Road.

61.7 Turn left onto River Road.

61.8 Turn right onto the Griggstown Causeway.

62.1 Turn right onto Canal Road.

65.1 Finish your ride back at the parking lot.

Local Events/Attractions

Round Valley Reservoir, part of the state's Round Valley Recreation Area, is a large lake surrounded by more than 500 acres of woods. In addition to boating and swimming on the lake, the area offers camping and a number of hiking trails. For details, visit www.state.nj.us/dep/parksandforests/parks/round.html.

Restaurants

Washington Street Station: 153 Washington Street, Rocky Hill; (609) 924-9872. Casual American cuisine.

Accommodations

Holiday Inn Princeton: 100 Independence Way, Princeton; (609) 520-1200.

Maps

DeLorme: New Jersey Atlas and Gazetteer: Pages 35 M28, 36 N3, and 42 A9.
New Jersey Bike Maps: Rocky Hill, Hopewell, Flemington, Raritan, Califon; www.njbikemap. com.

17 Assunpink Park Ramble

The Assunpink Wildlife Management Area is a beautiful 5,700–acre park that is an oasis for those who like to hunt, fish, or otherwise observe nature. This park is home to a good amount of wildlife and is a stopover for a number of migrating birds. This ride takes you on an easy loop in and around the park.

Start: Etra Lake Park parking lot on Disbrow Hill Road, Hightstown.
Distance: 18.8-mile loop.
Terrain: Mostly flat, with a few small hills. There is a short but steep 80-foot climb going into the Assunpink.

Traffic and hazards: Most of the roads traveled on this ride have light traffic and are easy to ride.

Riding past the farms on Etra Road

Getting there: Etra Lake Park is just outside of Hightstown. From exit 8 of the New Jersey Turnpike take Route 33 west toward Hightstown. You are on Franklin Street, which ends in a T at a fire station. Turn left onto North Main Street and go south until you see the Hightstown Diner on the left. Make a left onto Ward Street and then the next right onto South Main Street. Turn left onto Etra Road (County Road 571), which crosses the turnpike. After about a mile there is a lake on your left; this is Etra Lake. Make the next left onto Disbrow Hill. Etra Lake Park is just ahead on the left.

This is short ride with some nice scenery. It's a perfect route for a quick night-training ride or a leisurely afternoon trek.

This ride starts in Etra Lake Park, a small park with a few basketball courts next to the lake and some soccer fields. To start the ride, make a right turn out of the park onto Disbrow Hill Road and then make the next right onto Etra Road. Etra Lake is now on your right. This is a popular place to fish, so you will usually see a few people fishing from the banks of the lake or from boats. From here you will ride on back roads through a patchwork of small farms and newer housing developments.

After making a right onto CR 571 (Rochdale Avenue), go through the town of Roosevelt. Roosevelt was built in 1936 as part of President Franklin D. Roosevelt's New Deal. The town started as a garment factory that was owned and operated by the homeowners. Roosevelt looks much as it did in the late 1930s. The town is still composed of a series of small bungalow-style houses built close together. If you look closely at the park on the right as you go through the middle of the town, you will see a small bust of President Roosevelt.

Near the end of town, CR 571 turns left. Keep going straight here to enter the Assunpink Wildlife Management Area. There's a steep but very short hill as you enter the park. At the top of the hill, turn right at a T and follow the winding road through the park. Depending on the time of year, you may see hunters walking along the road and hear gunshots in the distance. There is almost no traffic on this road, so it feels like a big bike path. The road goes past an old farmhouse and continues to meander until you reach a large white house, which use to be the ranger's house but now seems abandoned.

Continue out of the Assunpink and go past a couple of horse farms. If you want to shorten the ride by a few miles, you can continue straight instead of making the left turn onto Imlaystown Road. This is Herbert Road and will rejoin the route where it turns onto Herbert Road at Mile 12.2.

You may encounter some traffic on County Road 524, so stay in the small shoulder on the right. Sharon Station Road starts with a nice little downhill here, so enjoy. At the bottom of the hill are some wetlands.

From Sharon Station turn left onto Herbert Road and ride past one of the many sod farms in the area. When Herbert Road ends at a T, make a right onto County Road 539, followed by a quick left onto Sharon Road. Watch the traffic here. Watch the miles, and don't miss the right onto Allens Road. If you cross over the turnpike, you have missed the turn.

After about a mile on Allens Road, you will see the Silver Decoy Winery. You are only a few miles from the end of the ride, so feel free to stop for a sample or two. Cross though a traffic light and continue on until you reach Cedarville, where you will make a left and retrace your path to Etra Lake Park.

Miles and Directions

0.0 Start at Etra Lake Park, and make right out of the park onto Disbrow Hill Road. N40° 15.137' / W74° 29.763'

0.2 Turn right onto Etra Road (Etra Perrineville Road).

0.6 Turn left onto Cedarville Road.

1.2 Turn left onto Windsor Perrineville Road.

1.7 Turn right onto Parkside Way.

2.1 Turn left onto Nurko Road.

3.5 Turn right onto CR 571 (Rochdale Avenue).

4.6 Go straight where CR 571 goes left onto Rochdale Avenue and enter Assunpink Park. There's a short but steep little climb here.

5.1 Turn right at the T onto Clarksburg Robbinsville Road (unsigned).

Assunpink Park Ramble

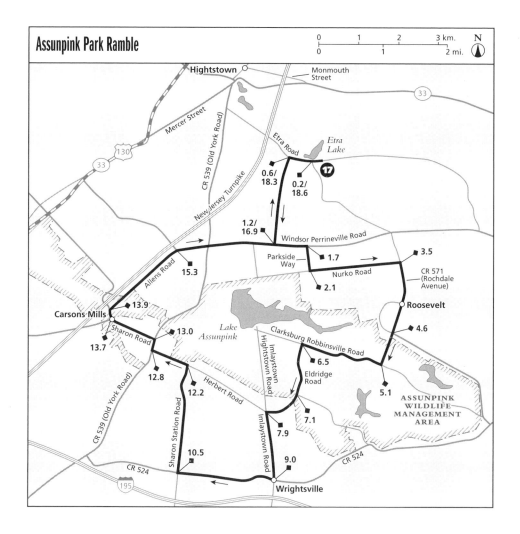

6.5 By the former ranger's house, turn left where the road becomes dirt onto Eldridge Road (unsigned).

7.1 Turn right at the T to stay on Eldridge Road.

7.9 Turn left onto Imlaystown Road.

9.0 Turn right onto CR 524.

10.5 Turn right onto Sharon Station Road.

12.2 Turn left onto Herbert Road.

12.8 Turn right onto County Road 539 (Old York Road).

13.0 Quick left onto Sharon Road.

13.7 Turn right onto Windsor Road.

13.9	Turn right onto Allens Road.
15.3	Bear right; the road becomes Windsor Perrineville Road.
16.9	Turn left onto Cedarville Road.
18.3	Turn right onto Etra Road (Etra Perrineville Road).
18.6	Turn left onto Disbrow Hill Road.
18.8	Turn left into Etra Lake Park to complete the loop.

Local Events/Attractions

The Assunpink Wildlife Management Area is a 5,700-acre park in the middle of Mercer County. It's a popular place for fishing, hunting, and horseback riding.

Restaurants

Slowdown Cafe: 110 Mercer Street, Hightstown; (609) 448-9900; www.slowdowncafe .com. A small cafe in the middle of Hightstown serving coffee, ice cream, and sandwiches.

Tavern on the Lake: 101 South Main Street, Hightstown; (609) 426-9345. Fine family dining in a casual lakeside atmosphere.

Accommodations

East Windsor–Days Inn Hightstown: 460 Route 33, E. East Windsor; (609) 448-3200.

Quality Inn East Windsor: 351 Franklin Street, Windsor; (609) 448-7399.

Maps

DeLorme: New Jersey Atlas and Gazetteer: Pages 42 N14 and 43 J15.

New Jersey Bike Maps: Hightstown, Allentown, Roosevelt; www.njbikemap.com.

18 Clarksburg Cruise

In the eastern part of Central Jersey, all roads lead to Clarksburg. Clarksburg is where a number of quiet country roads meet and is a convenient place to stop for a break. A number of bike clubs ride in this area, so in addition to some nice rolling roads, you also will find lots of company.

Start: Village Park parking lot, just off Maplewood Avenue, Cranbury.

Distance: 38.6-mile loop.

Terrain: Flat to rolling. Most of the roads in this area are relatively flat, with just enough rolling hills to keep it interesting. The only climb of the ride is up Stillhouse Road, a little over 100 feet.

Traffic and hazards: Most of the ride is on back roads with little traffic. The area around Cranbury can be a little busy at times, with moderate traffic.

Getting there: Village Park is in Cranbury, just off Maplewood Avenue. If you're coming from the south, take U.S. Highway 130 north and make a left at Cranbury Station Road then a right onto Main Street. Follow Main Street, turning right onto Westminster Place. The park is at the end of Westminster Place where it crosses Maplewood Avenue.

If you are coming from the north, take US 130 south and make a right onto Cranbury Half Acre Road then a quick left onto Maplewood Avenue. The entrance to the park is on the left just after the cemetery on the right.

Perrineville Road

Although this area of Central Jersey is continually losing farmland to development, there are some roads and areas that stay the same over time and make riding here easy and enjoyable. County Roads 571, 526, and 524 are the main east–west roads in this area of small towns and farmlands. Between these roads and the many other small roads in the area, it is easy to put together a variety of rides. This ride takes you on an easy loop of just under 40 miles that will show you some of the better roads in the area.

The ride starts at Village Park in Cranbury. To start the ride, exit the parking lot and turn left onto Maplewood Avenue. You will make a few turns and go through the town of Cranbury and eventually cross US 130. Watch the traffic in town—it can be hard to see around some of the corners.

After crossing US 130, cross over the New Jersey Turnpike and some railroad tracks as you continue heading mostly east. The roads get quieter as you continue, but be careful crossing Perrineville—the cross traffic is moving fast.

The roads wind around some houses and farms. When you make the right onto Iron Ore Road, stay to the right. This road will have moderate traffic. You are on this road only 0.5 mile before turning left onto Daum Road.

You will have some moderate traffic on Woodward Road, so stay to the right here, too. After you cross Route 33, the road gets quieter. From here you will be riding through some rolling hills as you continue on Lambs Lane and Baird Road.

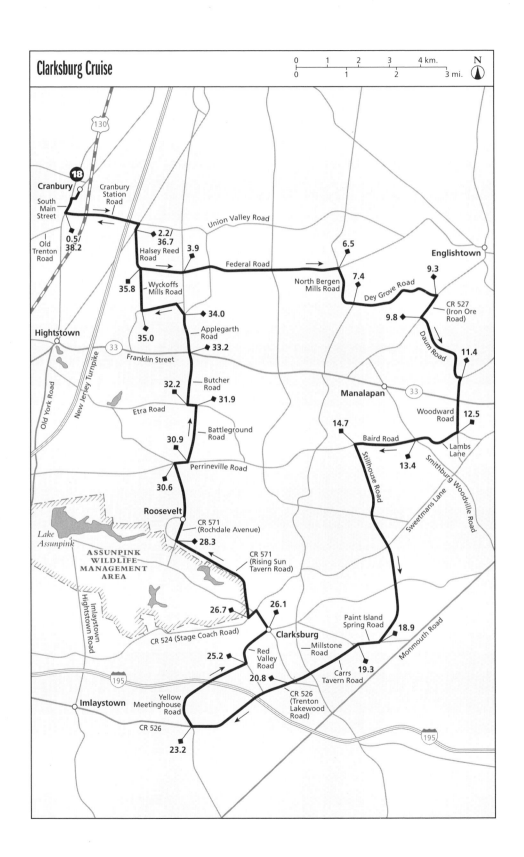

Clarksburg Cruise

0   1   2   3   4 km.
0   1   2   3 mi.

N

130

18

Cranbury

Cranbury
Station
Road

South
Main
Street

0.5/
38.2

Old
Trenton
Road

Union Valley Road

2.2/
36.7

Halsey Reed
Road

3.9

35.8

Wyckoffs
Mills
Road

Federal Road

6.5

7.4

North Bergen
Mills Road

Dey Grove Road

Englishtown

9.3

CR 527
(Iron Ore
Road)

9.8

Daum Road

11.4

Hightstown

33

Franklin Street

New Jersey Turnpike

Old York Road

34.0

35.0

Applegarth
Road

33.2

Butcher
Road

32.2

31.9

Etra Road

30.9

Battleground
Road

Manalapan

33

Woodward
Road

12.5

14.7

Baird Road

Lambs
Lane

13.4

Smithburg Woodville Road

Perrineville Road

30.6

Stillhouse Road

Sweetmans Lane

Roosevelt

CR 571
(Rochdale Avenue)

28.3

*Lake
Assunpink*

**ASSUNPINK
WILDLIFE
MANAGEMENT
AREA**

CR 571
(Rising Sun
Tavern Road)

Imlaystown
Hightstown Road

26.7

26.1

CR 524 (Stage Coach Road)

Clarksburg

Paint Island
Spring Road

18.9

25.2

Red
Valley
Road

Millstone
Road

Carrs
Tavern Road

19.3

195

Imlaystown

Yellow
Meetinghouse
Road

20.8

CR 526
(Trenton
Lakewood
Road)

Monmouth Road

CR 526

23.2

195

When you make the left onto Stillhouse Road, you encounter a series of rollers followed by a little climb. The top of the climb is 1.5 miles from the start of the road, at which point you will have climbed about 100 feet. At the top of the hill you are at the corner of Stillhouse and Sweetmans Roads, with a nice view of an old church to your left. There is a nice little hill here followed by some more rollers. When you cross CR 524 (Stage Coach Road), the road becomes much flatter. Continue along a few more roads on the back side of the town of Clarksburg, eventually reaching CR 526. CR 526 is a main east–west road in the area, with moderate traffic at times. The road has a shoulder most of the way; stay in it when you can.

This is a nice flat stretch—a good place to do some sprints or work on your rhythm. After 2.4 miles, you'll pass a lake on your right. Make the next right onto Yellow Meetinghouse Road. The road starts with a gentle uphill followed by a couple of rollers. Yellow Meetinghouse Road takes you to Red Valley Road, which ends at a strange intersection where it meets Spring Road and CR 524. There are two stop signs within about 50 feet. You want to go straight through the first stop sign and turn left at the second one onto CR 524 (Stage Coach Road). The Clarksburg Deli is at this intersection and makes a good stop. It's not a great deli, but it's got a good location and a place to sit outside. They will also let you use the restroom if you ask.

After your break, continue west on CR 524 past the Clarksburg Inn around a left bend, and then make the next right onto CR 571 (Rising Sun Tavern Road). The first 10 feet of this road are really steep, so if you're not in a low gear before you make the turn, you have a good chance of having to come to a complete stop, which can be a little dangerous.

Rising Sun Tavern Road has a fun series of rollers, with some good ups and downs. If you get the rhythm right, you can usually use the momentum from the downhill to get up the next uphill.

From here you will follow CR 571 through the town of Roosevelt. Continue on Route 571 until you come to a T-like intersection where CR 571 meets Perrineville and Windsor Roads. This can be a busy and confusing intersection for cars, because both the road you are on and Windsor Road come in at almost the same angle. Take a good look around before making a right onto Perrineville Road. Then take Battleground Road to Etra to Butcher Road and eventually cross Route 33 at a light. Continue straight through the light as the road name changes to Applegarth. The next mile or so will have moderate traffic, so stay to the right. After you cross over Route 33, Applegarth Road goes downhill past a firehouse and then a restaurant on your left. Right after the restaurant turn left onto Wyckoffs Mills Applegarth Road.

You'll wind around some protected land, and after 1 mile make a right at the corner of Wyckoffs Mills Applegarth Road and Wyckoffs Mills. Turn left at the next T onto Halsey Reed Road and wind through a new development before making a left onto Cranbury Station Road.

From here it's a straight shot back to Cranbury, and in a few more turns you will be back to Village Park where you started.

The area you just rode through has a lot of good bike roads that are relatively flat. This ride has taken you on some of the nicer roads, but there are a lot more out there. If you like the route, try exploring some of the other roads on your own.

Miles and Directions

0.0 Turn left out of the parking lot onto Maplewood Avenue. N40° 18.777' / W74° 30.784'

0.2 Follow the road around to the right onto Scott Avenue.

0.3 Turn left onto Main Street.

0.6 Turn left onto Cranbury Station Road (Station Road).

1.0 Cross US 130 and stay on Cranbury Station Road (Station Road).

2.2 Turn right onto Ely Road, which becomes Halsey Reed Road.

3.9 Cross Applegarth Road, which becomes Federal Road.

6.5 Turn right onto Bergen Mills Road.

7.4 Continue straight after a left bend onto Dey Grove Road.

9.2 Turn right at the T onto Iron Ore Road (County Road 527).

9.8 Turn left onto Daum Road.

11.4 Turn left at the T and then make the next right onto Woodward Road.

12.5 Turn right onto Lambs Lane.

13.4 Cross Smithburg Road. The road becomes Baird Road.

14.7 Turn left onto Stillhouse Road. There are a few small climbs ahead.

18.9 Turn right onto Paint Island Spring Road.

19.3 Bear left onto Carrs Tavern Road.

20.8 Turn left on to Spring Road followed by a right onto CR 526 (Trenton Lakewood Road).

23.2 Turn right onto Yellow Meetinghouse Road.

25.2 Turn left at the T onto Red Valley Road.

26.1 Turn left onto CR 524 (Stage Coach Road). (The Clarksburg Deli is at this turn and is a good place to take a break.)

26.7 Turn right onto CR 571 (Rising Sun Tavern Road).

28.3 Keep right onto CR 571 (Rochdale Avenue).

30.6 Turn right onto Perrineville Road.

30.9 Turn left onto Battleground Road.

32.0 Turn left at the T onto Etra Road.

32.2 Turn right onto Butcher Road.

33.2 Cross Route 33 at the light. The road becomes Applegarth Road.

34.0 Turn left onto Wyckoffs Mills Applegarth Road.

35.0 Turn right at the corner of Wyckoffs Mills Applegarth Road and Wyckoffs Mills.

35.8 Turn left at the T onto Halsey Reed Road.

36.7 Turn left at the T onto Cranbury Station Road.

38.2 Turn right onto Main Street.

38.3 Turn right onto Scott Avenue.

38.4 Scott Avenue bends to the left and becomes Maplewood Avenue.

38.6 Turn right into the parking lot to complete your ride.

Restaurants

Cranbury Inn: 21 South Main Street, Cranbury; (609) 655-5595. Award-winning historic colonial restaurant serving traditional American cuisine.

Cranbury Pizza: 63 North Main Street, Cranbury; (609) 409-9930. Pizza parlor with outside tables.

Teddy's Restaurant: 49 North Main Street, Cranbury; (609) 655-3120. Nice old-fashioned diner in the middle of Cranbury.

Accommodations

Residence Inn Cranbury South Brunswick: 2662 U.S. Highway 130, Cranbury; (609) 395-9447 or (888) 577-7005.

Maps

DeLorme: New Jersey Atlas and Gazetteer: Pages 43 F16 and 49 A20.

New Jersey Bike Maps: Hightstown, Jamesburg, Roosevelt; www.njbikemap.com.

19 Rues Road Roller-Coaster Cruise

The rolling hills of Central Jersey are a fun place to ride. Some of the roads have some quick ups and downs that give them a slight roller-coaster feel. This is an enjoyable ride in and around some beautiful farm country whose views have been frozen in time.

Start: Mercer County Park, Old Trenton Road (County Road 535) Road, West Windsor.
Distance: 39-mile loop.
Terrain: Flat, with a number of rolling hills. There will be a lot of ups and downs but no real climbs.
Traffic and hazards: Most of the roads for this ride are lightly traveled roads around farms. The roads around Mercer County Park can be a little busy, depending on the time of day, so traffic can be moderate at times. A good amount of the terrain on this ride is flat. There are some rolling hills, but none is a real climb.

Getting there: Mercer County Park is just off Old Trenton Road (CR 535) in West Windsor. Once you enter the park, continue past the tennis courts and ball fields and park next to the lake in the boathouse parking lot.

From north and south via Interstate 295: Take I-295 to exit 65A (Sloan Avenue). Turn east onto Sloan; at the third traffic light make a left onto Edinburg Road. After a couple of lights you will pass Mercer Community College. The entrance to Mercer County Park is your left.

From south via U.S. Highway 1: Cross the toll bridge into New Jersey on US 1. Make the first right onto Quakerbridge Road. Travel 2.2 miles and turn left onto Hughes Drive. Proceed on Hughes Drive to the first traffic light. Turn left onto Edinburg Road. After the next traffic light you will pass Mercer Community College. The entrance to Mercer County Park is on your left.

From south via U.S. Highways 130 and 206: Follow US 130 north to County Road 526 in Robbinsville. Turn left at traffic light onto County Road 526 and then right at the next light. From this point travel 3 miles to CR 535 (Edinburg Road). Turn left onto CR 535, and make the next right into Mercer County Park.

From north via US 1: Take US 1 south of Princeton to County Road 533 (Quakerbridge Road). Bear right off US 1 onto the exit ramp and cross over US 1 onto CR 533. Travel 2.2 miles and turn left onto Hughes Drive. At the first traffic light make a left onto Edinburg Road. After the next traffic light you will pass Mercer Community College. The entrance to Mercer County Park is on your left.

From north via New Jersey Turnpike: Take the turnpike south to exit 8 at Hightstown. Follow Route 33 west and turn right onto County Road 571. Travel on CR 571 for 2.2 miles to CR 535. Turn left onto Route 535 and proceed 3.4 miles. The entrance to Mercer County Park is on your right.

From south via New Jersey Turnpike: Take the turnpike to exit 7A. Travel west on Interstate 195 to exit 5B. Travel north on US 130 to second traffic light (CR 526). Turn left at the light and then right at the next light. Travel 3 miles to CR 535 (Edinburg Road). Turn left onto CR 535, and make the next right into Mercer County Park.

This nice cruise has a little bit of everything. During the ride you will go through parks, over rolling hills, through farmlands, and through some small towns. The terrain on this ride is constantly changing and has a few ups and downs. There are no real climbs, just a bunch of continuous rollers with some fun downhills.

This ride starts in Mercer County Park in the boathouse parking lot. Mercer County Park is a major recreation center for the county. There are numerous athletic facilities here. The park also has a nice set of mountain bike trails, although they are not well marked or advertised. The park hosts a number of athletic competitions throughout the year and on nice days is always fully of activity.

To start the ride, exit the boathouse parking lot and make a left onto the main road through the park. This road winds past the ice rink, baseball fields, and tennis courts and eventually takes you to the park exit on Old Trenton Road. Turn left here onto Old Trenton Road. This can be a busy intersection depending on the time of day and the activity in the park, so be careful here. Old Trenton Road is a main north–south road in the area and always has some traffic, so stay to the right. You won't be on the road long.

Make the next right onto Robbinsville Edinburg Road (CR 526). From here make the next left onto Meadowbrook Road and follow the road across US 130. Continue on this road until it ends where it meets Old York Road (County Road 539). Turn right here, staying in the shoulder. After about 0.75 mile, turn left just before the bridge over I-195. The bridge makes it a little hard for oncoming traffic to see you, so use caution here. You are now on County Road 524 just north of Allentown. The speed limit on this road is 50 miles per hour, and you will encounter some cars here, so stay in the small shoulder on the right.

You will be going east though some farmland. The road is mostly flat, but you will encounter a few small rollers. After you cross Imlaystown Road, you have a couple of small uphill sections. At the top of the hill on your left is the Horse Park of New Jersey. This world-class equine exhibition facility hosts a number of equine events and

Riding past the church on Emleys Hill

demonstrations throughout the year. On the right side of the road opposite the park is a carving of some horses.

After the road levels out, it bends right and then left and start a gentle downhill. Make the next right onto Chambers Road and start a slow uphill climb. The first road on your right is Tower Road; the next road on your right is Rues Road. The street sign on Rues Road is usually missing for some reason, so if you find yourself going downhill on Chambers, you have missed the turn to Rues Road.

Rues Road is a narrow, meandering road. The top part of the road has a couple of little ups and downs as well as a couple of hard left and right turns. This is a little-traveled road, but be on the lookout for the occasional car. The next part of this road is a nice screaming downhill with a couple of bumps that are easy to glide over. This is the roller-coaster part of the ride—if there are no cars, let 'er rip. The last part of the road is just a flat stretch that ends at a T on CR 526. Here, slightly to your right, is a Y in the road.

Veer left at the Y onto Imlaystown Road (Route 43). This road bends to the left and goes through the middle of Imlaystown. After a couple quick turns you will be on Davis Station Road and start a slow, easy uphill that will take you out of town past a tree farm. Once you make a left onto Emleys Hill Road you will encounter some more rolling hills. This is a scenic area, so take some time to enjoy the view. Toward

Rues Road Roller-Coaster Cruise

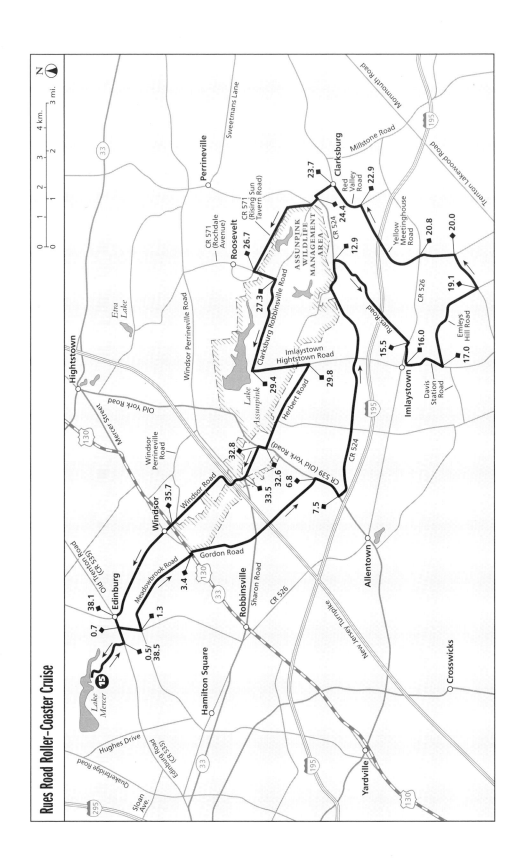

the end of the road is Emleys Hill Church. You can't miss the church—it's the only building at the top of the hill. This church was established in 1790, and from the look of it, nothing much has changed since it was built. This is a strangely quiet area; when there is a church service, you can hear the singing for miles.

Turn left at the church onto Burlington Path Road. There is a short but nice downhill here that goes past a large horse farm, Perretti Farms, that breeds thorough-bred horses. From here take Red Valley Road to Yellow Meetinghouse Road. Yellow Meetinghouse Road starts with a slow, steady uphill and then continues with a series of small rollers. After a little less than 2 miles, the road comes to a T. Turn left onto Red Valley Road. Don't worry—you aren't going in circles. This Red Valley Road has nothing to do with, and does not even intersect, the last Red Valley Road you were on. For some strange reason, it just has the same name.

Red Valley Road ends at an intersection where it meets Spring Road and Stage Coach Road (CR 524). Make a left here onto Stage Coach Road. If you want to take a break, the Clarksburg Deli is at this intersection and is a good place for a stop. It has a good selection of food and some chairs and tables outside where you can sit. They will also let you use the restroom if you ask.

Stage Coach Road can be a little busy at times, so stay to the right. The road bends around to the right and then left. After the left bend, you want to make a right onto Rising Sun Tavern Road (CR 571). The first 10 feet of this road are really steep. If you're not in a low gear before you make the turn, there's a good chance you'll have to come to a complete stop, which can be a little dangerous.

Rising Sun Tavern Road is a fun series of rollers with some good ups and downs. If you get the rhythm right, you can usually use the momentum from the downhill to get up the next uphill.

Here CR 571 goes to the right. Instead turn left and enter Assunpink Park. The entrance to the park is just ahead up a steep but very short hill. At the top of the hill, the road slowly levels out; it then goes downhill and comes to a T. Turn right here and enjoy a nice winding road through the Assunpink Wildlife Management Area. The Assunpink is a beautiful 5,700-acre park that is an oasis for those who like to hunt, fish, or otherwise observe nature. The road continues to meander until you reach a large white house that used to be the ranger's house but now appears abandoned. You have to make a left here—the road straight ahead, which leads to the lake, turns to dirt and is impossible to ride on a road bike.

Continue, leaving the Assunpink and riding past a couple of horse farms and sod farms. Watch out for traffic when you make the right onto Old York Road (CR 539). From here make a quick left turn onto Sharon Road; in about 0.75 mile make a right onto Windsor Road. You will be on Windsor Road for most of the rest of the ride, about 4 miles, until it meets Old Trenton Road at a light. Watch the traffic here as you make a left onto Old Trenton Road. The entrance to Mercer County Park is just ahead on the right. Turn right into the park and follow the main road back to the boathouse parking lot. Hopefully you have had a good workout and enjoyed the rolling hills of Central Jersey.

Miles and Directions

0.0 Turn left out of the boathouse parking lot. N40° 15.886' / W74° 38.289'

0.5 Turn left onto Old Trenton Road (CR 535).

0.7 Turn right onto Robbinsville Edinburg Road.

1.3 Turn left onto Meadowbrook Road.

3.4 Cross US 130 at a light. The road becomes Gordon Road.

6.8 Turn right at the T onto CR 539 (Old York Road).

7.5 Turn left onto CR 524, right before the bridge that goes over I-195.

12.9 Shortly after climbing a hill and passing a horse park, turn right onto Chambers Road.

13.1 Take the second right onto Rues Road. (If you start going downhill, you missed the turn.)

15.5 At the end of Rues Road there is a stop sign. Cross CR 526 and bear left at the Y onto Imlaystown Road.

16.0 Turn left at the next T onto Davis Station Road.

17.0 Continue out of Imlaystown and then turn left onto Emleys Hill Road.

19.1 Turn left at the church onto Burlington Path Road.

20.0 Turn left at the bottom of hill onto Red Valley Road.

20.8 Cross CR 526; the road becomes Yellow Meetinghouse Road.

22.9 Turn left at the T onto Red Valley Road.

23.7 Turn left at the intersection of Spring Road and CR 524 (Stage Coach Road). Clarksburg Deli is here if you want a to take a break.

24.4 The road bends around to the left. Make the next right turn onto CR 571 (Rising Sun Tavern Road).

26.7 Turn left at the stop sign onto Roosevelt Street.

27.3 Turn right at the top of the hill onto Clarksburg Robbinsville Road.

29.4 Turn left at the ranger's house onto Eldridge Road.

29.8 Turn right at the T onto Herbert Road.

32.7 Turn right onto CR 539 (Old York Road).

32.8 Quick left onto Sharon Road.

33.5 Turn right onto Windsor Road.

35.7 Cross US 130 at the light.

38.1 Turn left at the light onto Old Trenton Road.

38.5 Turn right into Mercer County Park.

39.0 Follow the park road to the boathouse parking lot and the end of your ride.

Local Events/Attractions

The Assunpink Wildlife Management Area
is a 5,700-acre park in the middle of Mercer
County. It's a popular place for fishing, hunting, and horseback riding.

Restaurants

Bill's Olde Tavern: 2694 Nottingham Way,
Trenton. Standard pub food in a casual
atmosphere.

Accommodations

East Windsor-Days Inn Hightstown: 460
Route 33, E. East Windsor; (609) 448-3200.
Quality Inn East Windsor: 351 Franklin Street,
Windsor; (609) 448-7399.

Maps

DeLorme: New Jersey Atlas and Gazetteer:
Pages 42 J8, 43 N18, and 49 A17.
New Jersey Bike Maps: Princeton, Allentown,
Roosevelt; www.njbikemap.com.

20 Mendokers' Bakery Ramble

Mendokers' Bakery is one of the best bakeries in the state and has a loyal following.
It's a favorite place to take a break while riding a bike, and this easy 28–mile ride will
hopefully burn off as many calories as you consume at the bakery. This ride takes you
from Cranbury to Jamesburg and back. Along the way you will visit some of the nicer
parks and lakes in the area.

Start: Village Park parking lot, just off Maple-
wood Avenue, Cranbury.
Distance: 28-mile loop.
Terrain: Mostly flat, with a few rolling hills.
Traffic and hazards: Most of the roads traveled
on this ride have light to moderate traffic and

are easy to ride. The center of Jamesburg,
where Mendokers' Bakery is, can have a lot of
traffic on a busy Saturday or Sunday afternoon,
so you will have to be patient here. There are
also a few intersections where you will need to
use a little extra caution.

Getting there: Village Park is in Cranbury, just off Maplewood Avenue. If you're coming from the
south, take U.S. Highway 130 north. Turn left at Cranbury Station Road and then right onto Main
Street. Follow Main Street and turn right onto Westminster Place. The park is at the end of Westminster Place where it crosses Maplewood Avenue.

If you are coming from the north, take US 130 south. Turn right onto Cranbury Half Acre Road
and then make a quick left onto Maplewood Avenue. The entrance to the park is on the left just
after the cemetery on the right.

This ride has one purpose: to eat some great baked goods. The exercise you will get
while riding the route is really secondary and only serves to reduce the guilt about
eating foods so high in sugar and fat.

This loop starts out in Village Park. Village Park contains a couple of ball fields
that get a lot of use. Depending on the time of day and year, it can be a busy place.
Be cautious as you ride out of the park, and watch for any cars or minivans rushing
kids to play baseball.

Mendokers' Bakery

The first few turns come pretty quick and serve to get you out of Cranbury onto Plainsboro Road. Cranbury is a pretty quiet town, so you shouldn't have many problems with traffic. Just make sure to follow the rules of the road and yield to traffic, especially at the light when you make a left onto Plainsboro Road.

Once you are on Plainsboro Road, you will be leaving Cranbury and entering Plainsboro. This used to be mostly farmland, but as the years go by more and more of it gets converted to apartments, condos, or houses. From here you will zigzag around the back end of the town of Plainsboro and end up on Friendship Road.

Friendship Road doesn't have much of a shoulder, so keep to the right. Pass New Road on your left. After about 1 mile, turn left onto Culver Road. Culver Road ends at a light where five different roads meet. As in most towns where the roads and intersections were established before the advent of modern traffic, it is a bit of a mess. It's not a hard intersection to navigate; when the light turns green, safely get into the left lane and make the left turn onto Georges Road.

Although Georges Road is a busy road, it has a wide shoulder to ride in most of the way, so traffic is not a problem. The one place you may hit a little traffic is where Georges and Deans Rhode Hall Roads intersect.

Georges Road crosses US 130 at a light. After the light, Georges Road loops back toward US 130. Right before it intersects the highway, make a right turn onto Riva Avenue. It's an easy road to miss, so if you run into US 130 again, you missed the turn. Once on Riva Avenue you will be entering Davidson's Mill Pond Park. There is a nice downhill here that ends at the waterfall where the mill used to be. The road has a sharp turn here at the bottom of the hill over a narrow bridge, so watch out for oncoming cars.

After you get over the next little hill, you will be riding along Farrington Lake. Long and narrow, Farrington Lake is a good place to fish and kayak.

As you continue on Riva Avenue, the road gets a little busier and a little rougher. Turn right onto Hardenburg Lane and start going uphill. Hardenburg Lane ends where it intersects Dunhams Corner Road at a light. Make a quick right here and then turn immediately left a few hundred feet down the road onto Fern Road. There is a left-turn lane you can wait in to make the turn onto Fern Road. Oncoming traffic is coming uphill around a turn, so be careful.

Take Fern Road to Old Stage Road, and eventually make a left onto Helmetta Boulevard. There is a nice downhill here before you enter the town of Helmetta and go through a swamp area with a bunch of reeds. Right after the swamp ends, turn right onto Maple Street. If you miss the turn, you will end up on Lake Avenue. Both roads run into the same street, so you won't get lost. At the end of Maple Street there is an old abandoned factory and a set of railroad tracks. Cross the tracks and make a right onto Main Street. This road isn't too busy, but there is not much of a shoulder, so keep to the right. The road takes you into the middle of Jamesburg. There may be some traffic here, so be careful when you make the left onto East Railroad Avenue. After the turn you will see a set of railroad tracks to your right. Make the next right, cross over the railroad tracks, and then make an immediate left. Mendokers' Bakery is a block ahead on the right.

Mendokers' is always busy no matter the time of day, so take a number from the dispenser when you walk in. There are usually a couple of tables outside the bakery where you can enjoy the food. You can also continue the route for another 0.5 mile and eat in the park just ahead. There is no restroom in the bakery, but the park has a couple of public restrooms.

Once you have finished your food, it's time to get back. Continue on past Medokers' until the end of the road. Turn right and then make a quick left into Thompson Grove Park. Stay to your left and continue along Lake Manalapan. As you go past the lake, the road bends to the right and you go up a short but annoying hill. As you are climbing the hill, make the next left and then bear right and continue to climb. This road winds around a little and takes you to Perrineville Road. Turn left onto Perrineville Road. This road is a little busy but has a small shoulder; stay to the right and you should be fine. After about a mile turn right onto Prospect Plains Road. There is a shopping center on the far right corner, which makes this intersection a little busy at times. Keep an eye out for cars entering or leaving the shopping center as you make the turn.

Continue on Prospect Plains Road for a little less then a mile. Where Prospect Plains meets Half Acre Road on the right, there are two stoplights really close together. Turn left at the second light onto Half Acre Road. Be extra careful here—the two lights make

Mendokers' Bakery Ramble

0   1   2   3   4 km.

0   1   2   3 mi.

N

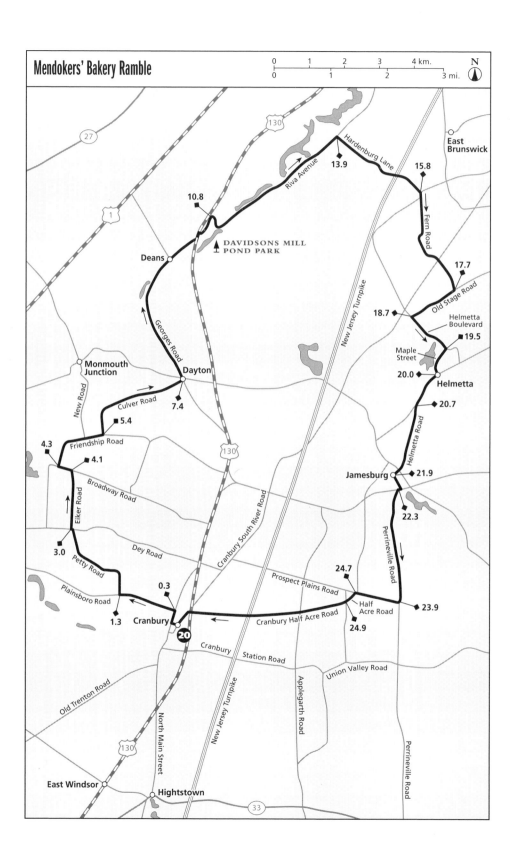

this intersection confusing, with cars entering and leaving the different parts of the intersection. After you make the left, go about 0.25 mile and then take the next right. It's now a straight run back to the start. In about 2.5 miles you will cross US 130 and then make the next left onto Maplewood Avenue, which takes you back to Village Park.

Miles and Directions

0.0 Go straight out of Village Park onto Westminster Place. N40° 18.797' / W74° 30.709'

0.1 Turn right onto North Main Street.

0.3 At the light turn left onto Plainsboro Road. This is a busy road, so stay to the right.

1.3 Turn right onto Petty Road.

3.0 Jog left onto Dey Road.

3.6 Turn right onto Rowland Road (Eiker Road).

4.1 Turn left onto Broadway Road.

4.3 Turn right onto Friendship Road.

5.4 Turn left onto Culver Road.

7.4 At the light turn left onto Georges Road. This is a busy intersection; be careful.

10.8 Turn right onto Riva Avenue.

13.9 Turn right onto Hardenburg Lane.

15.8 Jog right onto Dunhams Corner Road.

15.8 Make quick left onto Fern Road.

17.7 Turn right onto Old Stage Road.

18.7 Turn left onto Helmetta Boulevard.

19.5 Right after the swamp, turn right onto Maple Street.

20.0 After the railroad tracks turn right onto Manalapan Road (Main Street).

20.7 Keep left onto Helmetta Road.

21.7 The road bends right and changes to Augusta Street.

21.9 Turn left onto East Railroad Avenue. Use caution at this busy intersection.

22.1 Turn right onto Church Street and then left onto West Railroad Avenue. Medokers' is just ahead on the right.

22.3 Jog right onto County Road 612 (Forsgate Drive) and then make a quick left onto Lakeview Avenue. There are public restrooms ahead just after the gazebo.

22.6 As the road curves away from lake and climbs, turn left and then bear right.

22.9 After the road levels off and comes to a T, turn right and go through the baseball and soccer fields.

23.2 Turn left onto Perrineville Road.

23.9 Turn right onto Prospect Plains Road.

24.7 Take the second left at two closely spaced traffic lights onto Half Acre Road. Use caution here.

24.9 Turn right onto Cranbury Half Acre Road.

27.8 Turn left onto Maplewood Avenue.

28.0 Turn left into Village Park to complete the loop.

Restaurants

Cranbury Inn: 21 South Main Street, Cranbury; (609) 655-5595. Award-winning historic colonial restaurant serving traditional American cuisine.

Cranbury Pizza: 63 North Main Street, Cranbury; (609) 409-9930. Pizza parlor with outside tables.

Teddy's Restaurant: 49 North Main Street, Cranbury; (609) 655-3120. Nice diner in the middle of Cranbury.

Accommodations

Residence Inn Cranbury South Brunswick: 2662 U.S. Highway 130, Cranbury; (609) 395-9447 or (888) 577-7005.

Maps:

DeLorme: New Jersey Atlas and Gazetteer: Pages 42 F14 and 43 F16.

New Jersey Bike Maps: Hightstown, Monmouth Junction, New Brunswick, Jamesburg; www.njbikemap.com.

21 Rova Farm Cruise

As you ride around in Central Jersey, you never know what you are going to find among the farms and small towns. In this gentle cruise you ride through some rural farmlands and find a small piece of Russia in and amongst the farms.

Start: The corner of Main Street and County Road 526, Allentown.
Distance: 43.2-mile loop.
Terrain: Mostly flat, with a few rolling hills here and there.

Traffic and hazards: Allentown can be a little congested, but most of the roads have mostly light traffic. County Roads 528 and 524 may have moderate traffic, but these roads have shoulders most of the way.

Getting there: Take the New Jersey Turnpike to Interstate 195 west. Take exit 8 and head south on County Road 539 (Old York Road). This road turns into Main Street. Once you enter town, park anywhere along the street.

This ride is an easy cruise that offers a way to see some of the nicer farmland in the area without working too hard. The ride has a lot of long, straight stretches and is a good ride to start building up some miles.

The ride starts in Allentown. The Main Street area contains a number of historic houses as well as a number of antiques shops and restaurants. It can be a busy little town on a weekend afternoon.

The mileage for the ride starts at the intersection of Main Street and CR 526. Head south from here through the town and over the bridge. If the town is busy and congested, watch out for car doors as you ride through the town. Once you get to the south end of Main Street, you climb a small hill and then come to a Y. Stay left here. Pass a small park on your right. Make the next left onto Ellisdale Road and start heading toward the farmlands. Take Polhemustown Road to Holmes Mill Road, go through Cream Ridge, and pass a golf course. These are nicely wooded roads with a few rolling hills.

Russian church by Rova Farm

Be careful on Burlington Path Road at the intersection where you cross CR 539. This is a busy road, and cars are coming from the left and right pretty fast. As you continue on Burlington Path Road, you will be riding by some of the nicer horse farms in the area. Pass a beautiful small church with a graveyard behind it. You can't miss the church—it's the only building at the top of the hill. Turn right here onto Emleys Hill Road. Continue past some more farms and eventually cross County Road 537. This is a busy road, so use caution here.

There are a couple of rolling hills ahead. After 3 miles turn left onto CR 528. This is a road with a moderate amount of traffic, but it's a wide road with a shoulder most of the way. In 4 miles come to a traffic light where CR 528 and County Road 571 intersect. Turn left here onto CR 571. There are a couple stores here to the right, including a general store with a porch that's a good place to stop for a break.

You are now in an area called Rova Farms, a Russian American vacation community. Rova Farms was founded in the 1930s as a vacation playground after members of New York and Philadelphia Russian social clubs bought 1,600 acres of land in the historic Cassville section of the township.

This vacation community is not as active as it once was and is a little run down, but there is still a good Russian restaurant and a few Russian Orthodox churches here. You will see one of the churches on your left just before you make a right onto Freehold Road.

Rova Farm Cruise

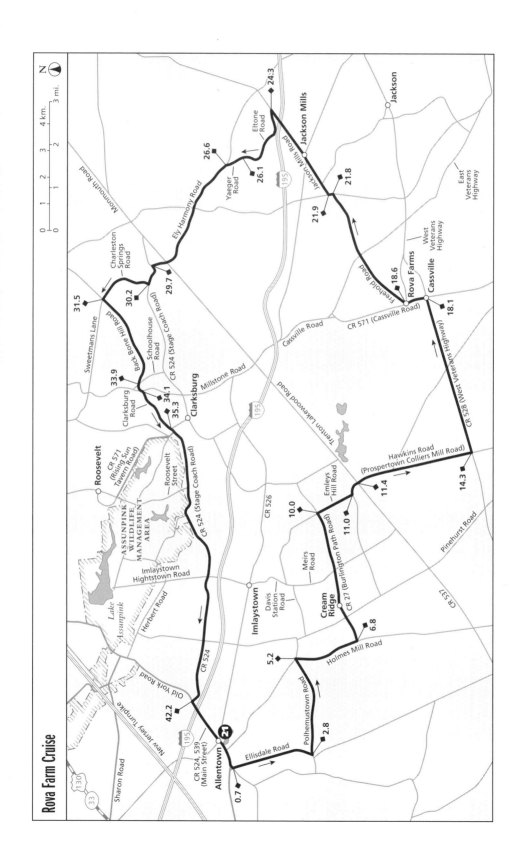

Once you are on Freehold Road, you leave the Rova Farms area and head toward Jackson Mills. Jackson Mills Road starts out as a quiet road and gets a little busier as you continue. As you approach County Line Road, the shoulder disappears and the road has two lanes in each direction. There are a couple of lights, with traffic entering from the left or right. The lanes are wide and there usually isn't a lot of traffic here, so just be careful as you go through these intersections. After Jackson Mills returns to a one-lane road, you cross an overpass that goes over I-195. Turn left just after the overpass onto Eltone Road. This road is before the stoplight, so if you go through the light you've gone too far.

Eltone, Yaeger, and Ely Harmony Roads are nice quiet roads that go through Turkey Swamp County Park. There are no particular sights here; these are just nice roads to ride.

After a little less than 3 miles on Ely Harmony Road, cross Monmouth Road (CR 537). This is a busy road with limited visibility to the right, so use caution when crossing the road. There is a little deli on the far right corner if you feel like a stop.

Continue on Ely Harmony Road to Stage Coach Road (CR 524) and make a right turn onto Charleston Springs Road. After a little over a mile turn left onto Back Bone Hill Road. Be careful as you make the left; oncoming traffic has limited visibility.

Back Bone Hill Road starts with a short little uphill then continues with a few rollers. Back Bone Hill Road ends where it meets Schoolhouse Road. Make a right here and then turn left at the T onto Millstone Road followed by a quick right onto Clarksburg Road. There is a little climb here, but there is a nice downhill on the other side. Clarksburg Road ends where it intersects CR 524 (Stage Coach Road). Go straight ahead on CR 524.

You will be CR 524 for about 7 miles. There may be a little traffic on this road, but most of the road has a shoulder, so stay to the right. There are a few rollers on this road, but most of it is flat, so this is a good road to try some sprints or work on your cadence. CR 524 ends where it intersects CR 539 (Old York Road). Make a left here, but be careful—there is an overpass for I-195 to your left with cars entering and leaving the highway.

Continue south on CR 539 and you will enter Allentown's Main Street and be back at the starting point. If you need to recharge after finishing the ride, check out some of the nice places to eat on Main Street.

Miles and Directions

0.0 From the corner of Main Street and CR 526 in Allentown, head south on Main Street. N40° 10.648' / W74° 35.065'

0.6 Go out of town up a small hill, and bear left at the Y onto South Main Street.

0.7 Turn left onto Ellisdale Road.

2.8 Turn left at the T onto Polhemustown Road.

5.2 Make a hard right turn (almost 180 degrees) onto Holmes Mill Road.

6.8	Turn left onto County Road 27 (Burlington Path Road).
10.0	Turn right by the church onto Emleys Hill Road.
11.0	Turn left at the T and continue on Emleys Hill Road.
11.4	Go straight across CR 537; the road changes to Hawkins Road.
14.3	Turn left at the light onto CR 528 (West Veterans Highway).
18.1	Turn left at the light on to CR 571 (Cassville Road).
18.6	Turn right onto Freehold Road.
21.8	Turn left onto Cedar Swamp Road.
21.9	Turn right onto Jackson Mills Road.
24.3	Turn left after the I-195 overpass onto Eltone Road.
26.1	The road name changes to Yaeger Road.
26.6	Bear left onto Ely Harmony Road.
29.7	Turn left onto CR 524 (Stage Coach Road).
30.2	Turn right onto Charleston Springs Road.
31.5	Turn left onto Back Bone Hill Road.
33.9	Turn right onto Schoolhouse Road.
34.1	Turn left onto Millstone, followed by a quick right onto Clarksburg Road.
35.3	Go straight at the stop sign onto CR 524 (Stage Coach Road).
42.2	Turn left onto CR 539 (Old York Road).
43.2	Arrive back at Main Street, Allentown.

Local Events/Attractions

Allentown, New Jersey, Web site: www
.allentownnj.com. Information about the town,
including a list of restaurants and shops.

Restaurants

Black Forest Restaurant: 42 South Main
Street, Allentown; (609) 259-3197. A quaint
eatery at the old mill, specializing in authentic
German cuisine.

Hoffmann's Bake Shoppe: 2 North Main
Street, Allentown; (609) 259-8442. Family
bakery offering a full line of breads, Danishes,
cakes, cookies, and coffee.

Rova Farm Resort: 120 Cassville Road, Jackson; (732) 928-0928. Not much to look at, it's
a good place for some authentic Russian food.

Accommodations

Peacefields Inn Bed & Breakfast: 84 Walnford Road, Allentown; (609) 259-3774; www
.peacefieldsinn.com/home.asp. An 1850
Georgian colonial farm estate situated on
a quiet country road adjacent to Historic
Walnford, a restored mill village on the
National Register of Historic Places.

Maps

DeLorme: New Jersey Atlas and Gazetteer:
Pages 43 N25, 48 A12, and 49 C15.
New Jersey Bike Maps: Allentown, Roosevelt,
New Egypt, Cassville, Adelphia; www.njbike
map.com.

22 Basic Training Challenge

Fort Dix and McGuire Air Force Base occupy a large area in south–central Jersey. There are no roads through the bases themselves, so this ride takes you around the bases for a long training ride that will get you into fighting shape.

Start: Peter Musical School parking lot, Ward Avenue, Bordentown.
Distance: 52.5-mile loop.
Terrain: Flat to rolling. The beginning and ending parts of the ride take you through some rolling terrain, including Hill Road, which has seven nice rollers in a row. The middle part of the ride is very flat as you skirt the Pine Barrens. The ride also takes you to the highest point in Burlington County, but at 234 feet it's really not much of a climb.

Traffic and hazards: Most of the ride is on backcountry roads with little traffic. You will pass through a few town centers that can be a little busy.

Getting there: From the north take the New Jersey Turnpike to exit 7a. Take Interstate 195 west to exit 5B and then U.S. Highway 130 south to Bordentown. After U.S. Highway 206 merges with US 130, make a U-turn at Route 528 and take US 130 north to Ward Avenue. Peter Musical School is on the right in 0.5 mile.

From the south take the New Jersey Turnpike to exit 7. Take US 206 north to Bordentown. After US 206 merges with US 130, turn right onto Ward Avenue. Peter Musical School is on the right in 0.5 mile.

Burlington County, the largest county in New Jersey, covers more than 827 miles. The county is mostly known for its agriculture and is a major producer of blueberries and cranberries. Burlington County is also home to Fort Dix and McGuire Air Force Base. Although these bases aren't as active as they once were, they still employ a lot of people in the area. This ride takes you from the northern end of Burlington County to the top of the Pine Barrens and back. Along the way you will see the outskirts of the military bases as well as some of the nice farmlands that surround the area.

The ride starts at the Peter Musical School. Make a right out of the school's parking lot onto Ward Avenue. You will be on this road for quite a while. Pass over the New Jersey turnpike and go through the town of Crosswicks. The road changes names a couple of times as you continue on. A mile after the road becomes Hill Road, there's a downhill followed by a sharp right bend in the road. Right before the bend, a road enters from the left—keep an eye out for incoming cars.

After the bend, Hill Road starts earning its name. There is a steep little 80-foot climb followed by six more rollers over the next 2 miles. It's a good workout. While you're working on the hills, make sure you take a look around. There are some nice views from the top of the hills.

Eventually Hill Road crosses Arneytown Hornerstown Road and the road name changes to Hutchinson Road. There is another steep little climb ahead, followed by a

Optional stop at McGuire Air Force Base

couple more little bumps. Hutchinson Road ends at a T where it meets Province Line Road. It's been 11 miles since you started the ride, and although the road has changed names, you actually haven't made a turn yet. Now make a couple of quick turns and ride through a residential community, eventually ending up on Route 528. This road can be a little busy at times, so stay to the right.

A few more turns will have you on Cookstown Browns Mill Road (Main Street) and take you through this small town. You are now right next to McGuire Air Force Base. The base holds a popular annual air show, which attracts a lot of people and creates some major traffic jams. If you want to attend the air show, consider biking to the base—it will allow you to beat most of the traffic. Although this ride continues straight on Cookstown Browns Mill Road, you can get to the base's main entrance by turning right at Wrightstown Cookstown Road.

As you continue south on Cookstown Browns Mill Road you will enter the area around Fort Dix and see signs telling you such. Most of the area that you are riding through is used for training, and you may see some military vehicles and personnel here. This is the only road in the area, so it can have moderate traffic at times. Continue past the base into a residential neighborhood surrounding Mirror Lake. This road winds around a little and after a few more turns brings you to the end of Clubhouse Road in the middle of Browns Mills.

This is a very busy intersection where a number of roads meet, so use extra caution here. Since this is the only real town you will see for the next 20 miles, it might be a good place to take a break. There is a Wawa and a couple of other stores to your right on Lakehurst Road, at the left half of the Y. This is a good place to stop—just watch the traffic. When you're done with your break, head back the way you came on Lakehurst Road. Go to the next light and turn right onto Junction Road.

This road starts out through a residential neighborhood that thins out as you continue. When you get to New Lisbon Road, you are at the top of the Pine Barrens and the riding is pretty flat. When you make the left turn onto Pemberton Vincentown Road, you are entering a large farming area.

Be careful crossing County Road 530 on Birmingham Road. CR 530 is a busy road with fast-moving traffic on a four-lane road, so be patient here. After crossing CR 530, you will wind around a residential neighborhood and eventually start a little climb. You are now headed to the highest point in Burlington County. It's only 234 feet, so it is not much of a climb. The climb ends where Birmingham Drive meets Arneys Mount Road. Turn left here and then turn right at the next intersection onto Juliustown Road (CR 669). If you look closely on the right after the turn, you will see a small windmill.

Continue on through the town of Juliustown then on to Jobstown. When you get to Route 537 (Monmouth Road), you begin a confusing series of quick turns. From Jobstown Juliustown Road turn right onto CR 537, make a quick hard left onto Jacksonville Jobstown Road, and then immediately bear right onto Columbus Jobstown Road. After another 0.5 mile, turn right onto Island Road and cruise past some farms. You may see a number of arrows on the road in this area as you make the next few turns. This is because the Princeton Freewheelers hold their annual bicycle event in this area and use the farm at the end of Island Road for one of their rest stops.

Continue along some of the back roads in this area and then cross Route 68. Route 68 is a busy road with fast-moving traffic, so be careful when you cross it. After crossing Route 68, go up a little hill and come to a T. Make a left here and then bear right onto Chesterfield Road.

You now have 2.7 miles of gentle rollers that will get you to Chesterfield. At Chesterfield the road comes to a T. Turn left and stay left onto County Road 528 (Bordentown Chesterfield Road). You are only a few miles from the end of the ride, but if you want a break there is a deli to your left right at the turn. Continue on CR 528 for 3 miles. Right after crossing the New Jersey Turnpike, make a right onto Hogback Road. Follow Hogback Road for 0.75 mile until it comes to a T. Turn left at the T onto Ward Avenue and follow it back to the school parking lot.

Miles and Directions

0.0 Make a right out of the school parking lot onto Ward Avenue. N40° 9.109' / W74° 41.344'

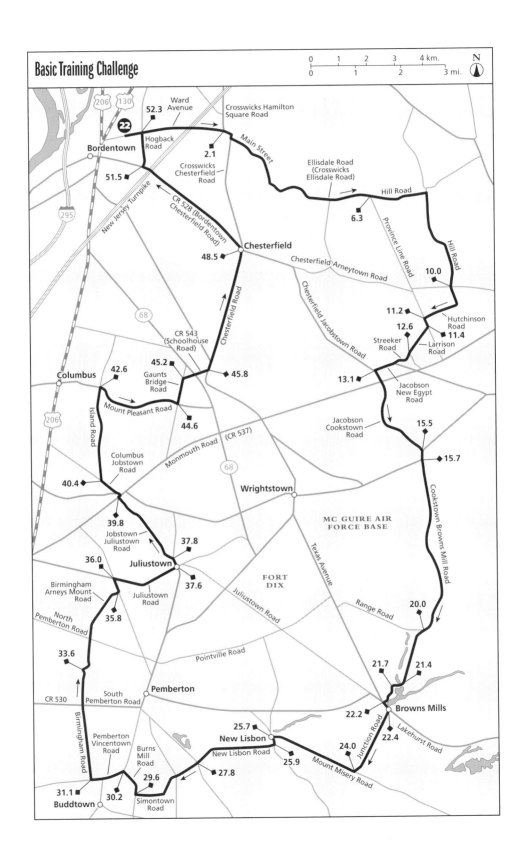

Basic Training Challenge

0 1 2 3 4 km.
0   1   2   3 mi.

N

206 130

22

52.3 — Ward Avenue

Crosswicks Hamilton Square Road

Hogback Road

Bordentown

2.1

Main Street

Crosswicks Chesterfield Road

Ellisdale Road (Crosswicks Ellisdale Road)

Hill Road

51.5

6.3

Province Line Road

Hill Road

New Jersey Turnpike

295

CR S-28 (Bordentown Chesterfield Road)

Chesterfield

48.5

Chesterfield Arneytown Road

10.0

11.2

Hutchinson Road

12.6

11.4

Chesterfield Road

Streeker Road

Larrison Road

68

CR 543 (Schoolhouse Road)

Chesterfield Jacobstown Road

13.1

45.2

45.8

Jacobson New Egypt Road

Gaunts Bridge Road

42.6

Columbus

Mount Pleasant Road

44.6

Jacobson Cookstown Road

15.5

206

Island Road

Monmouth Road (CR 537)

15.7

40.4

Columbus Jobstown Road

68

Wrightstown

MC GUIRE AIR FORCE BASE

Cookstown Browns Mill Road

39.8

Jobstown Juliustown Road

37.8

36.0

Juliustown

Texas Avenue

Birmingham Arneys Mount Road

37.6

FORT DIX

20.0

North Pemberton Road

35.8

Juliustown Road

Juliustown Road

Range Road

33.6

CR 530

South Pemberton Road

Pointville Road

Pemberton

21.7

21.4

Birmingham Road

Pemberton Vincentown Road

Burns Mill Road

25.7

New Lisbon

22.2

Browns Mills

22.4

Lakehurst Road

29.6

New Lisbon Road

25.9

24.0

Junction Road

31.1

30.2

27.8

Mount Misery Road

Buddtown

Simontown Road

2.1   Enter the center of Crosswicks, and continue straight. The road name changes to Main Street.

3.3   Continue straight as Main Street changes to Ellisdale Road (Crosswicks Ellisdale Road).

6.3   The road becomes Hill Road. It starts with a gentle downhill, then after a mile bends right and has some rolling hills.

10.0   Cross Route 27 (Arneytown Hornerstown Road). The road name changes to Hutchinson Road. There's another small climb ahead.

11.2   Turn left at the T onto Province Line Road.

11.4   Turn right onto Larrison Road.

12.1   Bear right at the Y onto Streeker Road.

12.6   Bear right and merge onto Jacobstown New Egypt Road (County Road 528).

13.1   Turn left onto Jacobstown Cookstown Road (County Road 665).

15.5   Turn right onto Main Street in Cookstown.

15.7   Leave Cookstown. The road changes names to Browns Mills Cookstown Road (Cookstown–Browns Mills Road).

20.0   Cross Range Road. Browns Mills Cookstown Road becomes East Lakeshore Drive.

21.4   Turn right onto Clubhouse Road.

21.7   Bear left at the Y where West Lakeshore Drive merges in from the right to stay on Clubhouse Road.

22.2   Turn left onto Lakehurst Road (a very busy intersection).

22.4   Turn right at the light onto Junction Road.

24.0   Bear right onto Mount Misery Road.

25.7   Turn left onto Four Mile Road.

25.9   Turn right onto New Lisbon Road.

27.8   Cross Magnolia Road, which becomes Simontown Road.

29.6   Turn right onto Burrs Mill Road.

30.2   Bear left onto Pemberton Vincentown Road.

31.1   Turn right onto Birmingham Road.

33.6   Turn right onto Brandywine Road, which eventually becomes to Birmingham Arneys Mount Road.

35.8   Turn left onto Arneys Mount Road.

36.0   Turn right onto Juliustown Road.

37.6   Turn left onto Georgetown Road.

37.8   Bear left at the Y onto Jobstown Juliustown Road.

39.8   Turn right onto Monmouth Road (County Road 537).

39.9   Make a hard left and then bear right onto Columbus Jobstown Road.

40.4   Turn right onto Island Road.

42.6   Turn right onto Mount Pleasant Road.

44.6   Turn left onto Gaunts Bridge Road.

45.2   The road bends to the right and becomes County Road 543 (School House Road). Be careful as you cross Route 68.

45.8 Turn left onto Chesterfield Road, then bear right to stay on Chesterfield.

48.5 Turn left onto Bordentown Chesterfield Road.

51.5 Turn right onto Hogback Road.

52.3 Turn left onto Ward Avenue.

52.5 Turn left into the school parking lot to complete the loop.

Restaurants

Mastori's Diner: 144 South U.S. Highway 130, Bordentown; (609) 298-4650. A popular diner with great food.

Accommodations

Comfort Inn Bordentown: 1009 U.S. Highway 206, Bordentown; (609) 298-9111; www .comfortinn.com.

Maps

DeLorme: New Jersey Atlas and Gazetteer: Pages 48 B5.

New Jersey Bike Maps: Trenton East, New Egypt, Browns Mills, Pemberton, Columbus; www.njbikemap.com.

23 Sandy Hook Ramble/Challenge

Sandy Hook is a beautiful 7-mile stretch of beach with a lot of history. It's a good place to spend a day. This ride takes you from Freehold to Sandy Hook (part of the Gateway National Recreation Area) and back and shows you some of the sites in and around Sandy Hook. This is a long ride of about 70 miles, which is why it is a challenge. If you are not up to the challenge or don't have the time, you can drive to Sandy Hook and do the 11-mile ramble that will give you a quick tour of the sights.

Start: Visitor center parking lot, Monmouth Battlefield State Park, Freehold (challenge); visitor center parking lot, Gateway National Recreation Area, Sandy Hook (ramble).

Distance: 65- to 70-mile loop (challenge); 11-mile loop (ramble).

Terrain: Mostly flat, with a few tough rollers near the beach.

Traffic and hazards: Most of the roads on these rides will have light traffic. Some of

the roads by Sandy Hook have moderate to heavy traffic, especially in summertime when the weather is nice. Weekend days can have bumper-to-bumper traffic around Sandy Hook for a few miles. There will also be some moderate traffic as you go through the towns of Freehold and Little Silver.

During summer this can be a hot ride. It's easy to get dehydrated in the hot sun, so be sure to drink a lot of water.

Getting there: For the challenge, start at Monmouth Battlefield State Park in Freehold. From the Garden State Parkway take exit 123 to U.S. Highway 9 south for 15 miles to Business Route 33 west. The park is located 1.5 miles on the right. Make a right into the park and park in the lot by the visitor center.

For the ramble start at Sandy Hook. From New York and northern New Jersey take the Garden State Parkway south to exit 117, then follow Route 36 east for 12 miles to the park entrance. Make a right into the park and park in the lot by the visitor center.

From Pennsylvania and southern New Jersey take the New Jersey Turnpike exit 7A to Interstate 195 east and then the Garden State Parkway. Take the Garden State north to exit 105 (Route 36). Follow Route 36 east for 11 miles to the park entrance. Make a right into the park and park in the lot by the visitor center.

Sandy Hook is a peninsula that juts out from New Jersey into Lower New York Bay. It's a place with a lot of history and natural beauty. In addition to the beach, Sandy Hook is also home to a U.S. Coast Guard station and historic Fort Hancock. The ramble part of this ride will take you on an 11-mile tour of all the sights of Sandy Hook. The ramble starts at Mile 27.0 of the directions below.

For the challenging ride, you will start at Monmouth Battlefield State Park and go on a 67.5-mile loop from the park to Sandy Hook and back. This challenge will not only show you Sandy Hook but also some of the nicer towns between Freehold and Sandy Hook.

To start the challenge, follow the road from the Monmouth Battlefield State Park visitor center back to Business Route 33. Make a left out of the park onto Route 33 and then the next left onto Wemrock Road. Because of the Freehold Mall, which is close by, this road can be busy on weekend mornings.

The next few turns will take you to the center of Freehold. Main Street is wide and rideable, but a number of roads cross Main Street and there is usually a moderate amount of traffic. If you stay to the right and watch out for cars, you should have no problem.

Continue on Main Street and come to a Y. Bear left here onto Route 79 (Broadway) and then make a right after about 0.5 mile onto Dutch Lane. You are now out of town and past traffic. You will be on Dutch Lane for quite a while—more than 5 miles—so relax and settle into a good pace. You will be going through some farmland and some nice residential areas.

When you make the left onto Route 34, stay in the shoulder as you go up a little hill. Make a few more turns and end up on Main Street/Newman Springs Road (County Road 520) in Holmdel. This is one of the main roads, so traffic may be a little heavier here. Continue on toward Red Bank. As you approach Red Bank you will see a river to your right and a bridge over the river ahead of you. Make a left here onto Hubbard Avenue; in a little over 0.5 mile, turn right onto Navesink River Road. As you continue on Navesink, you have some nice views of the river on the right. The road also has three or four tough rollers that you will have to get over. There are some really nice houses on this road. A number of baseball players and rock stars, including Jon Bon Jovi and Bruce Springsteen, are rumored to have houses here.

Make a few more turns and end up on Navesink Avenue. There is a slow, gradual uphill here that gets a little steeper toward the end. Halfway up this road on the right is Hartshorne Woods Park, a nice place to do some mountain biking.

At the top of the hill Navesink intersects Route 36. Sandy Hook is now in view and only a few miles away. Make a right here onto Route 36 to get to Sandy Hook. If you want to take a break and get some food before going to the beach, you can cross Route 36 and stop at a Quick Check.

Route 36 is a busy road, and on a nice summer day traffic can be bumper to bumper. There is a nice shoulder here, so stay in it as you ride down the hill on Route 36. At the bottom of the hill is a bridge that crosses the bay to Sandy Hook. There is no shoulder here, so stay single file and to the right. After crossing the bridge, stay to the right and follow the signs to Sandy Hook. You will be taking an exit ramp here that circles around to the right and leaves you heading north on Ocean Avenue. The entrance to Sandy Hook is ahead. If you are in a car you will have to pay to enter Sandy Hook, but there is no fee for bikes. Sandy Hook limits the number of people allowed into the park, so if you are driving to Sandy Hook and get there late on a nice day, there's a chance you won't get in.

After entering Sandy Hook, make a right into the first parking area. This is where the ramble part of the ride begins. There is a restroom here if you need one.

At the north end of the parking lot is the start of a multiuse path (MUP) that runs the length of Sandy Hook. To start the ramble or continue the challenge, head north on the MUP. This path more or less parallels Hartshorne Drive. You will be riding through the low woods of Sandy Hook. To your right is the ocean and to your left is the bay. If you look across the bay on top of the hill, you will see a pair of lighthouses. These twin lights of Navesink are now a maritime museum.

Continue on the MUP for a little over 1.5 miles to the visitor center. Feel free to stop here if you want to learn more about the history of Sandy Hook. You can also get food and drinks here.

Continue north on the MUP past some more beaches and some small missiles, which seem out of place at the beach. These are real but unarmed Nike missiles that were used for antiaircraft defense from 1954 until 1974.

Sandy Hook has played a major role in defending the New York area. Since the War of 1812, the United States has realized that it needs to defend its ports, including New York. Over the years the defenses on Sandy Hook were continually improved to help defend the entrance to New York Harbor. The northern part of Sandy Hook that you will be riding into is dominated by the remnants of Fort Hancock.

After about 6 mile on the MUP, you will come to what looks like the end of the path. This is Guardian Park, and there is a large missile in the field to your left. Leave the MUP and make a right onto Magruder Road. You are now in the Fort Hancock area and will be riding through some of the remnants of the base. Eventually come to an intersection where Magruder meets Hudson Road. Sandy Hook Lighthouse is

Leaving Sandy Hook

here. Originally this lighthouse was 500 feet from the ocean, but because sand continually builds up on the north end of Sandy Hook, the lighthouse is now 1.5 miles from the ocean. Turn right at the lighthouse onto Hudson Drive and follow Hudson past some of the old fortifications.

At the next T make a right onto South Bragg Drive. The roads on Sandy Hook are not marked really well, so it can be easy to get lost. You can't get too lost, though, because you will eventually run into either the bay or the ocean. At the next intersection turn left onto Ford Road. You will see some of the old mortar batteries here. These fortifications used to contain large mortars that could fire 1,000-pound projectiles at any ship trying to invade New York Harbor.

At the next intersection make a left onto Kilpatrick and the next right onto Canfield Road. You are now about as far north as you can get and will soon see the U.S. Coast Guard station. You cannot enter the station, so turn left here onto Kearny Road and start to head south. This road merges into Hartshorne Drive. You are now on the bay side heading south and will see a nice row of house on your left. There are a lot of little roads to explore in the Fort Hancock area. If you want to see more of the area, feel free ride around on your own.

When you're done exploring the Fort Hancock area, head south on Hartshorne Drive. This road will take you back to the MUP. Instead of using the MUP to head

Sandy Hook Ramble/Challenge

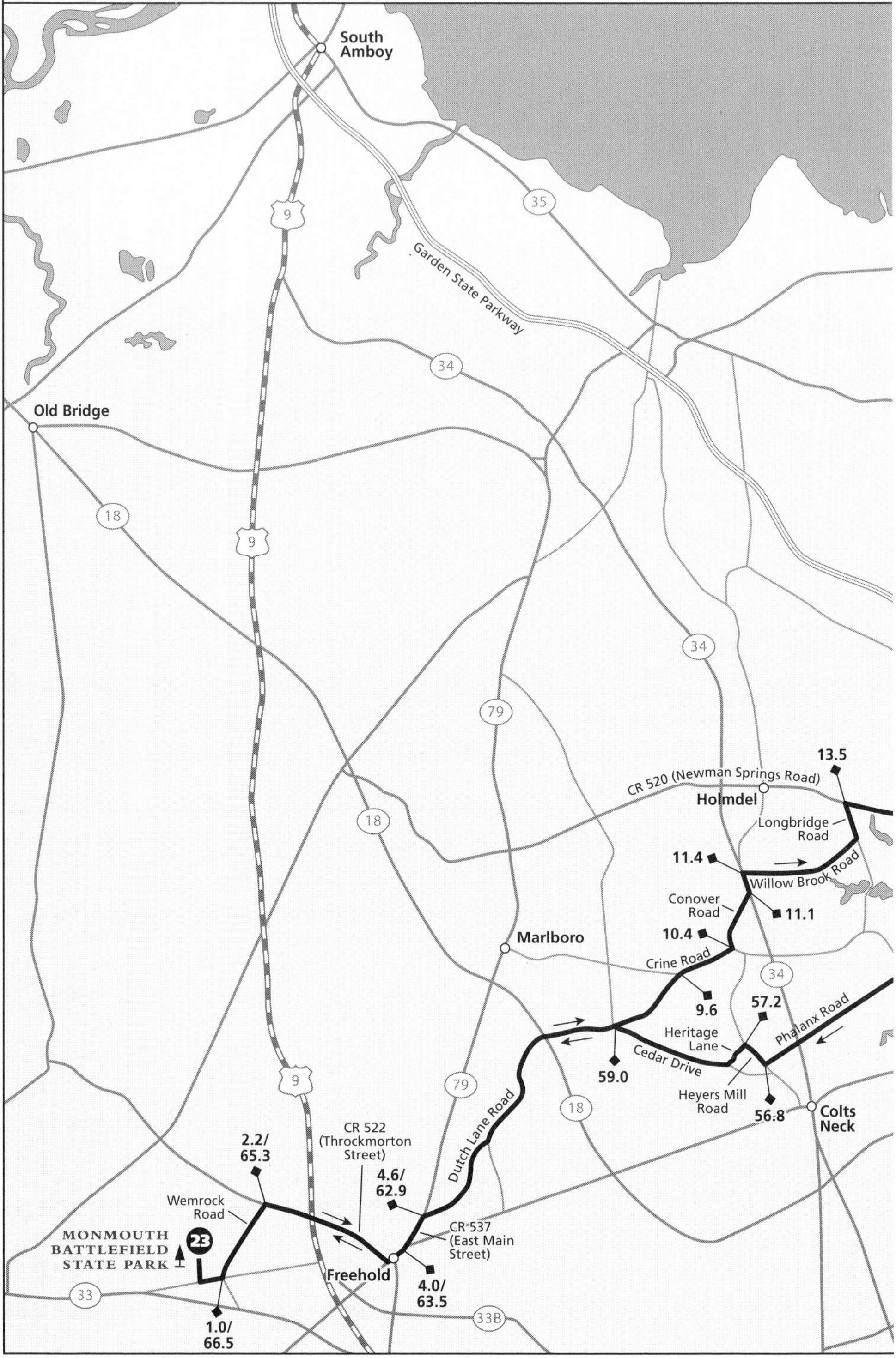

South
Amboy

9

35

Garden State Parkway

34

Old Bridge

18

9

18

79

13.5

CR 520 (Newman Springs Road)

Holmdel

Longbridge
Road

11.4

Willow Brook Road

Conover
Road

11.1

10.4

Crine Road

34

Marlboro

9.6

57.2

Heritage
Lane

Phalanx Road

59.0

Cedar Drive

Heyers Mill
Road

Colts
Neck

56.8

9

CR 522
(Throckmorton
Street)

2.2/
65.3

4.6/
62.9

Dutch Lane Road

79

18

Wemrock
Road

CR 537
(East Main
Street)

MONMOUTH
BATTLEFIELD
STATE PARK

23

Freehold

4.0/
63.5

33

33B

1.0/
66.5

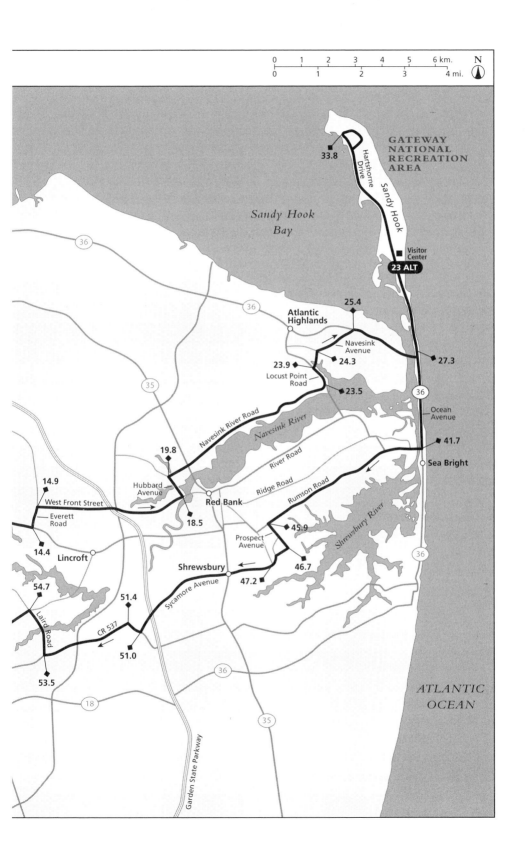

GATEWAY
NATIONAL
RECREATION
AREA

Sandy Hook Bay

Hartshorne Drive

Sandy Hook

33.8

Visitor
Center

23 ALT

25.4

Atlantic
Highlands

Navesink
Avenue

23.9

24.3

27.3

Locust Point
Road

23.5

36

Ocean
Avenue

Navesink River Road

Navesink River

River Road

41.7

19.8

Sea Bright

Hubbard
Avenue

Ridge Road

Rumson Road

14.9

Red Bank

West Front Street

18.5

Shrewsbury River

Everett
Road

45.9

14.4

Lincroft

Prospect
Avenue

46.7

54.7

Shrewsbury

47.2

36

Laird Road

51.4

Sycamore Avenue

CR 537

51.0

53.5

36

18

ATLANTIC
OCEAN

35

Garden State Parkway

N

0   1   2   3   4   5   6 km.
0   1   2   3   4 mi.

36

36

35

out of Sandy Hook, you could stay on Hartshorne Drive. This two-lane road doesn't have a shoulder, but if traffic is light it's OK to ride. If it's a busy beach day and traffic is heavy, you probably should use the MUP.

No matter which way you choose, just head south toward the entrance to Sandy Hook. If you are heading south on Hartshorne Drive, you will get a good view of the bay and a number of the small beaches on the bay. After about 5 or 6 miles of riding south, arrive at the entrance to Sandy Hook. This is where the ramble ends and the challenge starts the trip home.

Once you exit Sandy Hook you will be on Ocean Avenue. To continue south, bear left at the Y and continue over the overpass. This overpass circles around to the left. At the bottom of the overpass, make a right to stay on Ocean Avenue. This can be a very busy road in summer, since it runs along the beach. There is a small shoulder here, so stay to the right and watch out for traffic. There is a large seawall to your left that helps keep the ocean away from the houses.

After about 2 miles you will see a bridge to your right. Turn right here, go over the bridge, and start heading west. The ride back to Freehold will be flatter than the way in. There are no real rollers or hills to go over. The roads will busy here, especially in summer, with moderate traffic, but for the most part the roads are wide enough to accommodate both bikes and cars. After making the left onto Prospect Avenue, you enter the town of Little Silver. If you want to stop and get some food, there is a 7-11 here as well as a CVS and a pizza place.

Continue though the center of Little Silver. Traffic can be a little heavy here. After you pass Little Silver Train Station, traffic gets lighter as you leave town and ride through residential neighborhoods.

Continue through the back roads of Colts Neck and eventually get back on Dutch Lane. This is the road you came out on, so from here all you have to do is retrace the turns on the way out to get back to Monmouth Battlefield State Park. You will take Dutch Lane to Broadway (Route 79) back through downtown Freehold.

Since it will be later in the day when you come back through Freehold, traffic will be a little worse, so use caution. By the time you get back to the parking lot in the park you should have traveled between 65 and 70 miles. If you're hungry and want a good meal, check out some of the restaurants in Freehold. There are some nice outdoor restaurants that are a good place to unwind after a long ride.

Miles and Directions

0.0 Start in Monmouth Battlefield State Park by the visitor center. Take the entrance road out of the park. Challenge starting point: N40° 15.605' / W74° 19.130'

0.7 Turn left onto Business Route 33.

1.0 Turn left onto Wemrock Road.

2.2 Turn right onto Freehold Englishtown Road (County Road 522), which changes to Throckmorton Street.

3.9	Turn left onto Main Street (County Road 537).
4.0	Bear left onto Route 79.
4.6	Turn right onto Dutch Lane Road.
9.6	The road changes names to Crine Road.
10.4	Turn left onto Conover Road.
11.1	Turn left onto Route 34 north; stay in the shoulder.
11.4	Turn right onto Willow Brook Road.
13.0	Turn left onto Longbridge Road.
13.5	Turn right onto Newman Springs Road/Main Street.
14.4	Turn left onto Everett Road.
14.9	Turn right onto West Front Street.
18.5	Turn left onto Hubbard Avenue.
19.1	Turn right onto Navesink River Road; there are a few tough rollers here.
23.5	The road curves left and becomes Locust Point Road.
23.9	Turn right onto Locust Avenue.
24.3	Turn right onto Navesink Avenue for a slow uphill.
25.4	Turn right onto Route 36. There's a food stop across the highway.
27.0	Stay to the right and take the exit ramp to Sandy Hook.
27.1	At the bottom of the exit ramp, the road becomes Ocean Avenue.
27.3	Go through the Sandy Hook gate. The road becomes Hartshorne Drive.
27.4	Turn right into the first parking lot. (Note: The ramble begins here. Ramble starting point: N40° 24.018' / W73° 58.545')
27.5	Go to north end of parking lot, and enter the multiuse path (MUP).
32.0	Reach Guardian Park. Leave the MUP and turn right onto Magruder Road.
32.5	Turn right at the lighthouse onto Hudson Street.
32.9	Turn right at the T onto South Bragg Drive.
33.1	Turn left at the next intersection onto Ford Road.
33.3	Turn left at the next intersection onto Kilpatrick Road.
33.5	Turn right at the next intersection onto Canfield Road.
33.8	Turn left at the Coast Guard station onto Kearny Road.
34.1	Bear right at the Y onto Hartshorne Drive.
34.7	Continue south on Hartshorne Drive or if traffic is heavy get back on MUP and go south.
39.2	Go through the Sandy Hook gate onto Ocean Avenue. (The ramble ends here.)
39.4	Bear left at the Y and go over the overpass onto Ocean Avenue.
39.6	Turn right at the bottom of the overpass to stay on Ocean Avenue.
41.7	Turn right and cross the Shrewsbury River Bridge.
42.0	After crossing the bridge, the road name changes to Rumson Road.
45.9	Turn left onto Prospect Avenue.
46.7	Turn right onto Little Silver Point Road.

47.0	Turn left onto Willow Drive.
47.2	Bear right onto Sycamore Avenue.
51.0	Turn right onto Tinton Avenue (CR 537).
51.4	Turn left onto Colts Neck Road (CR 537).
53.5	Turn right onto Laird Road.
54.7	Turn left onto Phalanx Road.
56.3	Cross Route 34; the road name changes to Flock Road.
56.8	At the T turn right onto Heyers Mill Road.
57.2	Turn left onto Heritage Lane.
57.6	Turn right onto Cedar Drive.
59.0	Turn left onto Dutch Lane Road.
62.9	Turn left onto Broadway (Route 79).
63.5	The road merges with West Main Street (CR 537).
63.6	Turn right onto Throckmorton Street (CR 522).
65.4	Turn left onto Wemrock Road.
66.5	Turn right onto Business Route 33.
66.8	Turn right into Monmouth Battlefield State Park.
67.5	Complete the ride at the visitor center.

Local Events/Attractions

Monmouth Battlefield State Park was the site of one of the major battles of the Revolutionary War. The park is much the same as it was during the time of the battle. Fields, orchards, woods, and wetlands encompass miles of hiking and horseback riding trails, picnic areas, a restored Revolutionary War farmhouse, and a visitor center. Visit www.state.nj.us/dep/parksandforests/parks/monbat.html for more information.

Sandy Hook is a 2,044-acre barrier beach peninsula at the northern tip of the New Jersey shore. The national park includes 7 miles of ocean beaches, salt marshes, hiking trails, and a maritime holly forest. For details, visit www.nps.gov/gate/planyourvisit/thingstodosandyhook.htm.

Restaurants

Court Jester: 16 East Main Street, Freehold; (732) 462-1040. Serves a great array of appetizers, soups, salads, wraps, sandwiches, burritos, fajitas, hamburgers, full dinners, and much more in a casual atmosphere.

Doris & Ed's: 384 Shore Drive, Highlands; (732) 872-1565; www.dorisandeds.com. Regularly voted one of New Jersey's "10 Best" seafood restaurants, it's a great place for fresh seafood.

Accommodations

Days Inn Freehold: 4089 U.S. Highway 9, Freehold; (732) 462-3450 or (800) 329-7466 (reservations).

Sandy Hook Cottage Bed & Breakfast: 36 Navesink Avenue, Highlands; (732) 708-1923; www.sandyhookcottage.com.

Maps

DeLorme: New Jersey Atlas and Gazetteer: Pages 44 I1, 45 C15, and 39 N20.

New Jersey Bike Maps: Freehold, Marlboro, Long Branch, Sandy Hook, Long Branch East; www.njbikemap.com.

24 Belmar and Back Ramble/Classic

The Jersey shore is a great place to spend a warm summer day. There is nothing more relaxing than sitting on a beach soaking up the sun and listening to the music of the waves. Of course on summer weekends the beach can be a little crowded and congested, which is why taking the trip by bike can be a good idea. This ride gets you to the beach and back from two different starting points, allowing you to make it a short ramble or an all-day classic

Start: Village Park, just off Maplewood Avenue, Cranbury (classic); Manasquan Reservoir, Georgia Tavern Road, Howell (ramble).

Distance: 84.4-mile loop (classic); 28-mile loop (ramble).

Terrain: Mostly flat with a few rolling hills. The start and end of the ride have some rolling terrain but no climbs worth mentioning. The closer you get to the beach, the flatter it will be.

Traffic and hazards: Traffic will vary a lot on these rides. Most of the rides are on side roads with light to moderate traffic. You will go through a couple of small towns where even the side roads can be busy. This is especially true around Farmingdale. The last few miles into and out of Belmar can have heavy traffic, especially on summer weekends with good weather, so be prepared for some urban riding. Ocean Avenue along the beach is a wide road that is easy to ride, but there is a lot of activity here. Be on the lookout for people crossing the street, cars pulling in and out of parking spots, and other bikers.

Getting there: For the classic, from the south take U.S. Highway 130 north and make a left at Cranbury Station Road then a right onto Main Street. Follow Main Street and turn right onto Westminster Place. Village Park is at the end of Westminster Place where it crosses Maplewood Avenue.

From the north take US 130 south and make a right onto Cranbury Half Acre Road, then a quick left onto Maplewood Avenue. The entrance to the park is on the left just after the cemetery on the right.

For the ramble, take Interstate 195 to exit 28B. Follow U.S. Highway 9 north and turn right at the first traffic light onto Georgia Tavern Road in Howell Township. The entrance to Manasquan Reservoir is approximately 1 mile on right.

This fun ride will get you to the beach and back without having to worry about traffic or parking. There are two possible starting points, depending on how long a ride you want to take. If you are looking for a long ride, you can start in Cranbury and do the 84.4-mile classic. Although 84+ miles might seem like a really long ride, the terrain is mild. It's not a hard ride if you've been training and have done a few rides of 50 or 60 miles. The only thing that makes this ride hard is a stiff west wind, which can make the ride back from Belmar a real test of character.

If you're looking for something shorter, you can start at the Manasquan Reservoir and get to the beach and back in less than 30 miles. The start of the ramble is on

Manasquan Reservoir

Georgia Tavern Road at one of the Manasquan Reservoir parking lots (Mile 27.9 in the following directions).

Although the road gets a little congested by the beach, most of the route is on back roads that offer some nice scenery. The goal of the ride is to get to Belmar for some lovely views of the ocean and a little time in the sun at a nice outdoor food court.

To begin the long classic ride, make a left out of Village Park onto Maplewood Avenue. The next few turns come pretty quick and serve to get you out of Cranbury onto Cranbury Station Road. The road crosses US 130 and continues over the New Jersey Turnpike and across some railroad tracks. Right after the railroad tracks you enter a residential neighborhood and make a right onto Ely Road. Ely is a brand-new road as of this writing, so it may not appear on maps yet. The roads at this intersection have changed a lot over the last couple of years, so this area will be confusing until the maps are updated. Ely turns into Halsey Reed Road. From here continue west.

Once you cross Applegarth Road, you are riding past farmland on some of the quieter roads in the area. The next few turns onto England, Federal, and Bergen Mills Roads continue to take you farther east through more farmland. Bergen Mills Road goes downhill slightly and then bends to the left. Just past this bend, Bergen Mills makes a right. Stay straight here as the road becomes Gravel Hill and then Dey Grove Road.

When you reach Iron Ore Road, stay to the right—this road carries moderate traffic. From here you eventually get to Woodward and cross Route 33. Continue up a small hill and then make a right onto Sweetmans Lane. At the next intersection turn left onto Woodville Road followed by an immediate left onto Oakland Mills Road. Oakland Mills starts with a steep little downhill, then has a nice series of rollers with just enough ups and downs to make it fun.

After 2.4 miles on Oakland Mills Road, come to a stop sign where the road crosses County Road 537. Be extra careful at this crossing—cars will be coming fast from the left and right, and you don't have good visibility either way. Continue through some back roads and end up on Georgia Tavern Road approaching US 9. As you get closer to US 9, the road will have more traffic.

When you reach US 9 there will be a little shopping mall to your left. There is a Dunkin Donuts here if you need some food, but not much else. After you make the right onto Georgia Tavern Road, you will see Manasquan Reservoir on your left. There is a parking lot here, which is the starting point for the ramble. Manasquan Reservoir is more than just a place to store drinking water. The reservoir and surrounding land is also a great recreation area that offers boating, fishing, hiking, and other activities. (Check out the Web site listed under Local Attractions/Events for more information.)

After you pass the reservoir, turn left onto Windeler Road. Although this road follows closely along the shore of the reservoir, you will not be able to see the water through the trees. As you get close to Farmingdale, the roads will have moderate traffic, so stay to the right as much as possible.

Southward will take you to Main Street and the center of Farmingdale. There will be some traffic here. This is a good place for a food stop. Just ahead on your left is a shopping center with a bakery. A bagel shop on the right just across from the shopping center is another good place to stop.

After your break, continue down Main Street and make a right before the train tracks onto Railroad Avenue. You will eventually cross County Road 547 (Lakewood Farmingdale Road) by I-195 and go past Allaire State Park. This park is home to the historic village of Allaire, which was a bog iron–producing village in the nineteenth century. Part of the village has been preserved and today hosts craftspeople dressed in period garb who demonstrate the skills of the blacksmiths, carpenters, and tinsmiths of the time.

The turn onto Tiltons Corner Road can be a little difficult—there is a small shopping center here, making this a busy intersection.

You are getting close to the beach and the town of Sea Girt. In a few more turns, cross some railroad tracks and enter the center of town. Sea Girt Avenue bears left here; continue straight onto Washington Boulevard. There are a lot of little shops here with cars pulling in and out of parking spots, so keep your eyes open.

Belmar and Back Ramble/Classic

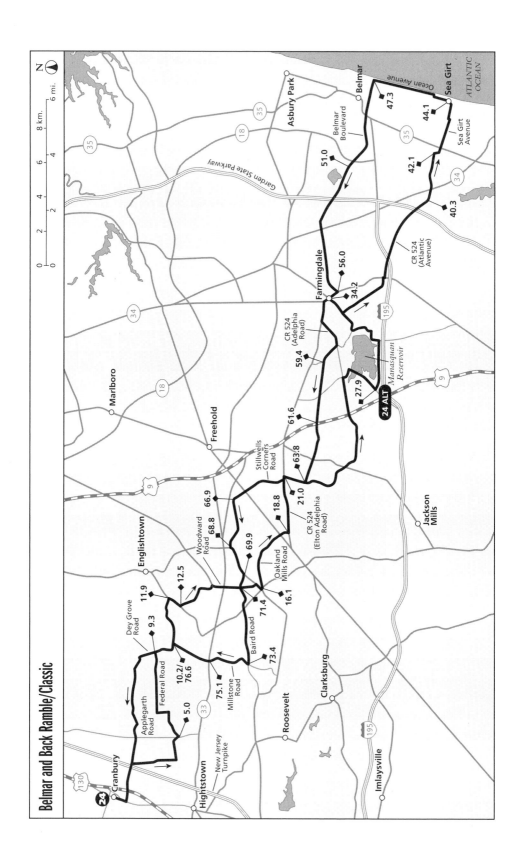

N

0 2 4 6 8 km.

0 2 4 6 mi.

Cranbury

Hightstown

Englishtown

Marlboro

Freehold

Asbury Park

Belmar

Sea Girt

ATLANTIC OCEAN

Roosevelt

Clarksburg

Jackson Mills

Imlaysville

Farmingdale

Manasquan Reservoir

Garden State Parkway

New Jersey Turnpike

Dey Grove Road

Applegarth Road

Federal Road

Millstone Road

Baird Road

Woodward Road

Oakland Mills Road

Stillwells Corners Road

CR 524 (Elton Adelphia Road)

CR 524 (Adelphia Road)

CR 524 (Atlantic Avenue)

Belmar Boulevard

Ocean Avenue

Sea Girt Avenue

5.0
9.3
10.2/76.6
11.9
12.5
16.1
18.8
21.0
27.9
34.2
40.3
42.1
44.1
47.3
51.0
56.0
59.4
61.6
63.8
66.9
68.8
69.9
71.4
73.4
75.1

24

24 ALT

130
33
9
18
35
34
195

After you pass though town, ride through a nice residential area. In a few more turns you will be on Ocean Avenue riding along the beach. You are now at the beach in Sea Girt riding north. Depending on which way the wind is blowing, this can be fun or painful. There are a lot of cars and people on this road, but it is very wide so it is easy to share the road. Just keep it slow and watch out for traffic.

In 2.3 miles you will be in Belmar at 17th Street. There is a nice set of food stores and outdoor tables between 16th and 17th Streets—a good place to stop and enjoy the beach for a while. If you want to dip your feet in the ocean, just cross the street and take a walk on the beach.

When you're done soaking up the salt air and sunshine, head out 17th Street. The first few miles will be congested. Once you cross Route 35 the road name changes to Belmar Boulevard. Continue to follow Belmar Boulevard west away from the beach. This road will have constant traffic on it. Parts of the road have a shoulder to ride it; others don't. The road is wide enough for both cars and bikes to share, but stay to the right as much as you can.

After crossing Route 18, you come to a part of Belmar Boulevard where you will have to bear left to stay on the boulevard. After almost 5 miles on Belmar Boulevard, cross Route 34 and leave most of the traffic behind you. Continue on Belmar Boulevard and follow it back to Main Street in Farmingdale. Go through the center of town and continue heading west through some nice rural roads. After less than a mile on Casino Drive, you will see Georgia Tavern Road on your left. If you are riding the ramble, turn left here and head back to your starting point, which is about a mile away. If you are on the classic ride, continue on Casino Drive.

Casino Drive eventually crosses US 9. There is a food store on the right if you need a stop. After crossing US 9, wind around some quiet roads and eventually enter the town of West Freehold. Traffic increases as you get closer to the center of town. Go through a couple of lights. After you cross Main Street the road becomes Wemrock Road. There is a small shopping center on your left if you want to stop for a break.

A little ways after the shopping center, turn left onto Gully Road at a light. Continue riding through some rolling hills in Millstone. Make a right onto Millstone Road and go down a nice long hill. At the bottom of the hill is a light where you will cross Route 33. After crossing Route 33, make a right at a T immediately after the light and then the next left onto Bergen Mills Road.

A few more turns will get you to Cranbury Station Road. Cross US 130 and you're back in the town of Cranbury. A few more turns will get you back to Village Park where you started.

I have done this route many times over the years in many different conditions— sunny, cloudy, hot, cold, and windy. It is always a fun ride for different reasons. I don't think my riding season would be complete if I didn't do this route a least once or twice. If you are looking for some fun miles, give this ride a try.

Miles and Directions

Starting point (classic): N40° 18.770' / W74° 30.766'
Starting point (ramble): N40° 10.703' / W74° 13.325'

0.0 Turn left out of Village Park onto Maplewood Avenue.

0.2 Follow the road around to the right onto Scott Avenue.

0.3 Turn left onto Main Street.

0.6 Turn left onto Cranbury Station Road (Station Road).

1.0 Cross US 130, and stay on Cranbury Station Road (Station Road).

2.2 Turn right onto Ely Road, which becomes Halsey Reed Road.

3.2 Turn right onto Wyckoffs Mill Road.

4.0 Turn left at the T onto Wyckoffs Mill Applegarth Road.

5.0 Cross Applegarth Road. The road changes names to Old Church Road.

6.0 Turn left at the T onto England Road.

6.7 Turn right onto Federal Road.

9.3 Turn right onto Bergen Mills Road.

10.2 Stay straight as Bergen Mills make a right. The road changes names to Gravel Hill Road/ Dey Grove Road.

11.9 Turn right onto Iron Ore Road (County Road 527).

12.5 Turn left onto Daum Road.

14.1 Turn left at the T and then bear right onto Woodward Road.

15.8 Turn right onto Sweetmans Lane (CR 527).

16.1 Turn left onto Woodville Road and make a quick left onto Oakland Mills Road.

18.5 Cross CR 537. The traffic is fast, so be careful.

18.8 Turn left onto Elton Adelphia Road (County Road 524).

21.0 Turn right onto Georgia Road.

26.0 Cross US 9. The road changes names to West Farms Road.

27.5 Turn right onto Lemon Road.

27.9 Turn right onto Georgia Tavern Road. (The ramble begins at a Manasquan Reservoir parking lot.)

29.2 Turn left onto Windeler Road.

30.8 Turn left at the T where Windeler Road meets Aldrich Road.

31.0 Turn left onto Old Tavern Road.

31.6 Turn left onto Manassa Road.

32.5 Turn right onto Southard Avenue.

34.0 Turn right onto Main Street (CR 547). If you need a break there's a shopping center on the left and a bagel shop on the right.

34.2 Turn right onto Railroad Avenue.

34.6 Bear right and merge onto Preventorium Road.

35.0 Turn left onto Squankum Yellowbrook Road (County Road 524A).

36.8 Cross Lakewood Farmingdale Road (CR 547) onto Allaire/Atlantic Avenue (CR 524). Stay on Atlantic Avenue.

40.3 Turn left to stay on Atlantic Avenue (CR 524 Spur).

40.8 Turn left onto Tiltons Corner Road.

42.1 Turn right onto Baileys Corner Road.

42.3 Turn left onto Sea Girt Avenue.

43.6 Cross railroad tracks, and continue straight onto Washington Boulevard.

44.1 Turn left onto Second Avenue.

44.2 Bear right. Stay on Crescent Parkway.

44.4 Turn left onto First Avenue.

44.9 Turn right onto Brown Avenue.

45.0 Turn left onto Ocean Avenue.

47.3 Turn left onto 17th Avenue. (There are food stores between 16th and 17th Avenues and a good place to enjoy the beach.)

48.0 Turn right onto Main Street.

48.1 Turn left onto 16th Avenue (Belmar Boulevard).

48.8 Cross Route 35. The road becomes Belmar Boulevard.

51.0 Bear left to stay on Belmar Boulevard. Continue to follow the boulevard.

56.0 Turn right at the T onto CR 547 (Main/Lakewood Farmingdale Road).

56.6 Follow the road around to the left to stay on Main Street (CR 524).

57.3 Turn left onto West Farms Road.

58.4 Turn right onto Casino Drive.

59.4 Pass Georgia Tavern Road. (Option: Turn left onto Georgia Tavern Road to return to the starting point of the ramble.)

61.6 Cross US 9. (There's a food store on the right before the light.)

62.9 The road becomes Stone Hill Road.

63.8 Turn right onto Georgia Road.

64.6 Turn left onto Elton Adelphia Road (CR 524).

64.7 Make a quick right onto Stillwells Corner Road.

66.3 Cross Main Street. The road changes names to Wemrock Road. (There's a food store on the left after the light.)

66.9 Turn left onto Gulley Road (Kinney Road).

68.8 Turn left onto Sweetmans Lane (CR 527).

69.9 Turn right onto Lambs Lane.

71.4 Go straight. The road changes names to Baird Road.

73.4 Turn right onto Millstone Road.

75.1 Cross Route 33; turn right at the T and then left onto Bergen Mills Road.

76.6 Turn left at the T onto Gravel Hill Road/Bergen Mills Road.

78.7 Turn left onto Union Valley Road.

81.3 Cross Applegarth; the road becomes Cranbury Station Road.

83.8 Turn right onto Main Street.

84.1 Turn right onto Scott Avenue.

84.4 Turn right into Village Park to complete your ride.

Local Events/Attractions

The Manasquan Reservoir is part of 1,204 acres that include woods and wetlands, a 5-mile perimeter trail, fishing and boating areas, and a visitor center. It is a great natural setting for people who enjoy outdoor recreational activities. For more details, visit www.monmouthcountyparks.com.

Restaurants

Cranbury Inn: 21 South Main Street, Cranbury; (609) 655-5595. Award-winning historic colonial restaurant serving traditional American cuisine.

Cranbury Pizza: 63 North Main Street, Cranbury; (609) 409-9930. Pizza parlor with outside tables.

Teddy's Restaurant: 49 North Main Street, Cranbury; (609) 655-3120. Nice diner in the middle of Cranbury.

Accommodations

Residence Inn Cranbury South Brunswick: 2662 U.S. Highway 130, Cranbury; (609) 395-9447 or (888) 577-7005.

Maps

DeLorme: New Jersey Atlas and Gazetteer: Pages 43 F16, 44 L1, 45 N18, and 50 A5.

New Jersey Bike Maps: Hightstown, Jamesburg, Freehold, Adelphia, Farmingdale, Asbury Park; www.njbikemap.com.

South Jersey is flat, rural, and a little strange. Its main features are its vast pineland forests and its many square miles of farmlands. There are also some very nice less-crowded beaches in the eastern section. It is very different from the other parts of the state and in some ways doesn't seem to be part of New Jersey at all. This area is the birthplace of the Jersey Devil and home to the Piney (New Jersey's version of a hillbilly), so there are a lot of strange stories coming from this neck of the woods.

The south is where New Jersey earns its name "the Garden State," with miles and miles of nothing but farmland. This area is not all rural, though. There are some congested areas in the west that are suburbs of Philadelphia. There is also Atlantic City, the gambling capital of New Jersey, with a nice beach in addition to casinos. And of course, if you want a romantic getaway, there's no better place than Cape May.

Biking in this area is pure joy. There are endless roads with no traffic, very few hills, and just enough civilization to make it interesting. This area may require you to drive a little farther to start the ride, but the scenery and quiet roads make it worth the effort.

25 Long Beach Island Ramble

Long Beach Island, or LBI as it is usually called, is an 18-mile barrier island on the southern coast of New Jersey. Its beautiful beaches and resort communities make it a popular vacation destination during the summer months. LBI is very bike friendly and a fun place to ride, especially if you like the smell of salt air. This ride takes you around the island and shows you the main sights.

Start: Richard A. Zachariae Recreation Center parking lot, Barnegat Avenue, Surf City.
Distance: 14- to 35-mile loops.
Terrain: Very flat. You are basically riding on a sandbar that is barely above sea level.
Traffic and hazards: This can be a very busy area, especially on summer weekends. This ride is best done in the off-season or on weekdays in summer. If you do ride this route on a summer weekend, try and get out early. The roads north of Route 72 all have wide shoulders to ride in. Near Beach Haven there are dedicated bike lanes on Beach and Atlantic Avenues. The area around Route 72 can be very congested during weekend mornings and afternoons when people are coming to and leaving the island. The best street for crossing this area is Barnegat Avenue. Long Beach Boulevard south of Route 72 has no shoulder and should be avoided when possible. Although most main roads have wide shoulders or bike lanes, these lanes are more like a multiuse path and can be filled with people walking, jogging, or skating during summer weekends.

Getting there: From the Garden State Parkway or U.S. Highway 9 take Route 72 east onto Long Beach Island. After coming over the last bridge onto the island, get in the left lane. If you are unfamiliar with LBI, stop at the information center and pick up a map. The information center is on the left between Barnegat and Central Avenues as you drive in on Route 72 east. Continue another block past the information center on Route 72 (Ninth Street) where it ends, and make a left onto Long Beach Boulevard. Go 5 or 6 blocks; turn left onto Fourth or Third Street and take it a couple of blocks to Barnegat Avenue. Make a right onto Barnegat and continue going north. Right after you pass First Street you will see a playground and boat launch ramp. Park in the lot next to the playground.

For those who like the beach and the smell of salt air, LBI has a lot to offer. There are a lot of nice beaches, plenty of good places to eat, and lots of things to do. This is an easy and enjoyable place to ride a bike. It can be crowded on summer weekends, so if you have a choice, try riding during the week in summer or any time during the off-season. This ride is basically composed of two loops: One goes north from Surf City to Barnegat Light and back; the other starts in Surf City and goes to the south end of the island and back. If you to do both loops, your ride will total about 35 miles. If you don't have the time or don't want to do the miles, you can do just one of the loops.

Both loops are more or less out-and-back loops. LBI is a very narrow island and doesn't have enough rideable roads to do a true loop, so it is very easy to adjust the length of the ride to fit the miles you want to do.

Couple on a recumbent bike

The milepoints for this ride assume that you are starting in the middle of LBI in Surf City, but your actual starting point will probably vary. If you are staying on LBI, the best thing to do is to start from were you are staying. It can also be nice to start in the north by Barnegat Light or down in the south end of the island by the Edwin B. Forsythe Wildlife Preserve. Both areas have places to park.

The main point of the Miles and Directions for this ride is to show you the best roads to ride on and how to connect them together. Just find the closest road to where you are, and start your ride from there.

No ride description of LBI would be complete without mention of the wind. Everyone who rides LBI on a regular basis knows that it is a windy place. Winds of 15 and 20 miles per hour are common. So even though the island roads are flat, the wind can sometimes make it feel like you are riding a constant uphill. If you are feeling strong and going faster than normal, it's probably because you have a tailwind. Make sure you save your energy for the return trip, because you'll be riding into a headwind. The winds on LBI are very changeable, so you may get a headwind going both ways.

This milepoints for this ride start at a playground parking lot by Barnegat Avenue and Division Street. Make a left out of the parking lot and head north on Barnegat. This northern loop will take you up Long Beach Boulevard, which is the main north–south street on the island. North of Route 72, it has wide shoulders and is easy to ride on. As you leave Surf City, the road is a little less congested because there aren't

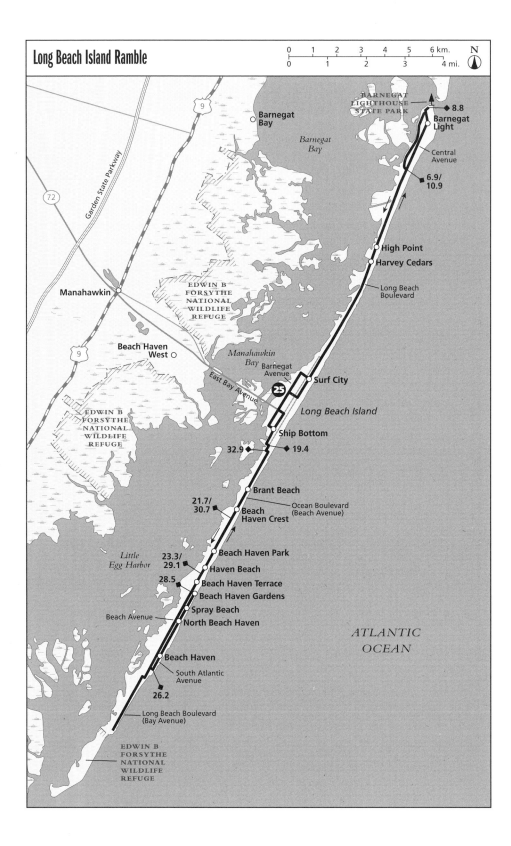

Long Beach Island Ramble

0 1 2 3 4 5 6 km.
0 1 2 3 4 mi.

N

Garden State Parkway

9

72

Manahawkin

9

Beach Haven West ○

EDWIN B FORSYTHE NATIONAL WILDLIFE REFUGE

EDWIN B FORSYTHE NATIONAL WILDLIFE REFUGE

Barnegat Bay ○

Barnegat Bay

Manahawkin Bay

East Bay Avenue

Barnegat Avenue

25

Surf City

Long Beach Island

Ship Bottom

32.9 ◆   ◆ 19.4

Brant Beach

21.7/ 30.7

Beach Haven Crest

Ocean Boulevard (Beach Avenue)

23.3/ 29.1

Beach Haven Park

Haven Beach

28.5

Beach Haven Terrace

Beach Haven Gardens

Spray Beach

Beach Avenue

North Beach Haven

Little Egg Harbor

Beach Haven

South Atlantic Avenue

26.2

Long Beach Boulevard (Bay Avenue)

EDWIN B FORSYTHE NATIONAL WILDLIFE REFUGE

BARNEGAT LIGHTHOUSE STATE PARK

◆ 8.8

Barnegat Light

Central Avenue

6.9/ 10.9

High Point

Harvey Cedars

Long Beach Boulevard

ATLANTIC OCEAN

as many stores. Continue riding, going through the town of Harvey Cedars and, after about 7 miles, reaching the town of Barnegat Light. Long Beach Boulevard becomes Central Avenue at this point. Here you will bear left at a Y onto Broadway, which takes you to the lighthouse. Along this road are a couple of nice places to eat. On the left is Mustache Bill's Dinner; ahead on the right is Kelly's Old Barney Restaurant. A lot of people ride their bikes to the restaurant for breakfast. The parking lot across the street from the restaurant makes a good alternative starting point.

At the end of the Broadway is the entrance to Barnegat Lighthouse State Park. If you haven't seen this lighthouse before, it's worth the stop. This is probably one of the most photographed lighthouses on the East Coast. For a small fee you can climb the 217 stairs to the top of the lighthouse and get a good view of the ocean, bay, and surrounding area. The park also has a visitor center, picnic area, and restroom.

From the state park start the trip back by heading south on Broadway. At Sixth Street make a right and then make the next left onto Bayview Avenue. The road takes you south along the bay. At 30th Street the road bends left and intersects Central Avenue/Long Beach Boulevard. Turn right here and continue south the same way you came north. When you reach the north end of Surf City, make a right from Long Beach Boulevard onto 24th Street. A few more turns will return you to the starting point.

Now the southern loop begins. Continue south on Barnegat Avenue. There will be a little more traffic, and you will not have a shoulder as you cross Route 72, so be cautious here. Barnegat Avenue ends at 19th Street. Turn left here, and then make the next right onto Central Avenue. Continue on Central until 27th Street. Make a left onto 27th Street and then the next right onto Long Beach Boulevard. You could continue on Central Avenue one more block to where it ends at 28th Street, but since a lot of cars will be making a right at the light from 28th Street onto Long Beach Boulevard, using 27th Street is easier and safer.

This part of Long Beach Boulevard doesn't have a shoulder, but the lanes are wide. As long as you stay to the right, you should have no problem with traffic. Continue on Long Beach Boulevard for 4 blocks; turn left onto 31st Street and then make the next right onto Ocean Boulevard. Continue south on Ocean Boulevard and Beach Avenue and go through Beach Haven, one of the older communities on LBI. This part of Beach Avenue has a nice dedicated bike lane, although it is also used by walkers, joggers, and skaters and can be congested on weekends.

As you go through the center of Beach Haven, you will have to stop at a couple of cross streets; watch out for cars as you cross. In Beach Haven you will see the Surflight Theater and the Beach Haven Bandshell where summer concerts are held.

Where Beach Avenue meets Dolphin Avenue is the turnaround point for the southern loop. If you want some extra miles, continue south on Beach Avenue until Liberty Avenue. Make a right onto Liberty followed by a left onto Bay Avenue and head south until you get to the Edwin B. Forsythe National Wildlife Refuge. This wilderness preserve protects more than 46,000 acres of coastal habitat and wetlands and is a popular place to do some bird watching. There is a parking lot at the refuge, with a restroom on the left side of the lot by the entrance. There is a deli on right-hand side before the parking lot. This extra trip adds 2 miles each way, so the option will add 4 miles to the southern loop. To get back to the main route, just retrace your steps back to Dolphin Avenue.

Heading north you will be riding along the ocean. Atlantic Avenue parallels Beach Avenue and, like Beach Avenue, has a dedicated bike lane. Atlantic Avenue ends after 2.4 miles at 34th Street. Make a left here and then the next right onto Beach Avenue; continue north until your reach a T at MacEvoy Lane. Make a right at the T followed by a quick left to stay on Beach Avenue.

Beach Avenue eventually turns into Ocean Boulevard and ends at 31st Street. Make a left here and then the next right onto Long Beach Boulevard. Watch the traffic here. After 4 blocks make a left turn on to 27th Street and then the next right onto Central Avenue. Continue on Central Avenue until 11th Street, where Central becomes a one-way street. Make a left onto 11th Street and then the next right onto Barnegat Avenue. Cross Route 72 and in a few blocks you will be back at your starting point.

Miles and Directions

0.0 Start at the Richard A. Zachariae Recreation Center. Turn left out of the parking lot onto Barnegat Avenue. N39° 39.410' / W74° 10.549'

0.1 Turn right onto First Street.

0.3 Turn left onto Long Beach Boulevard.

6.9 The road becomes Central Avenue.

8.3 Bear Left onto Broadway.

8.8 The road ends a Barnegat Light.

9.2 Leave Barnegat Light and head south. Turn right onto West Sixth Street.

9.3 Turn left onto Bayview Avenue.

10.9 Turn right onto Long Beach Avenue (Central Avenue).

16.2 Turn right onto 24th Street.

16.3 Turn left onto North Central Avenue.

16.9 Turn right onto 12th Street.

17.1 Turn left onto Barnegat Avenue.

17.8 Arrive back as starting point for the northern loop. Continue south on Barnegat Avenue to start the southern loop.

18.1 Cross Route 72; use caution at the intersection.

18.7 Turn left onto 19th Street.

18.9 Turn right onto Central Avenue.

19.3 Turn left onto 27th Street.

19.4 Turn right onto Long Beach Boulevard.

19.5 Turn left onto East 31st Street.

19.7 Turn right onto Ocean Boulevard.

21.7 The road name changes to Beach Avenue.

23.3 Turn right at the T onto MacEvoy Lane followed by a quick left back onto Beach Avenue.

26.1 Turn left onto Dolphin Avenue.

26.4 Turn right onto Liberty Avenue. Optional extension begins.

26.4 Turn right onto Bay Avenue (Long Beach Boulevard).

28.2 Reach the end of Bay Avenue and the entrance to Edwin B. Forsythe National Wildlife Refuge.

28.2 Leave the wildlife refuge and head north on Bay Avenue (Long Beach Boulevard).

29.9 Turn right onto Liberty Avenue.

30.0 Turn left onto South Beach Avenue.

30.3 Turn right onto Dolphin Avenue to rejoin route. Optional extension ends.

26.2 Turn left onto South Atlantic Avenue.

28.5 Turn left onto East 34th Street.

28.6 Turn right onto Beach Avenue.

29.1 Turn right onto MacEvoy Lane followed by a quick left to stay on Beach Avenue.

30.7 The road becomes Ocean Boulevard.

32.8 Turn left onto East 31st Street.

32.9 Turn right onto Long Beach Boulevard.

33.0 Turn left onto West 27th Street.

33.1 Turn right onto Central Avenue.

33.9 Turn left onto West 11th Street.

34.1 Turn right onto Barnegat Avenue and cross Route 72.

34.6 Arrive back at the starting point for the southern loop.

Local Events/Attractions

Barnegat Lighthouse State Park is home to Barnegat Lighthouse. The park contains a museum, picnic area, and places to fish. Visitors can climb to the top of the lighthouse for a small fee. For more information, visit www.state.nj.us/dep/parksandforests/parks/barnlig.html.

Edwin B. Forsythe National Wildlife Preserve is a wildlife refuge that protects more than 46,000 acres of coastal habitat and wetlands. This is a popular place for bird watching and contains a number of hiking trails. Check out www.fws.gov/northeast/forsythe for more information.

Restaurants

Kelly's Old Barney Restaurant: Third Avenue and Broadway, Barnegat Light; (609) 494-5115. One of LBI's favorite places for breakfast and lunch, it serves a wide variety of American classics.

Mustache Bill's Diner: Eighth Street and Broadway, Barnegat Light; (609) 494-0155. Good diner food.

Accommodations

Drifting Sands Oceanfront Motel: 119 East Ninth Street, Ship Bottom; (609) 494-1123 or (877) 524-7866 (reservations); www.dslbi.com.

Maps

DeLorme: New Jersey Atlas and Gazetteer: Pages 58 N11 and 59 D22.

Long Beach Island Visitors Map: This map can be picked up at the information center or online at http://resortmaps.com/Long_Beach_Island.

26 Cape May Ramble

Cape May is the oldest seaside resort in the United States and one of only five cities designated as a National Historic Landmark City. It's a picturesque place with large numbers of Victorian houses, beautiful beaches, and plenty of places to shop and eat. This ride takes you on a short ramble that shows you the main sights around town.

Start: Corner of Beach Road and Second Avenue, Cape May.

Distance: 15.8-mile loop.

Terrain: Flat. Cape May isn't much more than a big sandbar, so there are no real ups or downs on this ride.

Traffic and hazards: Cape May is a very crowded place, especially between Memorial and Labor Days. Beach Road, Broadway, and Sunset Boulevard will be congested with cars

and people as the day wears on. To avoid the worst traffic, try to ride early in the morning. Most hotels in Cape May are open from early April to late October, so if possible go during the off-season to avoid the worst crowds.

A lot of people ride bicycles in Cape May, so people in cars are used to sharing the road with bikes. As long as you are patient and polite and use some common sense, you should have no problem riding around the city.

Getting there: Take the Garden State Parkway south to the end and continue into Cape May. Continue straight on Lafayette Street to Madison Avenue. Turn left onto Madison Avenue and then right onto Beach Road where Madison ends. Take Beach Road to the end and find a parking spot by the beach.

Cape May is best known for its many historic Victorian homes, many of which serve as bed-and-breakfasts. This makes it a popular place for a romantic getaway. The city has a very historic feel, and it's easy to imagine what it must have looked like at the height of the Victorian era in the late 1800s.

Cape May has everything needed for a great seaside resort: beautiful beaches, good restaurants, places to shop, and just enough things to do to not get bored. It's a very popular place that gets very crowded on nice summer weekends. To avoid the traffic, try to get out early.

This easy ride will not only get you some exercise but also will show you the major sights around town. The ride starts at the southernmost end of Beach Road near Second Avenue. This is where people come at the end of the day to watch the sunset. If you look to the south you will see the Cape May Lighthouse in the distance. To start the ride, head north on Beach Road and then turn left onto Broadway.

Broadway is a busy road, so watch the traffic and keep to the right as much as you can. After 0.35 mile (about 5 blocks) make a left at the light onto Sunset Boulevard. Sunset Boulevard has a wide shoulder, so you can stay to the right and not fight with the traffic.

High-wheel bike riding the streets of Cape May

Continue on Sunset for 2.2 miles until the road ends. Along the way you will see a large meadow to your left that is part of the Cape May Migratory Bird Refuge. You will also pass the road to the Cape May Lighthouse, which you will ride by later.

At the end of Sunset Boulevard is Sunset Beach. As its name implies, it's a good place to watch the sunset. The flag ceremony performed right before sunset during summer is worth seeing. This beach has a couple interesting features. The first is the concrete ship that you can see just off the beach. The *Alantus* was built during World War I when a shortage of steel forced the government to experiment with concrete ships. The *Alantus* was towed to Sunset Beach in 1926 to be purposely sunk and used as part of a dock for ferry service, but the ship broke loose in a storm and got stuck on a sandbar. The ship could not be freed and has become part of the beach and a curious attraction.

The other interesting feature of this beach is the quartz crystal, or "Cape May Diamonds," that can be found in the sand. These crystals can actually be cut and polished to look somewhat like diamonds.

Once you're done looking around the beach, turn around and head back out Sunset Boulevard. In a little less than 0.5 mile, turn right onto Light House Avenue and head toward the Cape May Lighthouse. Continue straight on Light House Avenue

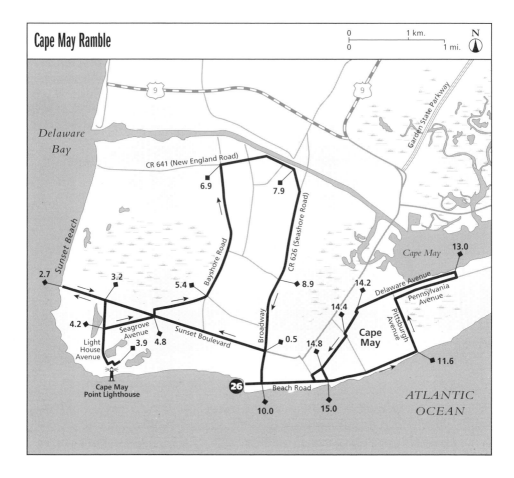

for 0.6 mile, and the lighthouse is on your left. Make a left into Cape May Point State Park to get a closer look at the lighthouse, which was built in 1859 and is still in operation today. The lighthouse was built tall so that the light could be easily seen at sea. The view from the top is spectacular, so if you have the time, climb the 199 stairs to the top for the view of Cape May and the surrounding area.

Once you're done at the lighthouse, head back out on Light House Avenue. After 0.35 mile make a right onto Seagrove Avenue. This road is unsigned but is easy to find, since it is the only road on the right after leaving the lighthouse.

This road will take you across Sunset Boulevard and continue past some houses and farmland. When you make the right onto County Road 641 (New England Road), you will be riding parallel to the Cape May Canal, which will be on your left as you continue. This canal was constructed during World War II to provide a protected route between the Delaware Bay and the inland waterway to avoid German U-boats.

As you continue along the canal you will see one of the bridges that crosses it. As you get closer to the bridge, New England Road curves to the right and merges with Seashore Road, which comes over the bridge. Seashore Road is one of the two roads that come into Cape May and is the better one to ride on. There is a bike lane on this road, so there is plenty of room to avoid any traffic. This road gets a little narrower and has more traffic as you get closer to the beach. The road name changes to Broadway and ends where it meets Beach Road.

You now have completed a big loop and are close to where you started. Turn left onto Beach Road to explore the other end of Cape May. You are now going to ride along the beach, passing through the busier part of Beach Road. On your left are a number of hotels, restaurants, and stores. On your right is the boardwalk, the beach, and the Atlantic Ocean. The part between Perry and Ocean Streets is especially busy, so be careful here.

As you continue down Beach Road, there will be fewer lights and less traffic, and the riding will be a little easier. You will be on Beach Road for 1.7 miles before turning left onto Pittsburgh Avenue. This is a nice, wide road with a dedicated bike lane. You are now riding through a newer residential section of Cape May. From here you will make a loop onto Pennsylvania Avenue to Delaware Avenue and go past the Coast Guard station.

When you are on Delaware Avenue, Cape May Harbor will be to your right and you will get some nice views of it as you ride along. Continue to ride through the residential area of Cape May. When you reach Columbia Street you will be back in the old part of Cape May and see some of the beautiful Victorian homes Cape May is famous for.

There is a nice little square where Columbia Street meets Gurney Avenue, and it's worth stopping here to take a look at some of the more elegant houses. Make a left here onto Gurney Avenue and then a right at the light back onto Beach Avenue. Continue on Beach Avenue until you are back at your starting point.

Although Cape May is a small town, it does have a lot of interesting sights and is a fun place to ramble around on a bike. This ride has shown you most of the sights, although it misses the Washington Street shopping area and some of the Victorian houses of Lafayette Street. These places are too crowded to ride. If you want to visit them, it is best to do it by foot.

Miles and Directions

0.0 Start at the end of Beach Road by the corner of Beach Road and Second Avenue. Head north on Beach Road. N38° 55.814' / W74° 56.055'

0.2 Turn left onto Broadway (watch the traffic).

0.5 Turn left at the light onto Sunset Boulevard, and go to the end of the road.

2.7 The road ends at Sunset Beach. (A concrete ship lies just off the beach.) Turn around and head back on Sunset Boulevard.

3.2 Turn right onto Light House Avenue.

3.8 Turn left into Cape May Point State Park to visit the lighthouse.

3.9 Leave the park and turn right onto Light House Avenue.

4.2 Turn right onto unsigned Seagrove Avenue (first road on the right).

4.8 Cross Sunset Boulevard. The road becomes Stevens Street.

5.4 Turn left onto Bayshore Road.

6.9 Turn right onto CR 641 (New England Road).

7.9 The road bends right and merges with Seashore Road (County Road 626); there's a bike lane on the right.

8.9 The road name changes to Broadway (no bike lane and the road gets narrower).

10.0 Turn left onto Beach Road.

11.6 Turn left onto Pittsburgh Avenue.

12.2 Turn right onto Pennsylvania Avenue.

12.9 Turn left onto Buffalo Avenue by the Coast Guard station.

13.0 Turn left onto Delaware Avenue.

14.1 Turn left onto Indiana Avenue, which becomes Michigan Avenue.

14.4 Turn left onto Madison Avenue.

14.4 Make a quick right onto Columbia Avenue.

14.8 Turn left onto Guerney Avenue.

15.0 Turn right onto Beach Road.

15.8 Complete your ride at the end of Beach Road.

Local Events/Attractions

Cape May: For the many sites and attractions on Cape May, check out the official Web site (www.capemay.com), or contact them at Cape-May.com, P.O. Box 2383, Cape May, NJ 08204; (609) 898-4500.

Restaurants

Check **CapeMay.com** for a comprehensive list of places to eat.

Accommodations

Check **CapeMay.com** for a comprehensive list of places to stay.

Maps

DeLorme: New Jersey Atlas and Gazetteer: Page 73 N20.

New Jersey Bike Maps: Cape May; www.njbikemap.com.

27 Fort Mott Challenge

Salem County lies right on the Delaware Bay in the southwestern part of New Jersey. This area is filled with quiet creeks, marshland, and lots of farmland. The pace of life is a little slower here, which makes it a nice place to ride. This ride takes you on a flat, nearly 57-mile loop around the nicer parts of the county.

Start: Fort Mott State Park parking lot off Fort Mott Road, Salem.

Distance: 56.8-mile loop.

Terrain: Very flat, with a small climb. There are some gradual inclines and declines but nothing that could be mistaken for a hill. The one hill (90 feet) on the route isn't really much of a climb.

Traffic and hazards: Most of the roads in this ride are quiet backcountry roads that have almost no traffic, but you will pass through a couple of towns with moderate traffic. Since the area that you will be riding in is mostly farmland and marshland, there is very little cover to provide shade, so avoid this ride on very hot, humid days.

Getting there: Take Interstate 295 or the New Jersey Turnpike to exit 1 at Pennsville and follow Route 49 east to Fort Mott Road. Turn right onto Fort Mott Road and travel 3 miles. Fort Mott State Park is located on the right.

Fort Mott State Park contains one of a couple of forts built to protect this part of the state from attack during the late 1800s. Today the park preserves the history of the fort and provides a great place to relax by Delaware Bay. If you look across the river you will see Delaware, but since there is a lot of industry along the river, the view isn't that nice.

You may think you are still in New Jersey, but technically you are in Delaware. Because of the strange way the boundaries of Delaware were specified, the small strip of land that Fort Mott sits on is officially owned by that state, although they don't pay any taxes on the land or provide any services.

The area of New Jersey by Delaware Bay is filled with a lot of little creeks and marshland and some very fertile farmland. The ride will take you around some of the quieter roads of this area and show you the sights. Although this is a long ride, it is mostly flat. If you've already done some 40- or 50-mile rides, this one won't be difficult.

To start the ride, turn left out of the parking lot onto Fort Mott Road. You will ride away from Delaware Bay past Finn's Point Lighthouse, a strange-looking lighthouse constructed of wrought iron. It's not the traditional type of lighthouse but part of what is called a range-light system. This lighthouse once worked in tandem with another one (now gone) on the bank of the Delaware River. Ship captains would line up the lights from the two lighthouses to find the center of the river.

After passing the lighthouse, ride along Lighthouse Road to where it intersects Route 49 and turn right. Follow Route 49 into the town of Salem and cross a bridge. Make a left turn immediately after the bridge onto Griffith Street (unsigned) and

Riding along the wetlands near Delaware Bay

go through an industrial area of town. After about 0.5 mile you will come to a light where Griffith intersects Route 45 (Market Street). Make a left here onto Route 45 and head out of town. This is a moderately busy road but has a shoulder that will get nicer as you get farther from town.

A couple miles out of town, turn left onto County Road 540 west, then make the next right to stay on CR 540 west. You are now away from the main roads and riding along some meadows and creeks. As you continue along CR 540 to Sunset Drive, you will start to see some farms. After 1.3 miles, turn right onto Marshalltown Road. There is no road sign here, but it's the only right-hand turn around. (If you go too far, Sunset Drive becomes a dirt road—if you hit dirt, you missed the turn.)

As you continue on Marshalltown Road, you'll see an interesting house on the right with a display of plants, boots, and other objects painted in bright polka dots. After you cross CR 540, Marshalltown Road will change names to Pointers Auburn Road. Then at 13.8 miles, you make a right onto Haines Neck Road. At Mile 14.5 the road curves to the right; turn left to stay on Haines Neck. There is no road sign here, but if you look down the road you should see a County Road 631 sign.

You are now in the heart of the area's farmland and can see why New Jersey is called the Garden State. Continue to ride through the farmland on some really empty roads. Approximately 0.5 mile after making a left onto Quaker Neck Road, you will enter the town of Alloway and come to a traffic light where Greenwich and Main Streets meet. If you need a break, there is a little deli a half block to the left on Main Street.

Continue through the town of Alloway, making a right onto Waterworks Road and then, after 1.2 miles, a left onto North Burden Hill Road. With a name that ends in the word "hill," you should expect a little climb ahead. About halfway down this road there are two small bumps that will require you to climb about 90 feet total. It's a pretty gentle climb but is a big change from the flats you have been riding on. This is the biggest climb in Salem County and the only real hill on the ride.

At the end of North Burden Hill, cross Route 49 and continue straight ahead on South Burden Hill Road. This is a nice little downhill that will give you a good view of the surrounding land. The smoke you may see in front of you is coming from the Salem Nuclear Power Plant; you will have various views of the plant as you continue the ride.

When you make a left here onto Jericho Road, you make encounter some light traffic on Jericho. This area is lightly forested, and the road has a number of rolling hills. Stay on Jericho Road for 3.4 miles and then, at the bottom of one of the bigger rollers, turn right onto Hell Neck Road. I'm not sure what a "hell neck" is, but this is a very tame road with a gentle uphill followed by a nice downhill.

Where Friendship Road intersects County Road 623 (Main Street) there is a nice food store on the corner if you need a break. Make a right onto Main Street and then the next left onto Long Bridge Road. This road and the next few turns will take you into some marshland

You may encounter some light traffic on Canton Harmersville Road (CR 623), as this is one of the main roads in the area. On Locust Island Road you will go by a small creek and pass the historic Hancock House. There are some nice views of the Intracoastal Waterway and marshland as you cross the bridge.

From here you will head back toward Delaware Bay and get some views of the river. Turning left onto Tilbury Road will take you back toward the town of Salem. Tilbury takes you past a boatyard and then bends around to the right and becomes Grieves Parkway (although there is no road sign here). At the next intersection make a hard left turn onto Front Street (unsigned) to go through the town of Salem. This road merges with Route 49 and you cross the bridge you crossed when you entered Salem on your ride out. You are now headed back to Fort Mott. Retrace your outbound route to get back to the parking lot.

Miles and Directions

0.0 Turn left out of the parking lot onto Fort Mott Road. N39° 36.132' / W75° 32.958'

1.2 Bear right onto Lighthouse Road.

1.4 Follow the road around to the right to stay on Lighthouse Road. (Finn's Point Lighthouse is on your right.)

3.6 Turn right onto Route 49 (South Broadway).

5.7 Turn left after crossing the bridge onto Griffith Street.

Fort Mott Challenge

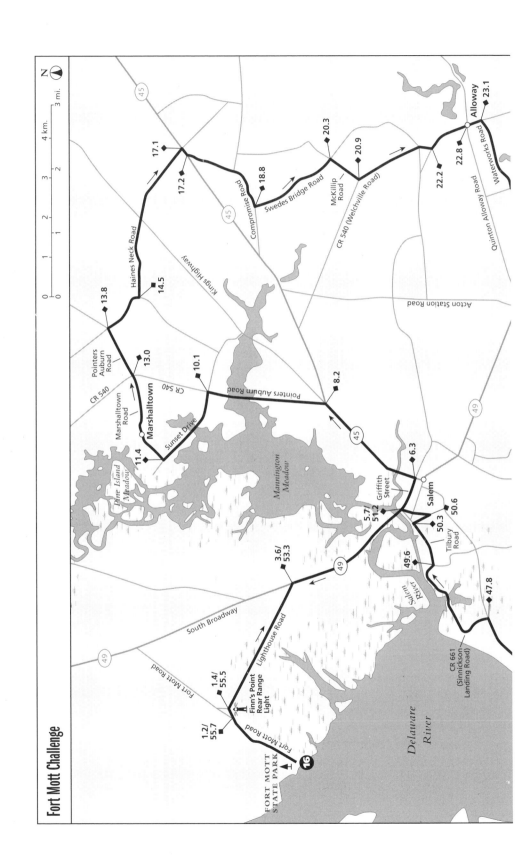

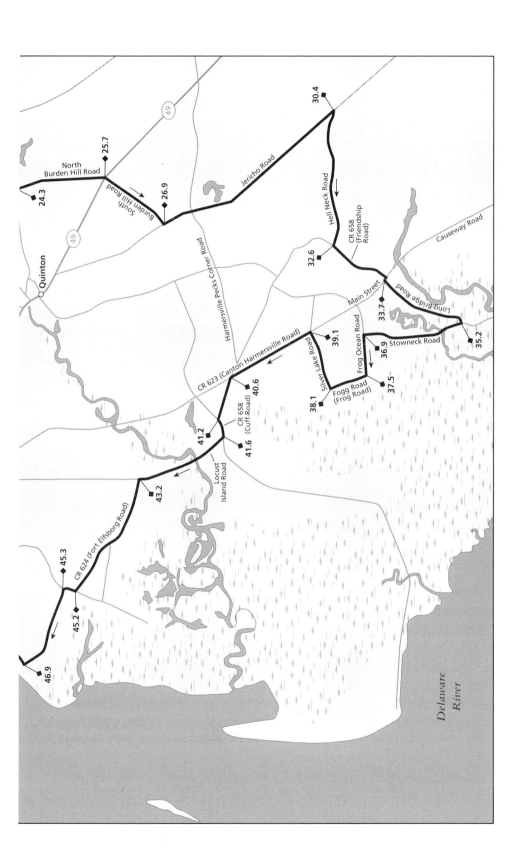

6.3   Turn left onto Route 45 (Market Street).

8.1   Turn left onto CR 540 (Bypass Road).

8.2   Turn right onto Pointers Auburn Road (CR 540).

10.1   Turn left onto Sunset Drive.

11.4   Turn right onto Marshalltown Road.

13.0   Cross CR 540. The road again becomes Pointers Auburn Road.

13.8   Turn right onto Haines Neck Road (CR 631).

14.5   Turn left to stay on Haines Neck Road (CR 631) (unsigned).

17.1   Turn right at the T onto Route 45.

17.2   Turn left onto Compromise Road (this is the second left).

18.8   Turn left onto Swedes Bridge Road.

20.3   Turn right onto McKillip Road.

20.8   Turn left at the T onto CR 540 (Welchville Road).

22.2   Turn left onto Quaker Neck Road (becomes Greenwich Road).

22.8   Reach Main Street in Alloway. (There's a deli a half block left on Main Street.)

23.1   Turn right onto Waterworks Road.

24.3   Turn left onto North Burden Hill Road (90-foot climb halfway down the road).

25.7   Cross Route 49. The road becomes South Burden Hill Road.

26.9   Turn left at the T onto Jericho Road.

30.4   Turn right onto Hell Neck Road.

32.6   Turn left onto County Road 658 (Friendship Road).

33.7   Turn right onto CR 623 (Main Street). (There's a food store on the corner.)

33.7   Turn left onto Long Bridge Road.

35.2   Turn right onto Stowneck Road.

36.9   Turn left onto Frog Ocean Road.

37.5   The road turns right and becomes Fogg Road (Frog Road).

38.1   The road turns right and becomes Silver Lake Road.

39.1   Turn left onto Canton Harmersville Road (CR 623).

40.6   Turn left onto CR 658 (Harmersville Road).

41.2   Turn left onto CR 658 Cuff Road.

41.6   Turn right onto Locust Island Road.

43.2   Turn left onto Fort Elfsborg Road (County Road 624).

45.2   Turn right to stay on Fort Elfsborg Road (CR 624).

45.3   Bear left to stay on Fort Elfsborg Road (CR 624).

46.9   Turn right onto Fort Elfsborg–Salem Road.

47.8   Turn left onto Sinnickson Landing Road (County Road 661).

49.6   Turn left onto Tilbury Road.

50.3   The road bends to the right and becomes Grieves Parkway.

50.6   Make a hard left turn onto Front Street (unsigned), which becomes Route 49.

51.2 Bear left and go over the bridge. Stay on Route 49.

53.3 Turn left onto Lighthouse Road.

55.5 Turn left onto Fort Mott Road.

56.8 Turn right into the parking lot at Fort Mott to complete your ride.

Local Events/Attractions

Fort Mott State Park: Fort Mott was part of a coastal defense system designed for the Delaware River in the late 1800s. Visitors can wander through the old batteries and learn about the fort's history. The shoreline offers good spots for walking and picnicking. For more information, visit www.state.nj.us/dep/parksandforests/parks/fortmott.html.

Accommodations

Comfort Inn and Suites: 634 Soders Road, Carneys Point; (856) 299-8282 or (877) 424-6423.

Maps

DeLorme: New Jersey Atlas and Gazetteer: Pages 60 G9, 61 I15, and 67 A19.
New Jersey Bike Maps: Delaware City, Salem, Canton; www.njbikemap.com.

28 Batsto Village Cruise

Beautiful Batsto Village, located in Wharton State Forest, is the site of a former bog-iron and glass-making community. The area around Batsto is surrounded by a number of preserved forests. The flat land and empty roads make this a great place to ride. This cruise takes you from Batsto to Oyster Creek and back. Along the way you will see forests, rivers, and coastland.

Start: Batsto Village, County Road 542, Hammonton.

Distance: 48-mile loop.

Terrain: Very flat. There are some gradual inclines and declines but nothing that could be mistaken for a hill.

Traffic and hazards: Most of the roads for this ride are through or around protected forest, so the roads have very little traffic. You will pass through a few town centers like Smithville, which will be a little congested.

Getting there: From southern New Jersey take the Garden State Parkway north to exit 50 (New Gretna), and follow U.S. Highway 9 north to a Gulf gas station. Turn left onto CR 542 and continue for 12 miles. Batsto Village is on the right.

From northern New Jersey take the Garden State Parkway south to exit 52 (New Gretna). Turn right at the stop sign onto East Greenbush Road. Make a left at the next stop sign. Cross two small wooden bridges. Pilgrim Lake Campground is on the right. Turn left onto Leektown Road and continue 2 miles to a stop sign. Stay straight on Leektown Road. Continue 3 miles to stop sign. Turn right onto CR 542 west and stay on CR 542 for approximately 9 miles. Batsto Village is on the right.

From the Trenton/Mount Holly area, take U.S. Highway 206 south to Mile Marker 3 and make a left onto County Road 613. Continue on CR 613 and then turn left onto County Road 693. Follow CR 693 until the road ends and then make left onto CR 542. Batsto Village is on your left.

NOTE: There is a fee to park at Batsto Village. If you don't want to pay the fee, continue past the entrance to Batsto for about a mile and park in the sand parking lot on the right. This lot is used by hikers/canoers to access some of the local trails and rivers.

Charles Reed founded Batsto Village in 1766 to produce iron, and the village produced iron and glass from 1766 to 1867. Today it is a historic village that preserves the past. Batsto Village also serves as a starting point for a number of hikes and canoe trips in the Pinelands as well as a starting place for bike rides.

To start the ride, turn left after you exit the parking lot onto Batsto Road. Most roads in the area are unsigned, but since the road you will be riding on is the only paved one, it is easy to follow. The road will change names a couple of times, and different maps call it by different names (Batsto, Tylertown, Bulltown). This is a quiet road with almost no traffic and feels like a wide bike path. The road winds around for over 5 miles, then you make a left onto CR 542 (Pleasant Mills Road). This road can have moderate traffic at times, so stay to the right. From here take Old Church Road to River Road, which takes you down to the Mullica River.

Ride along the river for a little less than 0.5 mile, and then make a right over a bridge that crosses the river. Pass through some swampland that eventually transitions to forest. A couple more turns will have you on County Road 624 (Clarks Landing Road), which will take you through some of the preserved forest in the area.

After about 6 miles, pass under the Garden State Parkway. There are a number of roads entering from the left and right and cars getting on or off the parkway, so be careful here. Make a few more turns and come to a T on Old New York Road where it meets U.S. Highway 9. Turn right here onto US 9.

Immediately after you make the right, you will see Lake Meone and Historic Smithville to your right. This is a good alternative starting point if you live in the area. Although Smithville sits near the site of the original town, only a small part of the original village remains. Today it is mostly a shopping village, with more than sixty small shops and places to eat. The road here can be a little busy because of the village, so be careful.

At the next intersection turn left at the light onto Moss Mill Road. Before you make the left, you may want to take a break. The rest of the ride goes through rural areas that don't have any stores. There are a few places to stop here. Smithville has a pizzeria and a bakery, or you can stop at the CVS on the far right corner or the convenience store that's just past the light on the left.

After making the left onto Moss Mill Road, you are heading east toward the coast. But after 1.3 miles you will make a right onto Leeds Point Road before you actually get to the water.

If you want to see Oyster Creek, which is part of the Intracoastal Waterway, continue straight instead of making the right and go to the end of the road. At the end are Oyster Creek and the south end of the Edwin B. Forsythe National Wildlife Refuge.

Parking lot at Oyster Creek

It's a pretty area and is worth a look—just don't stay too long. After about five minutes New Jersey's unofficial state bird, the greenhead fly, will find you and go for blood. They are very persistent and annoying. Once you're done, just head back the way you came in, now turning left when you get to Leeds Point Road.

Leeds Point is an unremarkable place but is famous for being the birthplace of the Jersey Devil. Look up the Jersey Devil online if you want the full story. It's pretty interesting.

Leeds Point Road starts taking you back to Batsto. Most of the route will be low traffic, but you may encounter moderate traffic when you get to Moss Mill Road, which is one of the busier roads in the area. When you make a right onto West Liebig Avenue, you will be back to low-traffic roads. There is a grid of roads here for no apparent reason. There are some houses here and there, but most of the area is just forested land.

West Liebig Avenue is a quiet, flat road that is only interrupted by the occasional stop sign. The cross streets are named for European towns. When you get to Frankfurt after 4.15 miles, make a left where West Liebig Avenue turns to sand. Then make the next right back onto Moss Mill Road (County Road 561A).

After 3.4 miles make a right onto Darmstadt Avenue and take it to Indian Cabin Road. Indian Cabin Road winds around some nice scenery for 5 miles before ending

Batsto Village Cruise

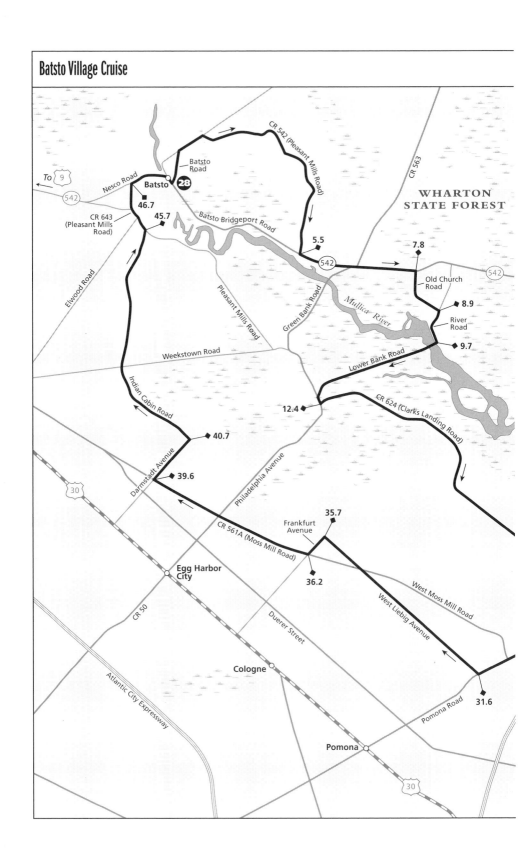

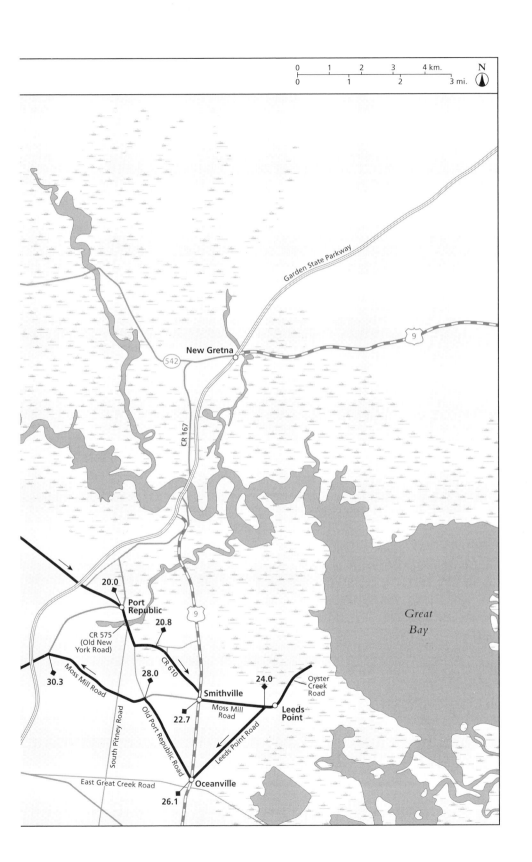

0   1   2   3   4 km.
0   1   2   3 mi.

N

Garden State Parkway

9

New Gretna

542

CR 167

20.0

Port
Republic

9

20.8

CR 575
(Old New
York Road)

CR 610

Moss Mill Road

30.3

28.0

24.0

Oyster
Creek
Road

Smithville

Leeds
Point

22.7

Moss Mill
Road

South Pitney Road

Leeds Point Road

Old Port Republic Road

East Great Creek Road

Oceanville

26.1

Great
Bay

at a T. Turn left here onto Pleasant Mills Road (County Road 643). After a mile this road also comes to a T. Turn right here onto CR 542. This is a busy road, so stay in the shoulder. In another mile you will see the entrance to Batsto Village on your left. Make the left into Batsto and you're back at the starting point. If you haven't been to Batsto before, the village is worth a look. There are also a number of hiking trails and rivers to canoe. Information about these activities is available in the visitor center.

Miles and Directions

0.0 Turn left out of the Batsto Village parking lot onto Batsto Road (also known as Bulltown or Tylerville Road). N39° 38.488' / W74° 38.696'

5.5 Turn left onto CR 542 (Pleasant Mills Road).

7.8 Turn right onto Old Church Road.

8.9 Turn right at the T onto River Road (County Road 652).

9.7 Turn right onto the bridge to Lower Bank Road.

12.3 Turn left onto County Road 563.

12.4 Turn left onto CR 624 (Clarks Landing Road).

20.0 Merge into Pomona Avenue followed by a quick right onto County Road 575 (Old New York Road).

20.8 Continue on Old New York, which is now called County Road 610.

22.6 Turn right onto US 9 (North New York Road). (Smithville Village is on your right if you need a stop.)

22.7 Turn left onto Moss Mill Road.

24.0 Turn right onto Leeds Point Road. **Optional extension begins:** To visit Oyster Creek, instead of turning right onto Leeds Point Road, continue straight on Moss Mill Road, which becomes Oyster Creek Road. After 1.4 miles the road ends at Oyster Creek. Turn around and head back on Oyster Creek Road. After 1.4 miles turn left onto Leeds Point Road. Optional extension ends.

26.1 Turn right and cross US 9 onto Old Port Republic Road.

28.0 Turn left onto Moss Mill Road.

30.3 Turn left onto South Pomona Road (CR 575).

31.6 Turn right onto West Liebig Avenue.

35.7 Turn left onto Frankfurt Avenue.

36.2 Turn right onto CR 561A (Moss Mill Road).

39.6 Turn right onto Darmstadt Avenue.

40.7 Turn left onto Indian Cabin Road.

45.7 Turn left onto CR 643 (Pleasant Mills Road).

46.7 Turn right onto Pleasant Mills Road (CR 542).

47.7 Turn left onto Batsto Road.

48.0 Turn left into the Batsto Village parking lot to complete your ride.

Local Events/Attractions

Batsto Village is a historic site located in the south-central New Jersey Pinelands. This historic site contains a number of original buildings. For more information, check out the Web site: www.batstovillage.org.

Historic Smithville and Village Greene comprises shops, restaurants, and cafes on the site of the original town and tries to preserve the colonial atmosphere. It's a good place to shop, eat, or just stroll the grounds. For more information, visit www.smithvillenj.com.

Restaurants

The Smithville Inn: 1 North New York Road, Smithville; (609) 652-7777; www.smithville inn.com. Good food in a colonial atmosphere with nice views of the lake.

Accommodations

Ramada Inn Hammonton: 308 South White Horse Pike (U.S. Highway 30), Hammonton; (609) 561-5700 or (800) 272-6232.

Maps

DeLorme: New Jersey Atlas and Gazetteer: Pages 64 E8 and 65 K15.

New Jersey Bike Maps: Egg Harbor City, Greenbank, New Gretna, Oceanville, Pleasant-ville; www.njbikemap.com.

29 Medford Lakes Cruise

The northern end of southern New Jersey is filled with small towns, rural farmland, and a lot of quiet roads. This ride takes you from Columbus to the top of the Pine Barrens through Medford and back. Along the way you will view scenic farmlands, a historic bike factory, and some cranberry bogs.

Start: Mansfield Community Park parking lot, County Road 543, Columbus.
Distance: 45.5-mile loop.
Terrain: Flat to rolling. This ride is mostly flat, with some occasional rolling hills. The ride will take you to the highest point in Burlington County, although it's really not much of a climb.
Traffic and hazards: Most of the roads in this ride are rural country roads. You will pass through a few town centers, which will be a little congested.

Getting there: Take the New Jersey Turnpike to exit 7 and then take U.S. Highway 206 south about 3.5 miles to Columbus. Exit US 206 when you see a sign for CR 543 Columbus. At the end of the exit ramp turn left, going over US 206. The entrance to Mansfield Community Park is on the right just after you enter the town.

Burlington County is a relatively flat quiet place to ride. The county marks the transition from Central Jersey to South Jersey and it still contains many rural farms. A number of towns you will ride through haven't changed much in the last fifty years, which is a welcome relief from constant new developments that are swallowing up other areas of the state.

To start the ride, turn left after you exit the parking lot onto Main Street (Mount Pleasant Road/Columbus Road). Go back through town and cross over US 206.

Historic bike shop at Smithville

After a mile, make a left onto Petticoat Bridge Road and start a long march south. Zig and zag on some quiet roads as you ride through farmland.

Two miles after turning onto Smithville Road, you will come to the historic village of Smithville. Smithville was an industrial village that produced woodworking machinery and high-wheel bicycles in the late 1800s. The building on the corner by the road has a display of some of the high-wheel bicycles produced here. If you pass by during visiting hours, you can stop and see how far bicycle technology has progressed in one hundred plus years.

Smithville Road will take you across Route 38 at a light and continue south. There is no street sign where you have to turn onto Eayrestown Road, but if you keep track of the miles from last turn, you can't miss it.

Continue south through more farmland and past some nice houses. After passing the golf course, you end up on Eayrestown Road, which can be confusing when mapping out the route, since there is another parallel Eayrestown Road just to the east.

Eventually cross Route 70 at a light. There is a gas station and Wawa on the left before the light if you need a break. After you cross Route 70, make a quick series of turns. First bear left at the Y onto Branin Road and then make the next left onto Chairville Road. Stay on Chairville for 0.4 mile and then bear right at a Y onto Hawkin Road.

Hawkin continues for 5.2 miles as the land transitions from farmland to forest. You are now at the top of the Pine Barrens. When you make the left onto New Road, there is a nice general store on the corner with some inviting rocking chairs that makes a good rest stop.

The turn onto New Road starts your trip back, and you are now heading mostly north. New Road can have moderate traffic, so stay to the right. Continue to travel through the north side of the Pine Barrens through some residential neighborhoods, and eventually cross Route 70. There is no light here, so watch out for traffic as you cross. On the other side of Route 70 the road's name changes to Big Hill. Don't worry about the road name—there are no real hills here, just a little roller or two. After about a mile you will see some cranberry bogs. New Jersey is a major producer of cranberries. If you ride this area in late September or early October, you may see the bogs flooded with water so that farmers can harvest their crop; otherwise you will just see cranberry plants in dry fields.

Continue to head north through some nice farmland. Be careful crossing County Road 530 (South Pemberton Road). This is a busy road with four lanes of traffic, so be patient. After crossing CR 530 you will wind around a residential neighborhood and eventually start a little climb. You are now headed to the highest point in Burlington County. It's only 234 feet, so it is not much of a climb. The climb ends where Birmingham Drive meets Arneys Mount Road. Make a left here and then continue straight through the next stop sign.

Continue zigzagging north through the farmland. You'll eventually end up on Mount Pleasant Road and back in the town of Columbus and the Mansfield Community Park parking lot where you started. Although this ride has shown you some of the better roads in Burlington County and Medford, there are a lot of other nice roads in the area. Feel free to vary the route to explore some other roads.

Miles and Directions

0.0 Turn left out of the parking lot onto Main Street (Columbus Road). N40° 4.306' / W74° 43.248'

1.00 Turn left onto Petticoat Bridge Road.

2.8 Turn left onto Jacksonville Jobstown Road.

3.1 Turn right onto Warner Road.

5.3 Turn right onto County Road 537 (Monmouth Road).

5.7 Turn left onto Smithville Road.

8.4 Cross Route 38. Continue on Smithville Road.

10.1 Turn right at the T onto Newbolds Corner Road.

11.6 Turn left onto Eayrestown Road (unsigned).

13.0 Turn right onto Bridge Road.

13.1 Turn left onto Country Club Drive.

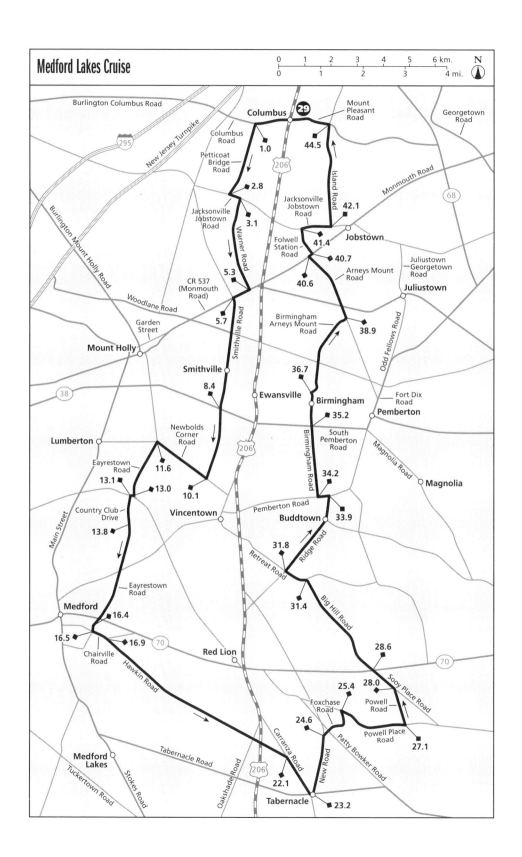

Medford Lakes Cruise

13.8	Continue straight. The road becomes Eayrestown Road.
16.4	Bear left onto Branin Road.
16.5	Turn left onto Chairville Road.
16.9	Bear right onto Hawkin Road.
22.1	Turn right onto Carranza Road.
23.1	Turn left onto County Road 532 (Chatsworth Road).
23.2	Quick left onto New Road (general store on right).
24.6	Turn right onto Foxchase Road.
25.4	Turn right onto Powell Place Road.
27.1	Turn left onto Powell Road.
28.0	Turn left onto Sooy Place Road.
28.6	Cross Route 70. The road becomes Big Hill Road.
31.4	Turn left onto Retreat Road.
31.8	Turn right onto Ridge Road.
33.9	Turn left onto Pemberton Road.
34.2	Turn right onto Birmingham Road.
35.2	Cross CR 530; use caution on this busy four-lane road.
36.7	Turn right onto Brandywine Road, which eventually changes to Birmingham Arneys Mount Road.
38.9	Turn Left onto Arneys Mount Road.
40.6	Turn right onto CR 537 (Monmouth Road).
40.7	Turn left onto Folwell Station Road.
41.4	Turn right onto Jacksonville Jobstown Road.
42.1	Turn left onto Island Road.
44.5	Turn left onto Mount Pleasant Road.
45.5	Turn left into the parking lot to complete your ride.

Local Events/Attractions

Smithville Park is home to historic Smithville Mansion and its grounds, which were part of a village that produced woodworking machinery and high-wheel bicycles in the late 1800s. The mansion and a number of the other buildings are open for tours. The park also offers hiking and other outdoor activities in the surrounding park. For more information, check the "Tourism" section of the Burlington County Web site: www.co.burlington.nj.us.

Restaurants

Mastori's Diner: 144 South U.S. Highway 130, Bordentown; (609) 298-4650. A popular diner with great food.

Accommodations

Best Western Bordentown Inn: 1068 U.S. Highway 206, Bordentown; (609) 298-8000

Maps

DeLorme: New Jersey Atlas and Gazetteer: Pages 48 G3, 55 A27, and 56 E1.
New Jersey Bike Maps: Columbus, Mount Holly, Indian Mills, Pemberton; www.njbikemap.com.

30 Belleplain Challenge

Belleplain State Forest lies in northern Cape May and western Cumberland Counties. This area comprises large amounts of forested land as well as marshland and coastal areas. This ride takes you through the forest and marshlands to East Point Light and back.

Start: Belleplain State Forest parking lot, Henkensifkin Road, Woodbine.
Distance: 53.4-mile figure eight.
Terrain: Very flat. There are some gradual inclines and declines but nothing that could be mistaken for a hill. The only "hill" you encounter will be a bridge over the Maurice River.
Traffic and hazards: The ride will be on a mix of county highways and back roads. The county highways will have moderate to heavy traffic, but all have wide shoulders to ride in, so traffic will be easy to deal with.

Getting there: From the north take the Garden State Parkway south to exit 17, then take U.S. Highway 9 north to County Road 550 west toward Woodbine. Follow the signs to the park. The entrance to the park is on Henkensifkin Road on the left about 1.8 miles after passing through Woodbine. Make a left on the Henkensifkin then a right into the parking lot.

From the south take the Garden State Parkway north to exit 13, then take US 9 North to Route 83 toward South Dennis. Route 83 merges into Route 47 north. Continue on Route 47 north until it meets Washington Avenue. Make a right onto Washington Avenue and then a left onto CR 550. The entrance to the park is on Henkensifkin Road on the left about 1.4 miles ahead. Make a left onto Henkensifkin and then a right into the parking lot.

The northwestern part of Cape May County is a quiet, undeveloped area. With no major attractions or large towns here, this is a relatively unknown area of the state. The large expanses of forest are broken only by occasional streams and coastal marshland. Although the forestlands here may look similar to the Pine Barrens, they are more diverse, with oak and Atlantic cedar in addition to the usual pine trees.

This ride is listed as a challenge because it is over 50 miles, but the terrain is flat and the roads are well maintained, so this should be an easy ride for anybody that has done a few cruises. This route is a figure eight that crosses the same point twice. If you want to shorten the ride, you can cut out the top part of the "eight" and reduce the distance by 20 miles.

To start the ride, turn right out of the parking lot on to Henkensifkin Road. You won't see any traffic until you're on Route 47 north. This can be a busy road, especially on summer weekends. The road has a wide shoulder, so although you may feel the wind as cars go by, there is no problem riding with the traffic. After a little over 0.5 mile, turn left to stay on Route 47. Continue on Route 47 through some farmland and forest for a total of 6.4 miles before making a left onto Glade Road. This road takes you through some marshland and then after 1.7 miles goes through a small town and changes its name to East Point Road. After another 2.6 miles the road

East Point Lighthouse

ends at a parking lot facing Delaware Bay. To your left is the southern part of Cape May County; to your right is the East Point Lighthouse.

East Point Lighthouse marks the entrance to the Maurice River. Although the East Point Lighthouse fell into disrepair in the '60s and '70s, the exterior of the lighthouse has been restored. In 1980 the Coast Guard installed a new beacon, so the lighthouse is again being used as a navigation aid.

Once you're done enjoying the view, head back out on East Point Road the way you came in. After 2.6 miles turn left onto Main Street and go through the small town of Heislerville. A couple more turns will take you along the Maurice River and through the small town of Leesburg.

Eventually come to a T on Main Street (County Road 616) where it meets Route 47. Make a left here onto Route 47 and then make a left at the light onto Mauricetown Crossway Road (County Road 670). This is very busy and confusing intersection where Route 47, County Road 347, and CR 670 meet, so watch the traffic. There is a Wawa on the left-hand side as you make the turn. It's the only place to stop for a break for the next 20 miles. This Wawa is the center of the figure 8. (If you want to shorten the ride, make a right at the light instead of a left and follow the directions from Mile 44.7.)

Once you're on the Mauricetown Crossway, continue for a mile and then cross the Maurice River. The bridge is a little rough to ride over, but it does have a small

Belleplain Challenge

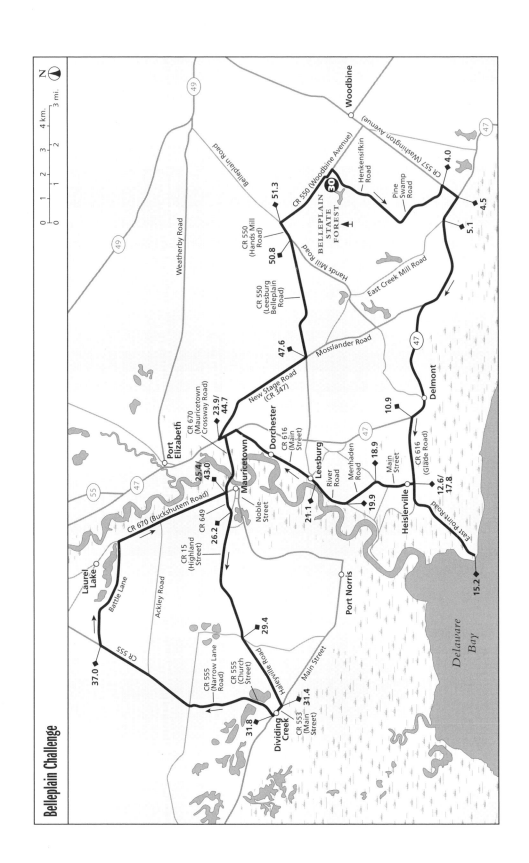

shoulder to ride in. Once over the bridge, continue straight through the blinking light, where the road name changes to County Road 649.

From here you will make a big 18-mile loop to the town of Dividing Creek and back. There is a lot of nothing out here, which makes the roads almost traffic free. You will be riding through some nice forests and by some artificial lakes. The lakes must be artificial and part of some chemical processing system, because they look a little too blue to be just water.

Pass through the small but quaint town of Dividing Creek and leave the town on Church Street. This road becomes Narrow Lane Road and continues through some more forest. This road has a few more ups and downs than other roads that you have been on. This wouldn't be worth mentioning except for the fact that the ride has been very flat up to this point.

After 5.28 miles, make a right onto Battle Lane. This road is unsigned, but it is one of the few non-sand roads; if you keep track of the mileage, it should be easy to find. If you go too far, you will run into Buckshutem Road and can just make a right to get back on track.

Battle Lane takes you through a small residential community that surrounds Laurel Lake. After this, turn right onto Buckshutem Road. This can be a busy road, so stay to the right in the nice, wide shoulder.

After just over 3 miles you will come to a blinking light that will look familiar. Turn left here onto Mauricetown Crossway and go back over the Maurice River. This road takes you back to Route 47 and the Wawa where you were about 20 miles ago. You have gone in a big loop, which could be cut out of the ride if you want fewer miles. At the light where Mauricetown Crossway crosses Route 47, continue straight and then make a right onto CR 347. Again, this is a moderately busy road, but the shoulder makes it very rideable.

In just under 3 miles turn left onto CR 550 (Leesburg Belleplain Road) as you head back toward the park. This is a much quieter road that goes along the northern side of the park. In another 3 miles this road merges with Hands Mill Road. Make a left here and then a right in just under 0.5 mile to stay on CR 550. In another 2 miles you will be back at the park entrance. Make a right at Henkensifkin Road, then another right back into the parking lot.

Belleplain Park has a nice lake, Lake Nummy, which is a good place for a swim. This is also a great area for hiking and bird watching, so if you have extra time, stick around and enjoy the other things the park has to offer.

Miles and Directions

0.0 Turn right out of parking lot onto Henkensifkin Road. Henkensifkin becomes Pine Swamp Road. N39° 14.939' / W74° 50.477'

4.0 Turn right onto Washington Avenue (County Road 557).

4.5 Turn right onto Route 47. This is a busy road, so stay in the shoulder.

5.1 Turn left to stay on Route 47.

10.9 Turn left onto Glade Road (CR 616).

12.6 Glade Road becomes East Point Road.

15.2 East Point Road ends by East Point Lighthouse. Turn around and head back out the way you came.

17.8 Turn left onto Main Street.

18.9 Turn left onto Menhaden Road.

19.9 The road bends right and becomes River Road.

21.1 River Road becomes Main Street (CR 616).

23.5 Turn left onto Route 47.

23.9 Turn left at the light onto Mauricetown Crossway (County Road 670). There's a Wawa on the corner. Option: This is the center of the figure 8. To shorten the route, make a right at the light instead of a left and follow the directions from Mile 44.7.

25.4 Continue straight at the blinking light. The road becomes CR 649.

26.2 Turn right onto Highland Street (County Road 15).

29.4 The road becomes Haleyville Road.

31.4 Turn right onto County Road 553 (Main Street in Dividing Creek).

31.8 Turn right onto County Road 555 (Church Street becomes Narrow Lane Road).

37.0 Turn right onto Battle Lane (unsigned).

39.9 Turn right onto Buckshutem Road (CR 670). This is a busy road, so stay in shoulder.)

43.0 Turn left at the blinking light onto Mauricetown Crossway Road (CR 670).

44.7 Turn right onto CR 347. Busy road; stay in the shoulder.

47.6 Turn left onto CR 550 (Leesburg Belleplain Road).

50.8 Turn left where CR 550 intersects Hands Mill Road to stay on CR 550.

51.3 Turn right onto CR 550 (Woodbine Avenue).

53.3 Turn right onto Henkensifkin Road.

53.4 Turn right into the parking lot to complete your ride.

Local Events/Attractions

Belleplain State Park is a 21,000+-acre park in Woodbine. A large forested area with a nice lake and campground, the park is a popular place for boating, fishing, and hiking. For more information, visit www.state.nj.us/dep/parks andforests/parks/belle.html.

Restaurants

Chiarella's Ristorante & Sidewalk Café: 100 East Taylor Avenue, Wildwood; (609) 522-4117. Casual family-owned restaurant with a good variety of food.

Urie's Waterfront Restaurant and Crab House: 588 West Rio Grande Avenue, Wildwood; (609) 522-4189; www.uries.net/index.htm. Steak and seafood with a nice view of the bay.

Accommodations

Cape Cod Inn Motel: 6109 Atlantic Avenue, Wildwood Crest; (609) 522-1177.

Coast Motel: 4000 Landis Avenue, Sea Isle City; (609) 263-1111 or (800) 804-6835.

Hyland Motor Inn: 38 East Mechanic Street, Cape May Court House; (609) 465-7305.

Maps

DeLorme: New Jersey Atlas and Gazetteer: Pages 66 K14, 68 M14, 69 M23, and 72 A6.

New Jersey Bike Maps: Woodbine, Heislerville, Port Norris, Port Elizabeth, Dividing Creek; www .njbikemap.com.

31 Pine Barrens Cruise

The Pine Barrens are a rural and somewhat mysterious area of New Jersey. This flat cruise takes you through the northern part of the Pine Barrens and shows you some nice small towns along the way.

Start: Visitor center parking lot, Brendan T. Byrne State Forest (formerly Lebanon State Forest), New Lisbon.
Distance: 43.9-mile loop.
Terrain: This ride is as flat as New Jersey gets. There are some gradual inclines and declines but nothing that could be mistaken for a hill.

Traffic and hazards: Most of the roads will have light traffic. The center of Medford Lakes will have moderate traffic. Almost half the roads on this ride have a dedicated bike lane, which makes riding easy. Just watch out for the Jersey Devil.

Getting there: From the New Jersey Turnpike take exit 7 and follow U.S. Highway 206 south to Route 38 east. Go to the second traffic light, and then turn right onto Magnolia Road (County Road 644). Follow Magnolia Road until you come to the Four-Mile Circle. From the circle take Route 72 east; at Mile Marker 1 make a left. There is a forest entrance sign on your left as you turn in. Go past the ranger house on the left and then take the first right. The visitor center is just ahead; turn left into the parking lot.

Many of New Jersey's stranger legends come from the Pine Barrens. A visit to this area of New Jersey seems like stepping back in time. The Pine Barrens are not really barren—just a large area of sandy, acidic, nutrient-poor soil that is not good to grow crops in. This area does, however, support a unique and diverse spectrum of plant life and is notable for its populations of rare pygmy pitch pines and other plant species that depend on fire to reproduce (fire is very frequent in the Pine Barrens). It's also the supposed home of the Jersey Devil, a large winged creature with hoofs that is mostly spotted by people with higher levels of alcohol in their blood.

The ride starts at the visitor center in Brendan T. Byrne State Forest. To start the ride, exit the parking lot and turn left onto Shinns Road. The roads are not well marked here. Shinns Road is the road on your left as you are facing the visitor center.

Shinns Road runs along the edge of the forest. It's a nice, quiet road with no traffic. After you leave the state forest, take Route 72 to County Road 563 to the town of Chatsworth. CR 563 has a bike lane, which continues when you make the right onto County Road 532.

CR 532 carries light to moderate traffic. You will be on this road for almost 14 miles; having the bike lane makes the riding easy. Pass Chatsworth Lake as you ride through the Pine Barrens. You'll see the forest on both sides of the road and not much else. The few roads that intersect CR 532 in this area are sand. This is a popular area for hunting, so you will see a number of hunting and gun clubs along this road.

Riding through Tabernacle

After about 10 miles on CR 532, you come to a stop sign. This marks the center of the town of Tabernacle, named for a log church that was built by missionary John Brainerd. That church no longer stands, but you will see a number of other large churches as you continue.

Eventually cross US 206, and here is where the bike lane ends. Except for a couple spots ahead, the road continues to have a shoulder most of the way. You are now close to Medford Lakes. Medford Lakes and Medford are two of the premier suburbs of Philadelphia.

After almost 14.5 miles on CR 532, you finally make a turn. Where CR 532 meets Dixontown Road, bear right and head into the town. At the end of Dixontown Road you will see a little strip mall on you left. There's a Wawa and a couple of other places here where you can stop and get some food and drink.

After the stop, continue on Dixontown Road and make a right at the light onto Skeet Road to head out of Medford Lakes. After you cross Route 70 at a light, you will be riding on rural back roads past farmland.

If you need to stop, there is a Wawa right before you cross US 206. You are now traveling through Southampton Township. Seventy-four percent of the township is dedicated to the Pineland Preserve, so this is a very rural area and a quiet place to bike through. Continue to ride on some very rural roads. It is quiet and lonely here, and

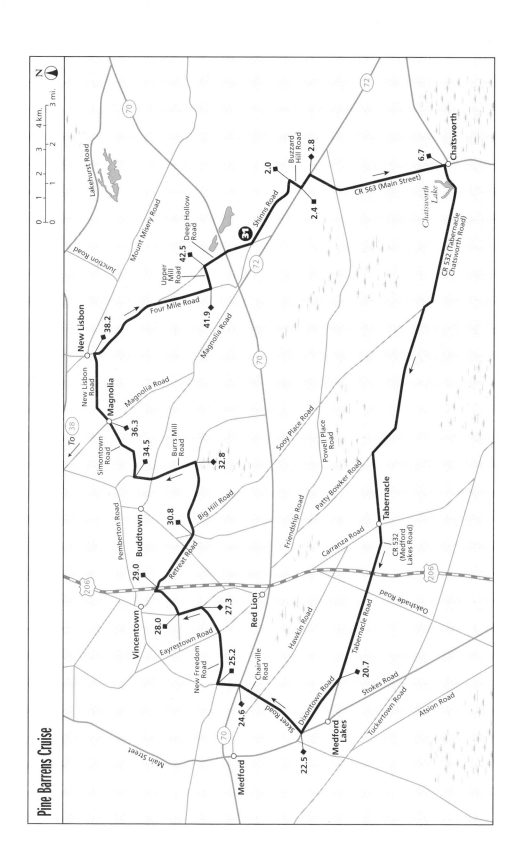

Pine Barrens Cruise

you can imagine how people could see some strange things on dark nights. From here you will head back into the Pine Barrens and eventually end up on Four Mile Road. There is a bike lane on this road that will take you most of the way back to the start.

You are back in the thick of the forest and surrounded by pine trees again. Be careful not to miss the turn in 3.7 miles onto Upper Mill Road or you will end up at the Route 70 circle. At the end of Upper Mill make a right onto Deep Hollow Road. In a little more than 0.5 mile, Deep Hollow crosses Route 70 and becomes Four Mile Road. Follow this for another 0.7 mile; the visitor center is on the right where you started the ride. If you are interested in exploring the Pine Barrens some more on foot, stop in the visitor center and pick up some information about hiking trails in the area.

Miles and Directions

0.0 Start at the visitor center. Turn left out of the west end of the parking lot onto Shinns Road. N39° 53.672' / W74° 34.476'

2.0 Turn right onto Buzzard Hill Road (unsigned) where Shinns Road becomes sand.

2.4 Turn left onto Route 72; stay in the shoulder.

2.8 Bear right onto CR 563.

6.7 Turn right onto CR 532 (Tabernacle Chatsworth Road).

20.7 Bear right onto Dixontown Road. (The strip mall ahead on left is a good place to take a break.)

22.5 Turn right onto Skeet Road.

24.6 Cross Route 70;the road becomes Chairville Road.

25.2 Turn right onto New Freedom Road.

27.3 Turn left at the T onto Red Lion Road.

28.0 Turn right onto Hilliards Bridge Road.

28.9 Turn right onto Main Street.

29.0 Cross US 206; the road becomes Retreat Road.

30.8 Bear left at the Y to stay on Retreat Road.

32.8 Bear left at the Y onto Burrs Mill Road.

34.5 Turn right onto Simontown Road.

36.3 Cross Magnolia Road; the road becomes New Lisbon Road.

38.2 Turn right onto Four Mile Road.

41.9 Turn left onto Upper Mill Road.

42.5 Turn right onto Deep Hollow Road.

43.2 Cross Route 70; the road becomes Four Mile Road.

43.9 Turn right into the visitor center parking lot to complete the loop.

Brendan T. Byrne State Forest (formerly Lebanon State Forest) is a 34,725-acre wilderness area within the New Jersey Pine Barrens. It is the state's second-largest state forest after Wharton State Forest. There are 25 miles of hiking trails and a camping area. Check out www.state.nj.us/dep/parksandforests/parks/byrne.html for more information.

Accommodations

Executive Inn: 7 West Hampton Street, Pemberton; (609) 894-8155.

Maps

DeLorme: New Jersey Atlas and Gazetteer: Pages 55 F28 and 56 C11.
New Jersey Bike Maps: Browns Mill, Chadsworth, Indian Mill, Medford Lakes, Mount Holly, Pemberton; www.njbikemap.com.

32 Zoo Cruise

Salem and Cumberland Counties are located in the southwest corner of New Jersey and are home to a lot of the state's farms. Riding is very pleasant in this area, with flat roads and almost no traffic. This ride takes you on a nice long loop through some of the more scenic roads in the area, as well through the Cohanzick Zoo for a look at a white tiger.

Start: Parvin State Park parking lot, 701 Almond Road, Pittsgrove.
Distance: 53.8-mile loop.
Terrain: Flat to rolling. There are no real hills to be found in this area, just some rolling terrain.
Traffic and hazards: Most of the roads on this ride are through the rural farmlands of Salem and Cumberland Counties, so there is very little traffic. A few town centers like Bridgeton and Centerton will be a little congested. This area is filled with a lot of open fields. There isn't much tree cover, so this isn't a ride you want to do on a sunny 90+-degree day.

Getting there: From Route 55 north or south, take exit 35 and follow the signs to the park. The park is located between Centerton and Vineland on County Road 540 (Almond Road).

Parvin State Park is a good place to spend a day fishing, hiking, or swimming. This area of New Jersey is fairly flat, traffic free, and filled with large farms and scenic roads. Riding in this area will help you understand why New Jersey is called the Garden State.

To start the ride, make a right after you exit the parking lot onto Almond Road. This road does not have a shoulder and can have moderate traffic at times, so stay to the right. Stay on this road for about 2 miles to the town of Centerton. The road comes to a T. Turn right here onto Centerton Road (County Road 553) and then bear left at the next intersection onto Dealtown Road.

From here you will pass Palatine Lake and head into farm country. You're soon surrounded by farmland for as far as the eye can see. Stay in the shoulder for the small stretch on Route 77—any car on this road will be moving fast. The left onto

South Jersey wheelmen riding through the farmland

Commissioner's Pike (County Road 581) takes you through the small rural town of Alloway. There is a general store on the right about halfway through town if you want to take a break. Three miles after going through Alloway, you will make a couple of quick turns through the town of Quinton.

When you get to Cross Road, you may see some plumes of white smoke to your right. This smoke is from the Salem Nuclear Power Plant, which is on the Delaware River. Some say the vegetables in this area grow a little bigger than normal...

As you get to Maskells Mill and Hell Neck Roads, the land becomes a little more forested. There is nothing evil about Hell Neck Road, just a little uphill section followed by a gentle downhill. From here you will wind your way through some more farmland toward the historic village of Greenwich.

Greenwich sits on the Cohansey River just 5 miles from Delaware Bay. During colonial times the town was a thriving seaport. Today it is a quiet and quaint bayside town with a number of Victorian houses and museums. If you are interested in colonial history, it's a place worth checking out.

As you go through the center of Greenwich and make a left onto Greenwich Bowenton Road (County Road 607), there is a general store on the far left corner if you need a break.

After leaving Greenwich, continue to ride past vast fields of farms. When you get to West Park Drive, you will start your approach to the town of Bridgeton and will encounter more traffic as you continue along this road.

In 0.5 mile you will cross Route 49. If you need a break, there is a store to your right just a little ways down Route 49. After 1.6 miles on West Park, cross West Avenue at a light and then go through Bridgeton City Park. Bear right at the Y onto Mayor Aitken Drive and then turn left into the parking lot of the Cohanzick Zoo.

Although Cohanzick Zoo is small, it's worth a quick stop, especially since the admission is free and there are restrooms here. The zoo has white tigers as well as bears, a golden eagle, and other animals.

Once you're done talking to the animals, make a right out of the parking lot and head back the way you came in. Bear left at the Y and then turn left onto West Drive. At the next intersection make a right onto West Avenue (Beebe Run Road), and then bear right at the next Y where the road becomes Beebe Run Road. Once on Beebe Run you will quickly leave town and be riding through some rural farmland again.

Silver Lake Road takes you by a lakeside residential community. Silver Lake crosses a couple of busy roads (Old Deerfield Pike and Route 77), so be careful here. At the end of Silver Lake, make a left followed quickly by a hard right onto Richards Road.

When Richards Road comes to a T intersection, make a left onto Parvins Mill Road. Parvins Mill carries moderate traffic, so stay to the right. After 2.2 miles Parvins Mill gets a little busier as you approach Parvin State Park. Eventually you will see Parvin Lake on your left. Make the next left onto Almond Road, which will take you back to the starting point.

There is nothing better than a swim after a long bike ride. If you remembered to bring your bathing suit, take a walk across the street from the parking lot and enjoy a dip in Parvin Lake.

Miles and Directions

0.0 Make a right out of parking lot onto CR 540 (Almond Road). N39° 30.678' / W75° 7.994'

2.2 Turn right at the center of town onto Centerton Road (CR 553), and then bear left onto Dealtown Road.

3.2 Turn left onto Olivet Road (County Road 690).

7.0 Turn left onto Route 77.

7.2 Turn right onto Friesburg Road (County Road 640).

8.2 Bear right to stay on Friesburg Road (CR 640).

10.3 Turn right onto Cohansey Road (County Road 635).

10.7 Turn left onto Remsterville Road (County Road 656).

13.1 Turn left at the T onto Alloway Aldine Road (County Road 611).

14.7 Turn left where the road merges with Commissioner's Pike/Main Street (CR 581). (There is a general store on the right as you pass through Quinton if you need a break.)

Zoo Cruise

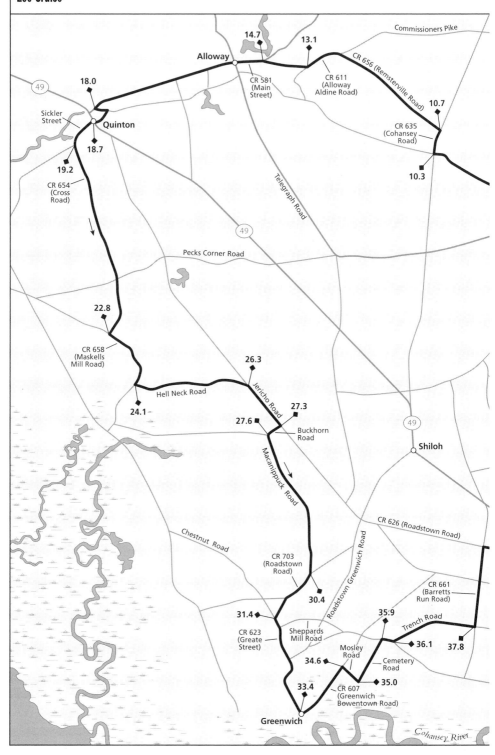

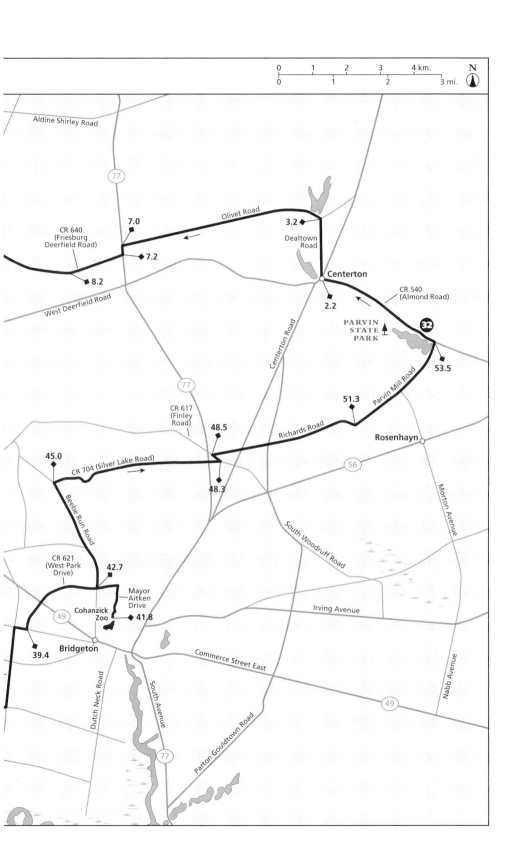

0   1   2   3   4 km.
0   1   2   3 mi.

N

Aldine Shirley Road

77

Olivet Road

CR 640
(Friesburg
Deerfield Road)   7.0

3.2

Dealtown
Road

7.2

Centerton

8.2

2.2

West Deerfield Road

CR 540
(Almond Road)

PARVIN
STATE
PARK

32

53.5

77

Centerton Road

Parvin Mill Road

CR 617
(Finley
Road)   48.5

51.3

Richards Road

Rosenhayn

45.0

CR 704 (Silver Lake Road)

48.3

56

Beebe Run Road

Morton Avenue

CR 621
(West Park
Drive)   42.7

South Woodruff Road

Mayor
Aitken
Drive

49   Cohanzick
Zoo   41.8

Irving Avenue

39.4   Bridgeton

Commerce Street East

49

Nabb Avenue

Dutch Neck Road

South Avenue

Parton Gouldtown Road

77

18.0 Turn left onto Waterworks Road.

18.3 Turn right onto Lake Avenue.

18.6 Turn right onto Route 49 (Quinton Marlboro Road).

18.7 Turn left onto Sickler Street (County Road 651).

19.2 Road name changes to Cross Road (County Road 654).

22.8 Turn left at the T onto County Road 658 (Maskells Mill Road).

24.1 Turn left onto Hell Neck Road.

26.3 Turn right onto Jericho Road (County Road 626).

27.3 Turn right onto Buckhorn Road.

27.6 Left at the Y onto Macanippuck Road.

30.4 Turn right onto Roadstown Road (County Road 703).

31.4 Turn left onto Greate Street (County Road 623).

33.4 Turn left onto Greenwich Bowentown Road (CR 607). (There is a general store on the far left corner as you make this left.)

34.6 Turn right onto Mosley Road.

35.0 Turn left at the end of the road onto Cemetery Road.

35.9 Turn right onto Sheppards Mill Road (County Road 650).

36.1 Turn left onto Trench Road.

37.8 Turn left onto Barretts Run Road (County Road 661).

39.2 Turn right onto Roadstown Road (CR 626).

39.4 Turn left onto West Park Drive (County Road 621).

41.5 Turn right onto Mayor Aitken Drive.

41.8 Turn left into the parking lot of Cohanzick Zoo. Enjoy the zoo.

42.0 Turn right out of the parking lot of Cohanzick Zoo onto Mayor Aitken Drive.

42.1 Bear left at the Y (same road you came in on).

42.2 Turn left onto Park Drive West.

42.7 Turn right onto West Avenue (Beebe Run Road).

42.9 Bear right onto Beebe Run Road.

45.0 Turn right onto Silver Lake Road (County Road 704).

48.3 Turn left onto Finley Road (County Road 617).

48.5 Turn hard right onto Richards Road (County Road 605).

51.3 Turn left onto Parvins Mill Road (County Road 645).

53.5 Turn left onto Almond Road (CR 540).

53.8 Turn right into the parking lot to complete your ride.

Local Events/Attractions

Cohanzick Zoo, New Jersey's first zoo, is located in Bridgeton's 1,100-acre city park. The small zoo has more than 200 birds and mammals from around the world, including white tigers, bears, leopards, ring-tailed lemurs, and eagles. Admission is free. For more information about the zoo, visit www.co.cumberland.nj.us/ tourism/cohanzick_zoo.

Situated on the edge of the Pine Barrens, **Parvin State Park** contains not only the pine forests typical of the area but also a swamp hardwood forest. The park has a diverse landscape, with many beautiful trees and more than 200 kinds of flowering plants. There are also numerous lakes for fishing and boating and a swimming area at Parvin Lake. For more information, check out www.state .nj.us/dep/parksandforests/parks/parvin.html.

Restaurants

Ye Olde Centerton Inn: 1136 Almond Road, Pittsgrove; (856) 358-3201. Traditional American food with a twist in a romantic 18th-century setting.

Accommodations

Comfort Inn: 29 West Landis Avenue, Vineland; (856) 692-8070.

Days Inn: 1001 West Landis Avenue, Vineland; (856) 696-5000.

Maps

DeLorme: New Jersey Atlas and Gazetteer: Page 61 K28, 62 M6, and 67 A19.

New Jersey Bike Maps: Elmer, Alloway, Salem, Canton, Shiloh, Bridgeton; www.njbikemap.com.

33 Atlantic City Boardwalk Ramble

Atlantic City is a historic seaside resort on the Jersey shore. Its famous boardwalk has attracted people for more than a hundred years and inspired the game of Monopoly. Although the city has had many changes over the years, the one constant has been the boardwalk. It's a great place to walk along the beach and see the many attractions. It's also a fun place to ride in the early morning. This easy ramble takes you on a tour of the boardwalk and beyond. Along the way you will see casinos, stores, beaches, and a large elephant named Lucy.

Start: North end of the Atlantic City Boardwalk where it meets New Jersey Avenue, Atlantic City.
Distance: 11.6 miles out and back.
Terrain: Flat. The boardwalk is flat and level, although a little bumpy. The only road that you will ride on, Atlantic Avenue, is next to the beach and as flat as the boardwalk. There are no hills on this ride.
Traffic and hazards: Between the beginning of April and the end of October, bicycles are allowed on the Atlantic City boardwalk only between 6:00 and 10:00 a.m. The rest of the year bicycles are allowed on the boardwalk between 6:00 a.m. and 12:00 p.m. The boardwalk gets more crowded as the day wears on, so the earlier you get out, the fewer people you will have to ride around. The boardwalk is very much like a multiuse path that is shared by runners, walkers, and bicycles. This means the pace of the ride will be slow to avoid running into other users.

Most of the ride will be on a boardwalk, not a road. Although this part of the boardwalk is pretty well maintained, it is still somewhat bumpy and you need to keep an eye out for damaged boards or raised nails. Since it will absorb a lot more of the bumps, a hybrid or mountain bike is the best type of bike to ride the boardwalk, but there is no problem using a regular road bike.

Getting there: Take the Garden State Parkway south to the Atlantic City Expressway and follow it into Atlantic City. The expressway ends a few blocks from the boardwalk. If you are not staying at a hotel in Atlantic City, the best place to park is at one of the casinos. Located on Mississippi Avenue right by the end of the expressway, the Trump Plaza Hotel and Casino is one of the easiest to get to. Once you find a parking spot, just get on your bike and head to the boardwalk.

The directions for this ride start on the boardwalk just south of where it meets New Jersey Avenue. This is the current location of the Showboat Casino, the city's northernmost casino. The boardwalk is not as well maintained north of here, so it is harder to ride. There is constant construction in Atlantic City, so this may change. Since this ride is an out-and-back ride and not a loop, the actual starting point doesn't matter. You can start at any convenient spot along the boardwalk.

When I was a kid, my family would spend a few days to a week in Atlantic City each summer. My favorite memories of these vacations were flying a kite on the beach and riding a bike on the boardwalk. There was just something magical about gliding along the boardwalk on my bike early in the morning. Even though it had been more than thirty years since I last rode the boardwalk, I wanted to try it again as part of writing this book.

What I discovered is that riding along the Atlantic City boardwalk is still as fun and special as it was when I was a kid. I may now be a mature member of society, but this ride made me realize that I really never grew up. Although the landscape of the boardwalk has changed, especially with the addition of the casinos, the feel of riding along the boardwalk is timeless.

This isn't a ride I would go out of my way to do, but if you are in the Atlantic City area it's a fun ride, especially for a family.

The mileage for this ride starts near the northern end of the boardwalk by States Avenue. This is where the Showboat Casino is.

To start the ride head south along the boardwalk. The boardwalk does continue north of here, but is not as well maintained and, to be kind, the city north of here is not real pretty and could use some urban renewal.

As you ride south on the boardwalk, you will go by the Showboat and the Taj Mahal casinos, then pass a bunch of small stores selling saltwater taffy, T-shirts, and other stuff you probably don't need. These stores usually don't open until 9:00 or 10:00 a.m., so most of them will be closed as you ride by. Some cafes and other food shops will be open for breakfast.

The boardwalk is very wide here, so there is plenty of room to go around any other people or bikes. The boardwalk is usually kept in good shape, but is still a little bumpy to ride on. There are always a few damaged spots here and there, so keep your eyes open just as you would for potholes on a road.

As you continue, on your left you will see the famous Steel Pier. From 1898 to the late 1970s, this was the entertainment center of the city. Today there are still some rides on the pier, but it is mostly a food court and shopping mall.

As you continue south, you ride past the next group of casinos (Sands, Bally's, and

Lucy the Elephant in Margate

others). In this area you will also see the Atlantic City Boardwalk Hall, which was the venue for the Miss America pageant from 1940 until 2004. On the left is a little open-air theater. As you continue there will be some more shops and then the last of the big casinos (Tropicana and Hilton).

As you continue south on the boardwalk by Albany Avenue, the boardwalk gets a little narrower. You are at the south end of Atlantic City now and heading toward the town of Ventnor. This is a quieter part of the boardwalk, with fewer hotels and more houses. Although there is less to see here, it is still an enjoyable ride. You will encounter a good number of people, both young and old, riding a number of different kinds of bikes from old beach cruisers to mountain bikes to road bikes.

After 4.4 miles the boardwalk ends in the town of Margate. Turn right off the boardwalk onto Martindale Avenue, and then make the next left onto Atlantic Avenue. This is a nice, wide street with a bike lane to ride in. There is a stoplight at every corner, which can be a little annoying when the timing is off and you end up stopping a lot. I have seen bikers ride through the red lights, which is against the law and dangerous so please don't do it.

After 1.3 miles on Atlantic Avenue, you will see a large elephant named Lucy on your left at the corner of Decatur and Atlantic Avenues. This is not a mirage but a house in the shape of an elephant. James Vincent de Paul Lafferty built the house in

Atlantic City Boardwalk Ramble

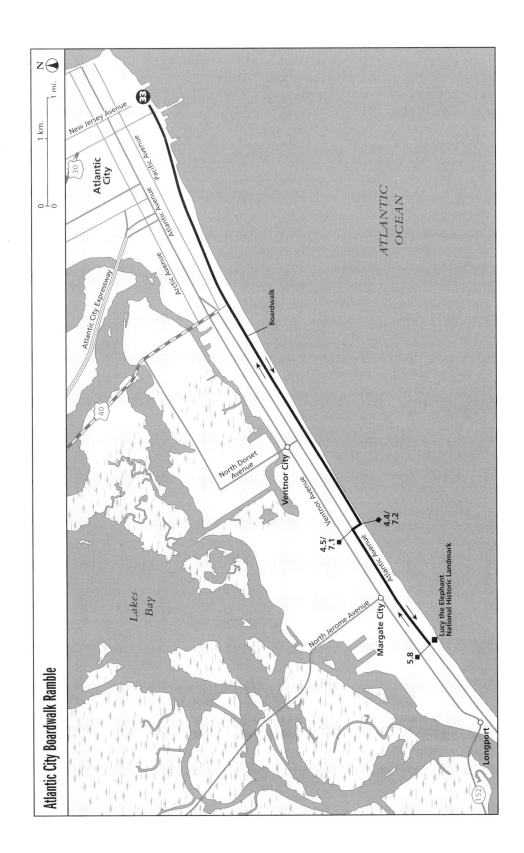

1881 as an attraction to help draw people to the area to buy the land he owned. Lafferty's real estate investments in the area never paid off, but Lucy survived numerous storms, a fire, and aging to become a beloved area attraction.

Lucy marks the southern end of this ride. Once you are done looking her over, turn around and head north on Atlantic Avenue back toward Atlantic City. When Atlantic Avenue meets Martindale Avenue, make a right and head back to the boardwalk. Then just follow the boardwalk north back to your starting point.

Once you are done with your ride, there are plenty of things to do in Atlantic City. You can relax on the beach, try out one of the many buffets, or try your luck at one of the casinos.

Miles and Directions

0.0 Start just south of where New Jersey Avenue meets the boardwalk. Head south on the boardwalk past casinos and the convention hall. N39° 21.588' / W74° 25.062'

4.4 The boardwalk ends in Margate. Turn right onto Martindale Avenue.

4.5 Turn left at Atlantic Avenue.

5.8 Turn left at Decatur to see Lucy the elephant.

5.8 Turn around and head north on Atlantic Avenue.

7.1 Turn right onto Martindale Avenue.

7.2 Turn left onto the boardwalk and head north toward Atlantic City.

11.6 Finish your ride back at the Showboat Casino.

Local Events/Attractions

Lucy the Elephant in Margate is a National Historic Landmark and a must-see if you are in the area. Tours of the inside of the elephant are available. For hours and more information, contact Lucy the Margate Elephant, P.O. Box 3336, Margate, NJ 08402; (609) 823-6473 or visit www.lucytheelephant.org.

Restaurants

Broadway Buffet: Trump Plaza Hotel and Casino, Mississippi Avenue and Boardwalk, Atlantic City; (609) 441-6000. One of the many good buffets in Atlantic City.

Accommodations

Showboat Casino Hotel: 801 Boardwalk, Atlantic City; (609) 343-4000.

Tropicana Casino and Resort: Brighton Avenue and Boardwalk, Atlantic City; (609) 340-4000.

Maps

DeLorme: New Jersey Atlas and Gazetteer: Page 85 H21.

New Jersey Bike Maps: Atlantic City, Ocean City; www.njbikemap.com.

The last two rides in this book don't belong to a particular area of the state but are rides to tour the entire state. The Cross-State Classic is a one-way west-to-east route that will take you across the center of the state from the Delaware River to the Atlantic Ocean. The Longest Day Ride is a marathon 232-mile north-to-south route that goes down the middle of the state. These tours come close to and overlap other rides in this book, so they can be combined with other rides to create a custom multiday tour.

34 Cross-State Classic

This ride takes you across the center of the state from the Delaware River east to the ocean in Belmar. This ride will give you a good look at the variety of terrain and towns in the state. Because this ride intersects and uses some of the roads of the other rides in this book, it can be used to create a longer multiday state tour.

Start: Washington Crossing State Park parking lot, Titusville.

Distance: 67.9 miles one-way.

Terrain: Hilly to rolling to flat. This ride starts off in the hills by the Delaware River with a few relatively easy climbs. After you cross U.S. Highway 1, the terrain will be flat to rolling. After you cross U.S. Highway 9, the roads will flatten out and it will be an easy run to the beach.

Traffic and hazards: For the most part you will be on quiet back roads with light to moderate traffic. Some town centers will be busy at times. The worst congestion and traffic will be from College Road, where you cross US 1, until you get past the town of Plainsboro and onto Cranbury Neck Road.

Getting there: Washington Crossing State Park is located just off Route 29 in Titusville. Take Interstate 95 south toward Pennsylvania and get off at exit 1, the last exit before crossing the Delaware River. Take Route 29 north for about 2.8 miles and then make a left at the short road leading to Washington Crossing Bridge, then turn right into the parking lot before actually crossing the bridge.

New Jersey's borders are defined by the Delaware River on west and the Atlantic Ocean on the east. New Jersey is not a very wide state (32 miles at its narrowest point), so it's easy to get from one side to the other. This ride will take you from historic Washington Crossing State Park on the Delaware to the ocean in Belmar. Although this is a long ride, it can easily be completed in a day if you have done some training and have someone to pick you up at the end. This ride takes you through a variety of places and terrains and gives you a good cross-sectional view of the state.

This ride can also be used as part of a multiday state tour. It intersects a number of other rides in the book, including the Longest Day Classic that runs the entire length of the state from north to south.

This ride starts at Washington Crossing State Park on the Delaware. This is the place where George Washington and his troops crossed the Delaware and marched to Trenton to defeat the Hessian troops on December 25, 1776. To start the ride, leave the parking lot and turn left onto Washington Crossing Pennington Road (County Road 546). Almost immediately cross Route 29 and start a long, gentle 120-foot climb. This road carries moderate traffic but has a good shoulder to ride in.

From here you will take Dublin to Pennington Titusville Road into the town of Pennington. Be careful as you cross Route 31 and head into town. You are now riding some of the roads of Ride 14 (Hill Slug Cruise) and are very close to the YMCA where that ride starts.

Headed toward Pennington

Continue out of Pennington and end up on Bayberry Road. There may be a sign here indicating that a bridge is closed, but this should not be a problem. The bridge has been closed for years to cars, but it is still open to pedestrians and bikes.

Bayberry is a pretty, rolling road with no traffic. When the road ends after 1.5 miles, make a hard left onto Hopewell Princeton Road. Be careful here—the visibility to the left is obscured by the curve in the road.

From here you will be following part of Ride 12 (Princeton Tour Ramble) through the back side of Princeton. When you make the right onto Cherry Hill Road, you have a nice downhill. At the end of the road is a light. Go straight through the light and cross U.S. Highway 206. Go to the T and turn left onto Mount Lucas. The road starts with a gentle uphill climb of 80 feet and then levels out and starts a slow downhill. You are now on the west side of Princeton.

A few more turns will have you on Route 27. You are now entering the town of Kingston. This section of Route 27 can be very busy, so stay to the right, especially while you are crossing the bridge over the river. Climb a short, steep hill here and then make a right at the top onto Academy Street. If you need a break, there is a deli on the left side of Route 27 just north of Academy Street.

Academy Street turns into Mapleton and takes you down a nice hill. You have now intersected Ride 35 (Longest Day Classic) and will be following the same roads for the next 6 miles. At next light, Mapleton goes to the right; continue straight here onto Seminary. Turn left at the next light onto College Road and cross over US 1. There is a shopping center here. Watch out for traffic; a number of roads merge onto and off this road from the shopping center and US 1.

After crossing over US 1 you will be riding through a large office park. The road is two lanes with no shoulder, but as long as you don't ride at rush hour during the week, there won't be much traffic on the road to bother you. Stay on College Road for 2.2 miles and then make a left onto Scudders Mill Road. Go over a bridge and take the next right onto Schalks Crossing Road. Because of the shopping center here, traffic will be a little heavy. Once you pass the shopping center, the riding will be easier with much less traffic.

After you pass the shopping center, you will make a series of short turns to head through the back roads of Plainsboro to get to Cranbury. Once on Cranbury Neck Road you have a nice, flat 3.7-mile stretch that takes you into the town of Cranbury. When you get to Cranbury you will be close to the starting point for Ride 12 (Mendokers' Bakery Ramble), Ride 18 (Clarksburg Cruise), and Ride 24 (Belmar and Back Classic), which start from Village Park here in Cranbury.

Cranbury Station Road takes you across U.S. Highway 130 and over the New Jersey Turnpike. After you cross over the turnpike, continue across some railroad tracks. Right after the railroad tracks, enter a residential neighborhood and turn onto Ely Road. Ely is a brand-new road as of this writing, so it may not appear on maps yet. The roads at this intersection have changed a lot over the last couple of years, so this area will be confusing until the maps are updated. Ely turns into Halsey Reed Road.

From here you will head mostly east through the quiet roads and area farmlands. Eventually you end up on Woodward Road and go across Route 33. After this, ride over some rolling hills for about 4.5 miles to West Freehold.

When you cross Main Street in West Freehold, there is a shopping center on your right if you need a break. After you cross Main Street, the road changes names to Stillwell Corner. Since you are in the middle of town, the road is busy; stay to the right. After you go through a couple more lights, the traffic eases up.

Wind around some residential neighborhoods, and after almost 5 miles cross US 9. Continue on a nice, quiet, flat road for another 3.1 miles. Make a few turns and end up on Main Street in Farmingdale. As you continue you will pass a number of stores. On the left is a shopping center with a bakery. There is also a bagel shop on the right just across from the shopping center. Either place is a good stopping point if you need a break.

After you pass the shopping center, continue over some railroad tracks. As you start to leave town, turn left onto Belmar Boulevard. This road will take you the rest of the way to the beach in just over 8 miles. The road starts out nice and quiet. Cross Route 34 and eventually go under the Garden State Parkway and then over Route 18. The road gets busier as you get closer to the beach. The road usually has a small

Cross-State Classic

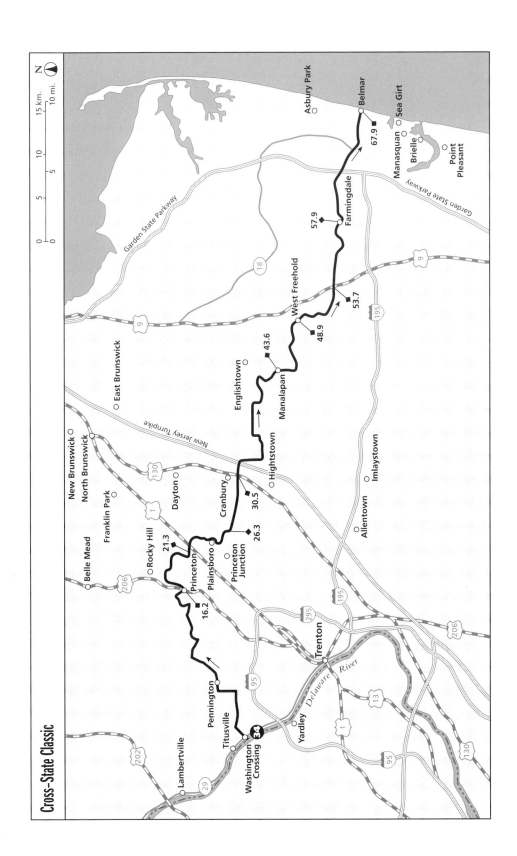

shoulder to ride in, but there are places where the road is a little narrow. There are a number of small shopping centers along the road, so watch out for cars entering and leaving them. After 7.2 miles cross Route 35; the road becomes 16th Street. Continue to the end of this road and you will be on Ocean Avenue in Belmar, where the ride ends. There is a nice group of food stores here with outdoor tables, so this is a good place to relax at the end of the ride. If you are lucky and the weather is good, you can get some beach time to recover from the ride.

Miles and Directions

0.0   Turn left out of the parking lot road onto Washington Crossing Pennington Road (Route 546). N40° 17.793' / W74° 52.032'

3.9   Turn left onto Dublin Road.

5.2   Turn right onto Pennington Titusville Road.

5.4   Cross Route 31. The road becomes Delaware Avenue.

5.9   Stay on Delaware Avenue and cross through the center of Pennington.

6.5   Bear left. The road becomes Pennington Rocky Hill Road.

8.8   Turn right onto Bayberry Road.

10.3   Make a hard left onto Hopewell Princeton Road.

10.7   Turn right onto Cleveland Road.

11.5   The road becomes Pretty Brook Road.

12.6   Make a left followed by a quick right to stay on Pretty Brook Road.

13.6   Turn left onto Great Road.

14.4   Stay to the right and then turn left onto Stuart Road.

15.2   Turn right onto Cherry Hill Road. Enjoy the downhill here.

16.2   At the light cross US 206. Go to the next intersection and turn left onto Mount Lucas Road.

17.2   Turn right onto Poor Farm Road.

17.4   Turn left onto Bunn Drive.

17.5   The road bends right and becomes Herrontown Road.

19.4   Turn left onto Route 27 (Lincoln Highway).

19.8   Turn right onto Academy Street.

20.8   Stay left at the light onto Seminary.

21.3   Turn left onto College Road and cross over US 1; watch for merging traffic.

23.5   Turn left onto Scudders Mill Road.

23.9   Turn right onto Schalks Crossing Road (shopping mall on right).

24.1   Cross Plainsboro Road; the road becomes Parkway Avenue.

24.3   Turn right onto Edgemere Avenue.

24.7   Turn left onto Maple Avenue.

25.0   Turn left onto Grovers Mill Road.

26.3   Turn left onto Cranbury Neck Road.

29.9 Turn left onto Main Street.

30.1 Turn right onto Cranbury Station Road.

30.5 Cross US 130; stay on Cranbury Station Road (Station Road).

31.7 Turn right onto Ely Road. Ely becomes Halsey Reed Road.

32.7 Turn right onto Wyckoffs Mill Road.

33.5 Turn left at the T onto Wyckoffs Mill Applegarth Road.

34.5 Cross Applegarth Road. The road becomes Old Church Road.

35.5 Turn left at the T onto England Road.

36.2 Turn right onto Federal Road.

38.8 Turn right onto Bergen Mills Road.

39.7 Stay straight as Bergen Mills goes right. The road changes names to Gravel Hill Road/Dey Grove Road.

41.4 Turn right onto Iron Ore Road (County Road 527)

42.0 Turn left on to Daum Road.

43.6 Turn left at the T, and then bear right onto Woodward Road.

44.7 Turn left onto Lambs Lane.

45.2 Turn left onto Sweetmans Lane (CR 527).

46.3 Turn right onto Kinney Road, which becomes Gulley Road.

48.4 Turn right onto Wemrock Road.

48.9 Cross Main Street in West Freehold. The road changes names to Stillwells Corner Road.

50.5 Turn left onto County Road 524 (Elton Adelphia Road).

50.6 Make a quick right onto Georgia Road.

51.4 Turn left onto Stonehill Road.

53.7 Cross US 9. Road changes name to Casino Drive.

56.8 Turn left onto West Farms Road.

57.9 Turn right onto CR 524. (Adelphia Road becomes Main Street when you enter Farmingdale.)

59.2 Turn left onto Belmar Boulevard (Route 18). Continue to follow Belmar as it crosses Route 34 and goes over Route 18.

66.5 Cross Route 35. The road becomes 16th Avenue.

67.9 Finish the ride at 16th and Ocean Avenues. (The food stores on the corner make a good place to relax.)

Local Events/Attractions

Just 8 miles north of Trenton, Washington Crossing Park is the site where George Washington and the Continental Army landed after their historic crossing of the Delaware River on Christmas night in 1776 and marched to Trenton to defeat the Hessian troops. Besides displaying a number of historical artifacts and buildings from colonial times, the park is also a great place for hiking, biking, fishing, and picnicking. For more information, check out the Web site at www.nj.gov/dep/parksandforests/parks/washcros.html.

Restaurants

Kliens Fishmarket, Waterside Cafe, and Grill Room: 708 River Road, Belmar; (732)

681-1177. Great seafood restaurant on the outskirts of Belmar with inside and outside dining.

Teddy's Restaurant: 49 North Main Street, Cranbury; (609) 655-3120. Nice diner in the middle of Cranbury.

Vitos: 2 North Main Street, Pennington; (609) 737-8520. Good pizza place in center of town.

Accommodations

Courtyard by Marriott: 360 Scotch Road, Trenton; (609) 771-8100.

Down the Shore Bed and Breakfast: 201 Seventh Avenue, Belmar; (732) 681-9023.

Residence Inn Cranbury South Brunswick: 2662 U.S. Highway 130, Cranbury; (609) 395-9447 or (888) 577-7005.

Maps

DeLorme: New Jersey Atlas and Gazetteer: Pages 41 H23, 42 E1, 43 G15, 44 M1, and 45 N15.

New Jersey Bike Maps: Lambertville, Pennington, Princeton, Hightstown, Jamesburg, Adelphia, Farmingdale, Asbury Park; www.njbikemap.com.

35 Longest Day Classic

The Longest Day is the name of the highest-mileage ride in New Jersey. The Central Jersey Bike Club sponsors this one-way ride from High Point to Cape May. The ride is usually done the second or third weekend of June, when the days are long. You have to be a special kind of crazy to do this kind of mileage in one day. This is a great route, though, and can be used to connect some of the rides in this book to create a multiday tour.

Start: At the parking lot just outside the entrance to High Point State Park near Montague (or in any of the park's parking lots).

Distance: 232 miles one-way.

Terrain: Hilly to rolling to flat. This ride starts in the hills of northern New Jersey, so the first 50 miles will have a lot of ups and downs. Since the ride starts at the highest point in the state, the steepest hills are downhills, and none of the climbs is a killer. After the first 50 miles the terrain is less hilly but still rolling. The farther south you get, the fewer hills you will encounter. The last 100 miles are essentially flat, with the only problem being the wind.

Traffic and hazards: This ride tries to keep to good rural roads, but it also travels through a number of populated areas where there will be some high traffic.

Getting there: High Point State Park is located just off Route 23 in Montague. To get there take Route 23 approximately 7 miles north of the town of Sussex, New Jersey, or 4 miles south of Port Jervis, New York. You can park in the parking lot just outside the entrance to the park or in any of the park's lots.

The Longest Day Classic follows a long route that goes down the center of the state. Although this route was developed for a one-day marathon ride, it is also a good route for touring the state. There have been a number of variations of this route. The route provided here is similar to the one posted on the New Jersey Department of Transportation Web site, with minor alterations.

If you are a mileage junkie, this route should satisfy your fix for a high-mileage ride and then some. Saner riders may want to break this route into a number of days and use it along with other rides in the book to design your own state tour.

Since this is a very long route, unlike the other rides in the book, the description for this ride provides a more high-level overview that will give the general terrain, trouble spots, sights to see, and other routes in the book along the way.

This ride starts by the monument at High Point State Park. Traditionally, Longest Day riders either ride up to or start the ride by the monument so they can say they rode from the state's highest point to the ocean in one day. The monument is a short but steep ride from any parking lot in the park. If you don't mind starting your ride with a tough climb, it's worth it for the view and bragging rights.

From the monument you will follow the main road out of the park back to Route 23 and make a right then the next left onto Sawmill Road. This is an easy turn to miss. Sawmill takes you to Deckertown Turnpike. This road is a little narrow with some very steep downhills, so be careful. At the end of Deckertown get onto County Road 519 and follow it to Newton. For the most part CR 519 is a rural country road with a shoulder to ride in some of the time. Traffic will be light to moderate, depending on the time of day. CR 519 is not a continuous road, so you will be making a number of turns to stay on it.

Stay on CR 519 until Newton, and then go through the town and end up on U.S. Highway 206. Newton is a good-size town and a good place for a rest stop. Although US 206 is a busy road, there is a wide shoulder here to ride in. While on US 206 you will pass Kittatinny State Park, where Ride 7 (Kittatinny Cruise) starts. Leave US 206 when you reach Andover; get on some nice back roads and pass a couple of lakes. Eventually you will be on Stanhope Road, which takes you into the town of Netcong.

Netcong is probably the worst part of this route as far as traffic goes. In the stretch from Brooklyn Road to US 206, there are a lot of intersections and highway entrance and exit ramps where US 206 goes under Interstate 80 and U.S. Highway 46. There is a shoulder here to ride in, but with all the cars entering and exiting the road, it is not a very comfortable place to ride.

Once on US 206 there will still be traffic, but you will have a wide shoulder to ride in. About 3.2 miles after crossing under I-80, you will go down a long hill and eventually come to an intersection with a light in Flanders. Make a left here onto Main Street. This will get you away from some of the traffic and back onto some back roads. These roads will take you down to the town of Chester, where you will get on Route 24.

Route 24 takes you through Mendham Township and into the town of Mendham. You will hit some moderate to heavy traffic in the middle of the town. Toward the end of town, turn right onto Tempe Wick Road and head back to some quieter

◀ *Start of the ride at High Point*

roads. The nicest road on this stretch is Hardscrabble, a beautiful winding road that is mostly downhill. This road and the next few turns are part of Ride 8 (Jockey Hollow Hilly Cruise). At this point you are also very close to the route of Ride 2 (The Great Swamp Ramble). The route continues through the town of Basking Ridge, which is a good place to take a break.

After Basking Ridge you will wind around the back end of Bernards Township. There are a couple of little pockets of traffic here, but for the most part you will be on decent back roads. As you get closer to Bound Brook, there are a quick series of turns to get into town that can be confusing. Bound Brook itself is a very busy, congested town, so you will hit traffic here. Once you cross the bridge over the Raritan River, the riding gets a lot easier. For the most part, from here on there are no more real climbs, just some rolling hills. After Bound Brook you will mostly be riding along the canal. Make a left off Amwell and enjoy a very nice 8+ miles of riding along the Delaware and Raritan Canal. This road is part of Ride 11 (D&R Canal Ramble). At the end of Canal Road, where it meets County Road 518, is the parking lot in Rocky Hill where Ride 15 (Lindbergh Long Hill Cruise) and Ride 16 (Round Valley Challenge) start.

Continue through the town of Kingston and across US 1. To get across US 1 you will go over an overpass into an office complex. It's a two-lane road with no shoulder, but as long as you don't ride at rush hour during the week, there won't be much traffic to bother you. Go through the town of Plainsboro. There is a tough intersection by the shopping center, but after that you will be mostly on back roads in West Windsor.

When you get to Cranbury Neck Road, the route in this book differs quite a bit from the route posted on the New Jersey Department of Transportation Web site. This variation in this book helps avoid crossing US 130 on a circle and the crowed center of Hightstown. If you continued on Cranbury Neck Road instead of turning onto Nostrand, you would end up in the town of Cranbury, the starting point for Ride 12 (Mendokers' Bakery Ramble), Ride 18 (Clarksburg Cruise), and Ride 24 (Belmar and Back Classic).

When you get to Windsor Road you will be about a mile away from Mercer County Park, where Ride 19 (Rue Road Roller-Coaster Cruise) starts. You are now halfway done with the route, heading mostly south. The next main town you will hit is New Egypt. From here you will head to Cookstown and then through Fort Dix, following some of the roads of Ride 22 (Basic Training Challenge) to get to Pemberton.

From here you enter the Pine Barrens as you pass through Brendan Byrne State Park, which is where Ride 31 (Pine Barren Cruise) starts. The rest of the route is flat, with only an occasional incline or decline. From Chatsworth to Egg Harbor you will be on County Road 563, which takes you through the heart of the Pine Barrens. The scenery is nice but gets a little boring after 20 miles of mostly pine trees.

There is a little deli where CR 563 crosses County Road 542. You are also very close to Batsto Village, the starting point for Ride 28 (Batsto Village Cruise).

Eventually you will reach the town of Egg Harbor City, and CR 563 changes to Route 50. This area is a little more crowded. Route 50 does have a shoulder to ride in most of the time, but you will hit pockets of traffic. Be careful as you pass under the Atlantic City Expressway and go through the town of Mays Landing.

Although Route 50 is still a busy road, once you are a few miles south of Mays Landing, there is less traffic and the road is a little more scenic. When you get to Woodbine Road and into the town of Woodbine, you are near Belleplain State Park, the starting point of Ride 30 (Belleplain Challenge).

From Woodbine take some bland back roads to the town of Cape May Court House. From Cape May Court House head back to Route 47 and take it to Railroad Avenue. It's now a straight shot south to Cape May. This road gets more congested as you continue south but has a decent shoulder to ride in. Railroad Avenue becomes Seashore Road and takes you over the canal and into Cape May. Make a right onto Sunset Boulevard and a left onto Light House Avenue to get to the lighthouse and the end of the ride.

Whether you did this ride in one day or several, it is one of those rides that make you really feel like you accomplished something and will always give you a few good stories to tell.

Miles and Directions

0.0 Start at the monument in High Point State Park. Turn left out of the parking lot onto Lake Street. N41° 19.238' / W74° 39.693'

1.7 Follow the park road to the entrance of the park and turn right onto Route 23. This is a busy road; stay in the shoulder. There are long downhill stretches ahead.

2.1 Turn left onto Sawmill Road.

6.6 Turn left onto Deckertown Turnpike. Caution: steep downhills ahead.

9.5 Turn right onto CR 519.

12.1 Turn right onto CR 519.

13.4 Continue straight. The road becomes CR 519 (Wantage Avenue).

19.5 Turn right, followed by a quick left onto CR 519 (Mill Street).

19.8 Turn right onto CR 519 (Newton Avenue).

19.9 Cross US 206. Continue straight onto CR 519 (Newton Avenue).

21.4 Turn left onto CR 519 (Newton Avenue).

23.5 Cross County Road 626. Continue straight onto CR 519.

26.4 Cross US 206/Route 94. Continue straight onto Trinity Street and enter the town of Newton (a good place for a rest stop).

26.7 Turn right onto Union Place.

26.8 Turn left onto Spring Street.

27.0 Bear right onto Sparta Avenue.

27.2 Turn right onto County Road 621 (Woodside Avenue).

27.6 Merge with US 206 (Woodside Avenue).

32.5 Turn left onto Lenape Road.

32.6 Continue straight; the road becomes Andover Mohawk Road.

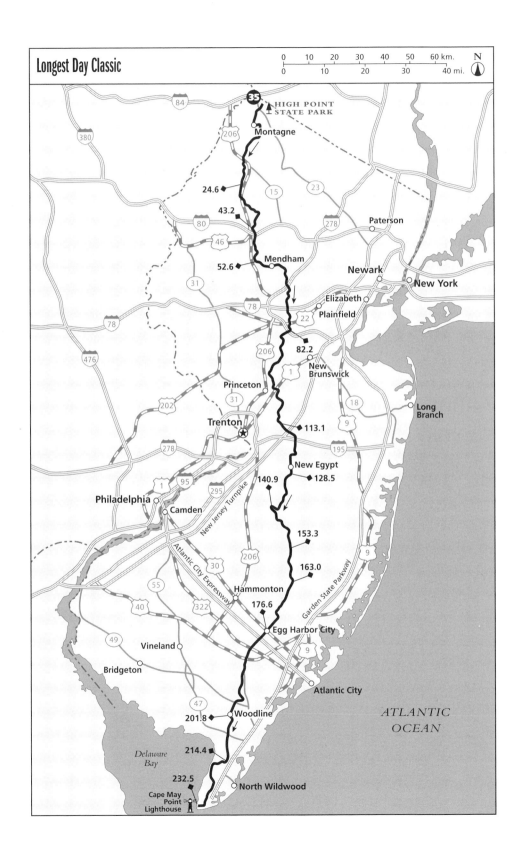

Longest Day Classic

| 0 | 10 | 20 | 30 | 40 | 50 | 60 km. |
| 0 | 10 | 20 | 30 | 40 mi. |

N

35 ↑ HIGH POINT STATE PARK

84

380

206

Montagne

24.6

15

23

43.2

80

Paterson

278

46

52.6 Mendham

Newark

31

New York

Elizabeth

78

Plainfield

22

78

476

206

82.2

1

New Brunswick

Princeton

31

202

18

Trenton

Long Branch

113.1

9

278

195

1

95

New Egypt

140.9

128.5

Philadelphia

295

Camden

153.3

30

206

163.0

55

Hammonton

176.6

40

322

Egg Harbor City

49

Vineland

9

Bridgeton

Atlantic City

47

201.8 Woodline

ATLANTIC OCEAN

214.4

Delaware Bay

232.5

North Wildwood

Cape May Point Lighthouse

33.0 Turn right onto Roseville Road.

36.8 Turn left onto County Road 607.

38.3 Turn right onto County Road 605 (Stanhope Road).

41.3 Continue straight; the road becomes CR 605 (Sparta Road).

42.1 Turn right onto County Road 602 (Brooklyn Road).

43.2 Bear left and merge with Route 183. This is a busy area; use caution.

43.7 Cross under U.S. Highway 46 then bear right to stay on Route 183 south. Cross US 46.

44.1 Cross under Interstate 80 (watch merging traffic). Continue on Route 183, which becomes US 206.

47.3 Turn left onto Main Street in Flanders.

47.4 Bear right onto Pleasant Hill Road.

47.8 Continue straight on Pleasant Hill Road. Stay to the right.

49.4 Continue straight; the road becomes Flanders Road.

49.5 Turn right onto Pleasant Hill Road.

52.2 Continue straight; the road becomes Hillside Road and enters the town of Chester.

52.6 Turn left onto Route 24 (East Main Street).

53.4 Turn right onto Route 24/County Road 510.

58.2 Cross County Road 525 and enter Mendam. Continue on Route 24/County Road 510 (food stores if you need a break).

58.8 Turn right onto County Road 646 (Tempe Wick Road).

61.0 Turn right onto Leddell Road.

61.7 Continue straight; the road becomes Jockey Hollow Road. There's a steep hill ahead.

62.7 Turn left onto Hardscrabble Road.

63.2 Bear left to stay on Hardscrabble Road.

65.2 Turn right onto Childs Road.

66.2 Make a left to stay on Childs Road.

66.4 Cross US 202; the road becomes Finley Avenue. Cross under Interstate 287 and enter Basking Ridge (food stores).

67.5 Turn left onto Henry Street.

67.6 Turn right onto County Road 657 (South Maple Avenue).

69.0 Turn right onto Cross Road.

69.6 Turn left onto South Finley Avenue.

69.8 Turn left onto Stonehouse Road.

71.2 Turn right onto County Road 512 (Valley Road).

71.8 Turn left onto Acken Road.

73.1 Cross over Interstate 78; the road becomes Dead River Road.

73.5 Turn right onto Mountainview Road.

73.6 Turn left onto Round Top Road. There's a steep downhill.

75.2 Continue straight; the road becomes Dock Watch Hollow Road.

76.5 Turn right onto County Road 616 (Washington Valley Road).

77.1 Turn left onto Vosseller Avenue.

77.7 Turn left onto Brookside Drive; this is a narrow road.

78.3 Turn right onto Stangle Road and a steep uphill.

79.1 Cross Hillcrest Road and continue straight; the road becomes Washington Avenue.

79.6 Turn right onto Woodland Terrace for a steep, winding downhill.

79.7 Turn right onto Middlebrook Road.

79.8 Turn left onto Cedarcrest Road.

80.3 Turn left and cross U.S. Highway 22 onto Vosseller Avenue. Enter Bound Brook. (There are food stores in town if you need a break.)

81.5 Turn left onto County Road 533 (Talmage Avenue).

81.7 Turn right onto Columbus Place.

81.8 Turn left onto CR 533 (West Main Street).

82.2 Turn right at the circle onto South Main Street. Cross the bridge over the Raritan River.

82.4 Turn right onto County Road 623 (Canal Road).

83.4 Cross under I-287 and continue on CR 623 (Weston Canal Road).

85.9 Turn left onto School House Road.

86.8 Turn right onto Mettlers Road.

87.5 Turn right and then make a quick left to stay on Mettlers Road.

88.7 Turn right onto County Road 514 (Amwell Road).

89.1 Turn left onto Market Street (deli on right just after the turn).

89.3 Turn right onto Elm Street, which becomes Canal Road.

93.0 Turn right to stay on Canal Road.

97.9 Cross County Road 518; the road becomes Kingston Rocky Hill Road/Laurel Avenue.

99.0 Cross Route 27.

99.1 Turn right on to Euclid Avenue.

99.3 Turn left onto Academy Street; the road becomes Mapleton.

100.3 Stay left at light onto Seminary.

100.8 Turn left onto College Road and cross over US 1. Watch for merging traffic.

103.0 Turn left onto Scudders Mill Road.

103.4 Turn right onto Schalks Crossing Road (shopping mall on the right).

103.6 Cross Plainsboro Road; the road becomes Parkway Avenue.

103.8 Turn right onto Edgemere Avenue.

104.2 Turn left onto Maple Avenue.

104.5 Turn left onto Grovers Mill Road.

105.8 Turn left onto Cranbury Neck Road.

106.6 Turn right onto Nostrand.

108.2 Cross County Road 571; to the road becomes Southfield.

109.6 Turn left onto Village Road.

110.6 Turn right onto South Lane.

111.8 Turn left onto Windsor Road.

113.1 Cross US 130.

115.3 Turn left onto Sharon Road.

116.0 Turn right onto Old York Road (County Road 539).

116.1 Quick left onto Herbert Road.

118.2 Turn right onto Imlaystown Road.

120.2 Left then quick right onto Davis Station Road.

120.3 Bear right to stay on Davis Station Road.

120.8 Bear right to stay on Davis Station Road.

121.3 Bear left onto Meirs Road.

122.5 Turn right onto Burlington Path Road (Route 27).

123.7 Cross CR 539; stay on Burlington Path Road (Route 27).

124.3 Turn right onto Holmes Mill Road (Route 27).

127.2 Cross County Road 537; the road becomes Evergreen Road.

128.5 Turn right onto Main Street in New Egypt.

128.7 Bear left onto County Road 528 Spur (Maple Road). (There's a Wawa on the corner if you need a break.)

130.6 Bear left onto County Road 667 (Main Street) in Cookstown.

130.9 Leave Cookstown. The road becomes Cookstown Browns Mills Road.

135.9 Cross Range Road; the road becomes East Lakeshore Drive.

136.6 Turn right onto Clubhouse Road.

136.8 Bear left to stay on Clubhouse Road.

137.3 Turn left onto Lakehurst Road.

137.5 Turn right onto Junction Road.

139.2 Bear right onto Mount Misery Road.

140.9 Turn left onto Four Mile Road.

144.6 Turn left onto Upper Mill Road.

145.3 Turn right onto Deep Hollow Road.

145.9 Cross Route 70; the road becomes Four Mile Road.

146.6 Turn left onto Shinns Road.

148.6 Turn right where Shinns Road changes to sand onto Buzzard Hill Road (unsigned).

149.0 Turn left onto Route 72; stay in the shoulder.

149.4 Bear right onto CR 563.

153.3 Cross County Road 532 in Chatsworth. (The food store here is the last place to stop for the next 15 miles.)

163.0 Bear right and stay on CR 563.

168.5 Turn right onto CR 542.

168.6 Make a quick left onto CR 563 (food store on corner).

169.0 Bear left and cross the Mullica River. Stay on CR 563.

170.6 Turn left into Weekstown; continue on CR 563.

171.8 Bear right to continue on CR 563.

175.1 Enter Egg Harbor City. Continue on CR 563 (Philadelphia Avenue).

176.6 Cross Route 30; the road becomes Route 50 (Philadelphia Avenue).

178.8 Cross under the Atlantic City Expressway; watch out for merging traffic. Continue on Route 50.

181.6 Cross over County Road 322 and continue on Route 50.

183.5 Enter Mays Landing. Stay on Route 50 (now also Route 40).

184.1 Turn left to stay on Route 50.

196.0 Turn right onto Route 49 in Tuckahoe.

197.4 Turn left onto County Road 557 (Woodbine Road).

201.8 Turn left onto Dehirsch Avenue in Woodbine (food store in town).

203.2 Turn right onto County Road 660 (Fidler Hill Road).

204.0 Turn left onto County Road 638 (Fidler Hill Road).

206.2 Turn right onto County Road 610 (Petersburg Road).

206.4 Make a quick left onto Route 47 (food store on corner).

208.0 Turn left onto CR 657 (Courthouse South Dennis Road).

212.9 The road becomes CR 657 (Dennisville Road).

214.0 Turn right onto US 9 (North Main Street), Cape May Courthouse.

214.4 Turn right onto County Road 615 (Mechanic Street).

214.7 Bear left onto County Road 612 (Dias Creek Road).

216.5 Turn left onto County Road 643 (Springers Mill Road).

218.0 Turn left onto Route 47 (South Delsea Drive).

223.2 Turn right onto CR 626 (Railroad Avenue).

223.6 The road becomes CR 626 (Seashore Road).

227.2 Bear left onto CR 626/County Road 162 (Seashore Road), and cross the Canal Bridge into Cape May.

229.5 The road becomes Broadway (CR 626).

231.2 Turn right onto Sunset Boulevard (County Road 606).

231.9 Turn left onto Light House Avenue (County Road 629).

232.5 Turn left into Cape May Point State Park. The ride officially ends at the lighthouse.

Local Events/Attractions

High Point State Park, Sussex County, is the location of the highest point in New Jersey. In addition to the monument at High Point, the park has a beautiful lake for swimming, camping facilities, a number of hiking trails, plus cross-country skiing in the winter. For more information, visit www.state.nj.us/dep/parks andforests/parks/highpoint.html.

For the many sites and attractions on Cape May, check out the official Web site (www .capemay.com), or contact them at CapeMay. com, P.O. Box 2383, Cape May, NJ 08204; (609) 898-4500.

Restaurants

Mastori's Diner: 144 South U.S. Highway 130, Bordentown; (609) 298-4650. A popular diner with great food.

End of the ride at Cape May Light ▶

Washington Street Station: 153 Washington Street, Rocky Hill; (609) 924.9872. Casual American cuisine.

Accommodations

Cape May accommodations: CapeMay.com, P.O. Box 2383, Cape May, NJ 08204; (609) 898-4500; www.capemay.com.

Comfort Inn Bordentown: 1009 U.S. Highway 206, Bordentown; (609) 298-9111; www.comfortinn.com.

Comfort Inn of Port Jervis: 2247 Greenville Turnpike, Port Jervis, NY; (845) 856-6611 or (888) 330-6611.

Executive Inn: 7 West Hampton Street, Pemberton; (609) 894-8155.

Holiday Inn Express Hotel & Suites Newton Sparta: 6 North Park Drive, Newton; (973) 940-8888 or (888) 465-4329 (reservations).

Holiday Inn Princeton: 100 Independence Way, Princeton; (609) 520-1200.

Ramada Inn Hammonton: 308 South White Horse Pike, U.S. Highway 30, Hammonton; (800) 272-6232.

Maps

DeLorme: New Jersey Atlas and Gazetteer: Pages 19 C20, 24 D1, 30 A5, 36 A11, 42 A9, 43 M15, 48 H14, 49 A16, 56 A12, 64 C14, 65 A15, 70 A4, 72 A10, and 73 I22.

New Jersey Bike Maps: Port Jervis South, Branchville, Newton West, Stanhope, Chester, Mendham, Bernardsville, Bound Brook, Monmouth Junction, Princeton, Hightstown, Allentown, New Egypt, Browns Mill, Pemberton, Chatsworth; www.njbikemap.com.

Appendix: Bicycling Resources

There is a lot of good information available about bike riding in New Jersey. This section contains a brief list and description of some of the best resources available to help you learn more about the bicycling in the state.

New Jersey Bike Map

For those looking to explore new roads in New Jersey, their first stop should be to visit New Jersey Bike Map (www.njbikemap.com), or NJBikeMap as it is commonly known. This site was started in 2002 by Dustin Farnum and is your best source of information about bikeable roads in New Jersey. The Web site contains more than 190 detailed street-level maps of New Jersey and the surrounding area showing the information a biker needs when creating bike routes. The maps contain a wealth of information, including types of roads, location of parking areas, where to stop for food, and so much more. Although these maps contain a lot of information, they are very compact, well organized, and easy to read. Best of all, the information on this site is updated on a regular basis and is totally free.

When you go to the Web site, you will see the main page, which has a set of links on the left. To get to the maps, click on the "Go to the Map" link. This will take you to a picture of the state of New Jersey showing all its counties as well as all the counties in surrounding states. If you look closely you will see that the map is divided into three sections: North, Central, and South. Clicking on one of these sections will bring you to a more detailed view of that section.

The detail view will show you a grid of maps for that section of the state. Each cell in the grid shows the name of the main town on that map. If you do not see the town that you are looking for, or don't know which map to choose, you can use the link at the bottom of the grid to find which map contains a specific town.

Once you click on one of the maps of the grid, you will see a detailed street-level map of that area. This map may look simple and plain compared to other commercial maps, but don't let its plainness fool you. This map is ingenious in its simplicity.

The first thing you will notice about the map is its color-coded roads:

- Green roads are country roads that are easily rideable.
- Purple roads are suburban roads that can be ridden but are more congested. Purple roads contain more intersections and traffic and are a little harder to ride.
- Red roads are usually main highways with high-speed traffic and should be avoided if possible.
- Green roads with yellow backgrounds are country roads with scenic views.
- Some green and purple roads will have red backgrounds where they go through the center of towns. This does not mean the roads are not rideable. There may be a little more traffic here, but there are probably businesses and food available.

- Roads outlined in brown are dirt roads.
- Gray roads are roads that have not been field-checked, so the type is unknown.

In addition to the color coding, the thicker the line on the map, the busier the road. For the most part, the color coding is very accurate. The purple roads are the most variable. Some aren't too bad to ride on, while others can be very congested at times.

A number of roads are not shown on the map. These include:

- Roads that go nowhere or are dead ends
- Congested roads in major cities like Newark and Camden
- Roads that are sand in South Jersey

This was done to reduce map clutter. This does make it a little harder sometimes to determine where you are while riding, but it's a good trade-off that helps keep the maps small and more readable.

The map contains a lot of symbols and markings to help you find things that are important while riding. The map contains red F's to show where you can get food and a shopping cart symbol to show where shopping centers are. A car-with-a-bike-on-top symbol shows places where you can safely park your car and start a ride. There are also symbols to show the location of bike paths, hospitals, covered bridges, and many other features. For a complete list of the map symbols, click on the "Map Key" link on the main page.

One of the most ingenious markings on the map is the way it shows the elevations of the climbs. Instead of using markings of a typographical map to show elevation, every road that is a significant climb has a circle at the bottom of the climb and a flag at the top of the climb. Between these two marks is the elevation of the climb. In North and Central Jersey, any climbs over 100 feet are marked. In South Jersey any climb over 50 feet is marked. Although this marking system doesn't show the actual grade of the climb, this can usually be inferred from the distance between the circle and flag.

One thing you will notice about the maps is that maps next to each other don't line up and contain some overlap. This was done on purpose to make it hard for people to take the maps and create larger maps on their own. The overlap is actually a nice feature, since it means roads that are hard to read on the edge of one map will be an inch or two in on another map.

As you continue to explore the Web site and its different maps and lists, you will realize what a great resource it is. The bikers of New Jersey owe Dustin a debt of gratitude for creating and maintaining this site. It was a great help in writing this book and saved me countless hours of research. I'm sure anybody biking in New Jersey would find the site useful.

Maintenance of the Web site is a lot of work. Dustin does it because he is passionate about biking and maps and enjoys exploring and finding new roads. He also enjoys hearing from other bikers. If you have any comments or corrections to the map or ideas to make it better, just send him an e-mail through his Web site.

New Jersey Bike Clubs

Joining a bike club is the best way to safely learn the roads in a particular area and pick up valuable bike-riding skills. Novice bike riders will especially benefit from riding with the many experienced riders in a club and quickly become better riders. Joining a bike club is also a great way to socialize with people of like minds who enjoy biking.

Below is a list of the bike clubs in New Jersey. No matter where you live, you will find one close to where you live or want to bike. Bike clubs are usually a loose association of people who want to ride together. Most usually publish a monthly newsletter containing a list of available rides for the month. The rides will be different lengths, speeds, and terrains. Most clubs will let nonmembers ride on club rides a few times before they require you to join the club. The hardest part of joining a club for new members is finding the right leader and group of people to ride with. The best thing to do when you first join a club is to try three or four different rides to find a compatible group. Most people overestimate their abilities, so start off with easier rides and then move up as you become confident that you will be able to keep up with the other riders.

Atlantic Bicycle Club (Racing/Touring)
P.O. Box 330
Allenwood, NJ 08720
(908) 528-7198
www.atlanticbicycleclub.org

Bicycle Touring Club of North Jersey
446 Ellis Place
Wyckoff, NJ 07841
Membership hotline: (201) 891-6786
www.btcnj.org

Bedminster Flyers Cycling Club
P.O. Box 341
Far Hills, NJ 07931
(908) 876-9096
www.bedminsterflyers.com

Central Jersey Bicycle Club
P.O. Box 2202
Edison, NJ 08878
(732) 225-HUBS
www.cjbc.org

Central Jersey Cycling Team (Racing)
P.O. Box 185
Neshanic Station, NJ 08853
(908) 369-4522

Century Road Club of America
c/o Knopps Bicycle Shop
38 Spring Street
Princeton, NJ 08542
(908) 704-6985

Doubles of the Garden State
231 Brookside Avenue
Laurence Harbor, NJ 08879
www.d-o-g-s.org

G. S. Park Ridge Cyclesport (Racing)
1 Hawthorne Avenue
Park Ridge, NJ 07656
(201) 391-5269

Jaeger Wheelmen Club (Racing)
35 Sunset Avenue
Ewing, NJ 08628
(609) 882-7956

Jersey Shore Touring Society
P.O. Box 8581
Red Bank, NJ 07701
(732) 747-8206
www.jsts.us

Major Taylor Cycling Club NY/NJ
71 South Orange Avenue
South Orange, NJ 07079
majortaylornynj.com

Mercer-Bucks Cycling Club/Harts Racing
Harts Cyclery
7 North Route 31
Pennington, NJ 08540
(609) 7373008

Morris Area Freewheelers Bicycle Club
25 North Star Drive
Morris Township, NJ 07960
(973) 397-9975
www.mafw.org

New Jersey Road Club
www.njroadclub.com

North Jersey Mountain Bike Club
223 Taylor Road
Paramus, NJ 07652
(201) 214-2004
www.dwmorrison.com/njmbc.htm

Outbike NJ
http://pweb.netcom.com/~lavillas/OUTBIKE.html

Outdoor Club of South Jersey, Inc.
P.O. Box 455
Cherry Hill, NJ 08003-0455
(609) 427-7777
www.ocsj.org

Princeton Freewheelers
P.O. Box 1204
Princeton, NJ 08542
(609) 882-4PFW (4739)
www.princetonfreewheelers.com

Shore Cycle Club
P.O. Box 492
Northfield, NJ 08225
www.shorecycleclub.org

South Jersey Wheelmen
P.O. Box 2705
Vineland, NJ 08362-0725
(856) 691-3936
www.sjwheelmen.org

Summit Cycling Club
14 Nedsland Avenue
Titusville, NJ 08560
(609) 737-2373

Western Jersey Wheelmen
31 Mark Drive
High Bridge, NJ 08829
(908) 638-6172
www.bikewjw.org

Other Resources

- The New Jersey Department of Transportation maintains a great Web site (www .state.nj.us/transportation/commuter/bike) with a lot of good information about biking in New Jersey. On this site you will find information about bicycle laws, safety and commuter tips, as well as some bike tours that can be downloaded.
- *Bicycling* magazine. The magazine's Web site (www.bicycling.com) is the best place to start your search for bike rides, bike gear, and training and fitness tips.
- MapMyRide.com (www.mapmyride.com). This Web site allows users to plot maps of their rides. The maps are shown using Google Maps, and they can be shared and searched. This a great site for planning rides and sharing them with friends.

Ride Index

About the Author

Born and raised in New Jersey,
Tom Hammell has been riding
a bike as long as he can remember. For the past eighteen years
he has lived in central New
Jersey and explored most of
the roads of the state via bike.
As an avid bike rider and ride
leader with the Princeton Freewheelers, he rides thousands of
miles a year leading other riders through the beautiful back
roads of New Jersey. You can
follow his latest bike adventures
on his blog at http://frisket
.blogspot.com.